Eden's Endemics

UNDER THE SIGN OF NATURE: EXPLORATIONS IN ECOCRITICISM

Serenella Iovino, Anthony Lioi, and Kate Rigby, Editors

Michael P. Branch, SueEllen Campbell, and
John Tallmadge, Senior Advisory Editors

Eden's Endemics

NARRATIVES OF BIODIVERSITY
ON EARTH AND BEYOND

Elizabeth Callaway

University of Virginia Press
Charlottesville and London

University of Virginia Press
© 2020 by the Rector and Visitors of the University of Virginia
All rights reserved
Printed in the United States of America on acid-free paper

First published 2020

9 8 7 6 5 4 3 2 1

Library of Congress Cataloging-in-Publication Data
Names: Callaway, Elizabeth, author.
Title: Eden's endemics : narratives of biodiversity on earth and beyond / Elizabeth Callaway.
Description: Charlottesville : University of Virginia Press, 2020. | Series: Under the sign of nature: explorations in ecocriticism | Includes bibliographical references and index.
Identifiers: LCCN 2019058282 (print) | LCCN 2019058283 (ebook) | ISBN 9780813944562 (hardcover) | ISBN 9780813944579 (paperback) | ISBN 9780813944586 (ebook)
Subjects: LCSH Literature and science. | Biodiversity. | Biodiversity conversation. | Human ecology and the humanities.
Classification: LCC PN55 .C35 2020 (print) | LCC PN55 (ebook) | DDC 809/.9336—dc23
LC record available at https://lccn.loc.gov/2019058282
LC ebook record available at https://lccn.loc.gov/2019058283

Cover art: Echinidea, plate 30, Ernst Haeckel, *Kunstformen der Natur.* (Leipzig: Verlag des Bibliographischen Instituts, 1904)

For Bill

Endemic, n. an organism that is restricted or peculiar to a locality or region

—*Merriam-Webster*

Contents

Acknowledgments xi

Introduction: Accounting for Biodiversity 1

1. Natural History at the End of the World: Seed Banks, Database, Apocalypse 25

2. Cross Sections of the Tree of Life: Visualization and Evolutionary Supertrees 53

3. A Bird in Hand: Species Encounters in Competitive Birding 80

4. Islands in the Aether Ocean: Speculative Ecosystems in Science Fiction 106

5. Biodiversity Within: The Human Microbiome 130

Coda: Nature Writing by Artificial Intelligence 161

Notes 173

Bibliography 191

Index 201

Acknowledgments

THE SEEDS THAT LATER GREW into this book were sown when I wrote my very first (undergraduate!) essay about biodiversity on Octavia Butler's *Dawn* and Bruce Sterling's *Schismatrix* at Stanford University in 2006. Since then, I have worked on this book while living in California, Colorado, New Jersey, and Utah. I have been extremely fortunate to have found rich academic communities at every institution and in every position I have held throughout the course of completing this work.

The Department of English at the University of Utah has been the most vibrant community from which to finish this book. I'd like to thank all my colleagues for their insightful and challenging questions, their welcome critiques, and their generous donation of time and expertise. Special thanks to Lisa Swanstrom, David Roh, Scott Black, and Steve Tatum for their feedback on different aspects of this book and their mentorship more broadly.

The Environmental Humanities Graduate Program at the University of Utah provided a stimulating interdisciplinary space that helped propel my thinking about environmental concepts and texts. Thanks go to Jeff McCarthy not only for discussing portions of this book with me on many occasions but also for cultivating the environmental humanities (EH) community at the university and in the region, making this such an intellectually exciting place to work. This work also benefited from wide-ranging discussions with the members of the EH Research Interest Group: Brett Clark, Sylvia Torti, Steve Tatum, Andy Hoffman, Carlos Santana, Alejandro Quin, Julia Corbett, Diana Leong, Katharina Gerstenberger, and Jeff McCarthy. Thanks are also due to my EH graduate students who participated in my course on biodiversity narratives and let me test out some of the ideas contained here: Tiana Birrell,

Zak Breckenridge, Laura George, Charity Jessop, Keith Scott, Heather Tourgee, and Cleo Warner.

I have been fortunate to have found a second interdisciplinary family in digital humanities (DH). Though it makes less of an appearance in this book, digital humanities and the DH centers I have been part of have contributed to my modes of scholarship in innumerable ways. Thank you to Digital Matters at the University of Utah. David Roh, Rebekah Cummings, Anna Neatrour, and Marissa Snyder have enriched my thinking on digital culture, digital humanities, and metadata. Thank you to the Center for Digital Humanities at Princeton for being my unofficial hosts and my intellectual home while I was living in New Jersey, especially Natalia Ermolaev, Phillip Gleissner, Claude Willan, and Jean Bauer.

I'd like to thank, at UC Santa Barbara, Tess Shewry, Peter Alagona, Jeremy Douglass, and especially Stephanie LeMenager for their engaged feedback on my work and for their continuing mentorship. My undergraduate years at Stanford were unbelievably enriched by having Ursula Heise as my adviser. I not only took every class she offered but have never stopped following the trails she blazes.

Many peers have given me incredibly valuable feedback on chapters and portions of this book. Diana Leong, Kyle Bucy, Rachel Mason Dentinger, and most especially Roberta Wolfson, who has read nearly as many versions of this book as I have. Without their keen eyes, careful critiques, and the energy of our writing groups, this book would not exist.

I am also tremendously indebted to the anonymous reviewers of this manuscript, whose profound insights and reasoned evaluations were instrumental in pushing me to shape nascent arguments into a coherent whole.

Finally, I would like to sincerely thank the many people who took care of my twin daughters so I had time to write this. It has become a truism in acknowledgments to assert that writing is not the product of a lone effort. Raising children is even less so. I was able to concentrate on this project for uninterrupted hours only because I knew I was leaving my children in the unmatched care of professionals, family, and friends. My deepest gratitude goes to Janet Fredricks Winters, Hannah Winters, Martha Ann Rogers, Manon Bowers, Heather Duggan, Nanda deFigueiredo, Maggie Love, Mike Anderegg, and my parents, Edward and Lynn Callaway. Most of all, I thank my husband, Bill Anderegg, who not only sacrificed his own work hours to cover gaps in childcare while I wrote this but also provided the best interdisciplinary conversations and unwavering encouragement.

A version of chapter 4 was originally published in *Contemporary Literature* 59, no. 2 (2018): 232–60. © by the Board of Regents of the University of Wisconsin System. Reprinted courtesy of the University of Wisconsin Press.

Eden's Endemics

Introduction

Accounting for Biodiversity

Biological diversity must be treated more seriously as a global resource, to be indexed, used, and above all, preserved. Three circumstances conspire to give this matter an unprecedented urgency. First, exploding human populations are degrading the environment at an accelerating rate, especially in tropical countries. Second, science is discovering new uses for biological diversity in ways that can relieve both human suffering and environmental destruction. Third, much of the diversity is being irreversibly lost through extinction caused by the destruction of natural habitats, again especially in the tropics.

—E. O. Wilson, *Biodiversity*

BIODIVERSITY DISCOURSE IS FULL of seemingly straightforward exhortations to stem the irreversible loss of threatened species, genes, and landscapes. Here, the renowned biologist and biodiversity advocate E. O. Wilson clearly states the problem, highlights its urgency, and lists its causes. But what seems like a simple statement with an overabundance of support actually conceals damaging stories about what biodiversity is, what threatens biodiversity, and what is at stake in preserving biodiversity. With its air of dry and unequivocal certainty, this quotation masks a dramatic narrative. The detached tone urges the reader to take its series of claims about biodiversity at face value: biodiversity loss is urgent though not treated seriously enough; it is accelerating; it is irreversible; and it is a problem that is located in the tropics, or at least "especially in the tropics." While Wilson's account originally appears to be a routine statement of mundane fact, it is actually too simple, not much more complicated than an easily digestible children's fairy tale, complete with a protagonist, a villain, and even a damsel in distress.

The character in need of rescue is biodiversity itself, and the practices that are threatening it are an "exploding human population" and "environmental destruction." Wilson locates these villains "especially in the tropics." Here is the first troubling story told in the excerpt: the tropics are a place of danger for biodiversity. The choice to cite a rise in population rather than runaway consumerism as the first threat to biodiversity squarely places the onus of action not on reader-consumers from the United States and the Global North but on people living in the tropics. The other threat to biodiversity, "destruction of natural habitats," is similarly located in the tropics, but the cause of the destruction is glaringly missing. In the absence of a specific claim about demand for palm oil, beef, or soy in the United States and Europe, trade agreements, or neo-imperialist extractive practices, one is left only with the implication that the danger to tropical biodiversity arises from the tropics themselves and the people who live there.

But this troubling conception of the tropics as a place of inherent danger to biodiversity is only one narrative that we need to rethink. In addition, in this quotation Wilson portrays science as the hero and savior of the story. It is telling that the passage positions "human suffering" as a scientific problem rather than a social, ethical, or equity problem: "Science is discovering new uses for biological diversity in ways that can relieve both human suffering and environmental destruction." Human suffering and its relief, then, become simplified. Suffering is now not only a solvable problem but one solvable by a single discipline. The complex affective, emotional, and social process called "suffering" is assumed to be a universal experience that does not account for the cultural variety that may lead different societies to read "suffering" differently. Science is also portrayed as exceptionally potent. Not only is it here described as capable of alleviating human suffering acting all on its own, but science also uses biodiversity to save biodiversity. In this circular narrative where science finds uses for biodiversity that mitigate the "environmental destruction" that decimates biodiversity, science is both a strangely powerful protagonist and a doomed one, needing only the thing it aims to save in order to save it.

This narrative of a savior science rescuing biodiversity from "the tropics" (a surrogate for the Global South in general) is only one of the prevalent narratives told about biodiversity, and in fact it is only one of the narratives running beneath the surface of this quotation. We could also examine the way this excerpt defines biodiversity as a resource and its assumptions about who should have access to this resource. Clearly, this passage is not proposing that biodiversity be preserved for the use of tropics-dwellers to feed large families. Biodiversity's use seems reserved for U.S.-based, Western science. The consequence is that biodiversity is framed as a resource for the enjoyment and enrichment of citizens of the Global North, whose scientific uses for biodiversity are defined as a "non-use" even as different types of use by different groups of people come to be labeled as destructive abuses of the environment. *Eden's Endemics* is fundamentally interested in moments like this, where the choices made in representations of biodiversity have consequences to what spaces, species, and people are positioned as contributing to biodiversity. The project of *Eden's Endemics* is to extend the critical examination, begun here, of the narratives drawn upon when biodiversity is "indexed, used, and above all preserved."

E. O. Wilson is just one scholar offering one perspective on biodiversity, but his work instantiates the types of biodiversity stories that I am tracing in this book. The excerpt that begins this introduction is paradigmatic as one of the first of its kind. It is the opening passage of *Biodiversity*, the book that came out of the first scientific meeting on biodiversity, the National Forum on BioDiversity, which was held in 1986 in Washington, D.C. Three decades after the National Forum on BioDiversity, one can still find prominent examples of biodiversity discourse that resonate with the narratives of Wilson's foundational definition. For example, a section of the World Wildlife Fund's (WWF) 2014 *Living Planet Report* focuses on ecotourism in Virunga national park, a gorilla refuge situated in the Democratic Republic of the Congo on the Ugandan border. In this section of the *Living Planet Report*, threats to biodiverse locations are similarly portrayed as coming from the tropics themselves: "Tourists come from all over the world to see gorillas in their natural habitat, and the revenues help fund gorilla conservation and community projects. Ultimately, local people gain more from preserving their natural resources than from exploiting them in the short term."[1] Although the report does not immediately describe what forms this local "exploitation" takes, several paragraphs later the report points to the practice of fetching drinking water from park streams as the activity that previously endangered gorillas: "Women and children used to collect water from streams within the national parks. Not only was this an arduous and potentially dangerous chore, but the presence of large numbers of people posed a threat to the gorillas and other wildlife."[2]

Fetching drinking water is categorized as a "threat" to animals and ecosystems at the same time that ecotourism is described in hyperbolically positive terms: "Gorilla tourism has transformed communities in the region—like Nkuringo, an isolated mountain town in Uganda. The town is home to the Clouds Mountain Gorilla Lodge, a community owned boutique hotel that welcomes 1,200 guests a year. It directly employs more than 40 people, but the benefits extend to more than 30,000 others living in nearby villages," the report states. This lodge is owned by Jonathan and Pamela Wright, who live outside the Ugandan capital, Kampala, about three hundred miles away.[3] While they may or may not be community members, calling the hotel "community owned" implies that the community itself collectively owns the business. The description of the ownership of the Clouds Mountain Gorilla Lodge and its ability to benefit thirty thousand people while directly employing only forty point to a tendency to amplify the benefits of ecotourism in the discourse of conservation nonprofits like the WWF.

In the 2014 *Living Planet Report*, as in the Wilson excerpt, one type of use (ecotourism, in this case, instead of scientific research) is portrayed as a non-use, whereas other types of use (sustenance) are described as "threats" to the environment. In this formulation, ecotourists are virtuous protectors of the environment who help nature *and* local communities even as they travel for their own enjoyment. They invest in this self-aggrandizing image despite the clear costs to the environment that ecotourism poses in carbon, road building, and infrastructure development. The case of the rhetoric of conservation nonprofits is an especially powerful example of how narratives shape what future biodiversity will look like. Since the WWF is carrying out more than 1,300 conservation projects worldwide, if it (in practice) defines biodiversity as "gorillas plus ecotourists" but not "gorillas plus water fetchers," then that is what protected areas will look like. The WWF will preserve the biodiversity that its story describes, thereby sculpting the world into an image of the story.[4]

These two bookended biodiversity stories—one from the origins of biodiversity and one from its present—are specific instantiations of definitions of biodiversity that spring from the term's more open scientific definition. In the most widely deployed scientific definitions, biodiversity tends to be described in sweeping yet vacuous terms. The United Nations "Convention on Biological Diversity" defines biodiversity as "the variability among living organisms from all sources including . . . terrestrial, marine and other aquatic ecosystems and the ecological complexes of which they are part: this includes diversity within species, between species and of ecosystems."[5] Covering all diversity on all scales, the term is commonly used to denote the variety of life on Earth or within some other designated spatial boundary. As capacious as the term already seems from this overarching definition, scientists now recognize many dimensions of biodiversity that can each be measured in different ways. In addition to classic species diversity measured by a simple sum of species present, one can measure or preserve phylogenetic diversity (which emphasizes evolutionary uniqueness); genetic diversity (which maximizes the diversity of genes); functional diversity (which focuses on the different ecological roles played by species); temporal and spatial diversity (which capture diversity changes throughout time or across space); interaction diversity (which counts the types of interactions between organisms); and landscape diversity (which counts landscape types).[6] The meaning of biodiversity, however, is not found exclusively in scientific definitions; rather, as scholars like Timothy Farnham,[7] David Takacs,[8] and Ursula Heise[9] have shown, biodiversity has become a term with wide-ranging implications outside the sciences.

The bourgeoning subfield of extinction studies furnishes much of the critical conversation around the cultural meanings of species and their loss. Ursula Heise's foundational book *Imagining Extinction* explores the stories that people use to make meaning out of endangered species, the political lives of threatened organisms, and ideas of multispecies justice. Though especially interested in extinction and endangered species, Heise's work also establishes the cultural reach of biodiversity in general, as biodiversity is addressed in databases, laws, and fiction. Other scholars have explored the meanings of species and extinction in a variety of cultural contexts. Thom van Dooren makes present the cultural and ethical repercussions of extinction even as he poetically invokes encounters with endangered organisms themselves.[10] Deborah Bird Rose uses the endangered dingo as a touchstone to investigate the capacity to form ethical relationships with nonhuman others and looks beyond Western cultures when exploring the cultural meanings and relationships between human and nonhuman organisms.[11] These authors and more have shown that biodiversity (within the context of extinction) is not the exclusive province of the sciences but is a term whose meaning is negotiated among all sorts of cultural artifacts.

It remains urgently necessary to extend this fundamental work on extinct and endangered species to considerations of biodiversity as it is described not only in the scientific literature but in wider discourses. Investigating the cultural meanings of the concept of biodiversity—that is, the variety within, among, and between species (and kinds)—comes with its own unique challenges that are somewhat different from considering extinction. In its focus on the meanings of biodiversity *itself*, prior to interrogating extinction, *Eden's Endemics* can be read as complementary to—rather than part of—extinction studies.

One major difficulty that arises when considering biodiversity in particular are the substantial representational challenges of temporal, spatial, and numerical scales. Rob Nixon has cogently argued in *Slow Violence and the Environmentalism of the Poor* that other environmental disasters, like climate change, oil extraction, and the slowly degrading toxins left by war, characterize a type of violence that both exceeds the attention spans cultivated by current spectacle-driven news cycles and also resists traditional representational strategies due to extended timescales and displaced effects.[12] Climate change, in particular, unfolds on more-than-human timescales, while actions taken in one part of the world can have climate consequences thousands of miles away. Jesse Oak Taylor has written about how the idea of climate itself is an abstraction that is difficult to conceptualize and even harder to feel viscerally.[13] Biodiversity creates a similar representational challenge, though to the issues of abstraction, extended timescales, and displaced effects, biodiversity adds overwhelming quantities. If scientists are quick to point out that biodiversity is not "about" any particular array of organisms but instead "about" the *differences between* them, then it is a concept that can only be portrayed by many organisms at once. This means that in order to engage with biodiversity, a text has to do more than focus on a handful of individuals or species (threatened or otherwise). Rather, to conceptualize biodiversity, a text has to engage with dozens, if not hundreds or thousands, of species (or other groupings of kinds).

In assembling this book's archive to reflect the narratives we use to understand biodiversity, I selected media objects that gather together appearances of hundreds or thousands of kinds of organisms, or else feature entire planets' worth of creatures. The texts I consider take on the representational obstacle of numerical scale by narrating species in their multitudes. This considerable challenge is aligned with that of "big data" in that biodiversity may be an object that is simply too big to be condensed into any one media object. Even texts that portray thousands of kinds of organisms barely scratch the surface of the millions of kinds of living beings that reside on Earth. The objects I consider take up this perhaps insurmountable representational challenge and, in the process, draw upon narratives and genres that affect how people perceive species and spaces.

At the broadest scale, this book contends that the ways in which we talk about environmental concepts affect how those concepts frame the world and then work to remake the world to fit their image. In Karen Barad's terms, narrative functions like the "apparatuses" she examines, which makes sense, since she argues that "apparatuses *are* discursive practices" that "enact what matters and what is excluded from mattering."[14] Biodiversity narratives perform "agential cuts" to create discrete entities with determinate boundaries out of the indeterminate, never-separate intra-acting phenomena. These perceived entities then have properties and can be accounted for in environmental decisions. The discursive formulations that environmental discourses draw upon are important to what is visible and what remains invisible of the nonhuman others who share our planet; they create the "conditions of possibility and impossibility of mattering."[15] This book is an argument for a careful reading of the narratives and genres employed (often unknowingly) to talk about environmental concepts (like biodiversity) and a call to question whether those formal choices achieve the desired results. Are our current environmental narratives making visible the organisms and places we find valuable in the natural world? Are they creating a just discussion of what we value? What "we's" are invited to the conversation?

On a finer scale, I choose to query biodiversity as an environmental concept not only because (along with climate change, sustainability, and the Anthropocene) it is one of the dominant frameworks through which we understand the more-than-human world but also because it registers many of the effects of the other current major environmental crises. The consequences of environmental degradation are felt most keenly in their devastation of living systems. Climate change, for example, is a concern in that it impacts living systems. Although the physics and the chemistry of climate change can be fascinating, the consequences that people tend to care about most are its effects on living beings (human and otherwise). Similarly, the land use changes, diversion of sediment, atomic testing, and distribution of species that all potentially mark the Anthropocene in the geological record (in addition to rising atmospheric carbon dioxide levels) are troubling in their impact on planetary life. In examining the stories that are intertwined with biodiversity, this project interrogates the tropes we use to understand a foundational concept that encompasses what is most valued in the more-than-human world.

The title of this book references two of the specific tropes drawn upon often in biodiversity discourse: the golden-age paradise (Eden) and endemism (which pays attention to endemic species: species that are found in only one location on Earth). These widely used tropes highlight "the tropics" as a synecdoche for the Global South, then reify those tropical places, defining them exclusively as places of nature and biodiversity. Using the frame of endemic species combined with Edenic myths, common descriptions of biodiversity locate diversity exclusively in sites imagined as island paradises (whether these be real islands or remote continental ecosystems). This not only limits the meanings of biodiversity, establishing biodiversity as something that is located far away from daily activities in the Global North, but it also limits the meanings of these locations themselves. At the same time as biodiversity becomes a problem that is solved somewhere else, these narratives also conveniently make islands into little biodiversity reservoirs for the enjoyment of denizens of Europe and North America. My title also draws attention to the world-encompassing aspirations of biodiversity surveys bequeathed to them by the concept's roots in imperial natural history. Since biblical tradition holds that every species was represented in Eden, then Eden's endemics would be the entire biota of Earth, the naming and indexing of which continues to be a priority for scientific biodiversity research today.

While the title references biodiversity's affiliation with natural history, *Eden's Endemics* argues that current mobilizations of biodiversity tend to draw upon another register simultaneously: that of science fiction. One can detect these two genres of natural history and science fiction in the E. O. Wilson quotation with which I began this introduction. The idea that biodiversity is a resource that must be "indexed" and "used" comes straight from colonial natural history, the project of which was to index and organize the entire natural world for the use and profit of the colonizing power.[16] At the same time, the quotation strays into the realm of science fiction when Wilson projects imagined futures. Depicting population as exploding at an accelerating rate extrapolates demographic trends into the future (a projection that proved accurate in the decades since Wilson wrote the passage but at the time was still a speculative forecast). Similarly, the description of science as finding new uses for biodiversity posits a future where biodiversity has provided science with unimaginable insights into the natural world as well as the human body, as human suffering is also relieved in this future.

The opening quotation flirts with science-fictional imaginings that are developed more fully in other texts examined in *Eden's Endemics* as well as in Wilson's later work. One of Wilson's repeated tropes in later writing is a thought experiment in which he imagines sentient alien life arriving on Earth.[17] In his 2014 book *The Meaning of Human Existence*, he writes extensively of these hypothetical alien visitors: "The extraterrestrial visitors would know [much], from robot probes and the principles of evolutionary biology. They could not immediately fathom Earth's full history of organic evolution, with its extinctions, replacements, and dynastic rise and fall of major groups—cycads, ammonoids, dinosaurs. But with their super-efficient fieldwork and DNA-sequencing and proteonomic technology, they would quickly learn Earth's fauna and flora at the present moment, and the nature and ages of forerunners, and calculate patterns in space and time of life's evolutionary history."[18] The alien visitors and their methods of discovery (robot probes, advanced proteonomics, interstellar travel) are straight out of science fiction. However, the natural history of the first quotation runs under the surface of this excerpt as well. The passage allows Wilson the opportunity to paint a brief, sweeping portrait of the history of biodiversity on Earth. Instead of focusing on the spatial distribution of biodiversity as "especially in the tropics," this minicensus focuses on temporal variation from early cycads to current flora and fauna but makes similar claims about the importance of biodiversity. The alien visitors' enthusiasm for generating knowledge about life on Earth bestows biodiversity with universal (or at least galactic) interest. Simultaneously, the passage implicitly rebukes human societies for knowing so little about the history, trends, and diversity of life on their own planet. Moreover, Wilson's hypothetical aliens are natural historians par excellence who survey current life, look for patterns, and glean insight about evolutionary history from current configurations. The combination of science fiction and natural history allows Wilson to imagine biodiversity as an attribute of ecosystems that preexists its discovery, needing only more advanced techniques to be adequately quantified and turned into useful information.

In the texts I examine throughout the chapters of *Eden's Endemics,* biodiversity is thought of in the same modes of natural history and science fiction. Biodiversity is described as existing in colonial island paradises, consisting of a perfectly balanced nature, and located in re-created Edens *at the same time* as it is imagined in terms of apocalyptic futures or as a terraforming project. In specific instances, the media examined in this book combine the two registers into powerful conceits. Biodiversity is at times a mechanism of time travel to the precise moment of first European, colonial contact with a landscape and at other times an updated book of nature: a living database of pure information that must be preserved to protect future scientific discoveries.

While the "book of nature" is an idea straight from natural history, I see this impulse to view biodiversity as *information* rather than a feature of *embodied organisms* as a version of the science-fiction dream/nightmare of the downloaded consciousness, a trope that appears in early cyberpunk fiction like William Gibson's *Neuromancer* (1984)[19] as well as recent speculative fiction like Neal Stephenson's *Fall; or, Dodge in Hell* (2019).[20] In these works, characters' personalities and memories, their very essences, are uploaded to computers through "brain scanning" or other means. There they solve problems, build worlds, and live forever or beg to be shut off. Just as the human self is here preserved as informational patterns in digital code, there is a tendency to view the essence of biodiversity as bodiless information that is contained within (but independent from) the plant, animal, and microbe bodies that make up biodiversity. Usually the type of information that an organism is depicted as containing is either genetic information (useful genes that can be spliced into other organisms) or evolutionary history (information that gives scientists a picture of the history of life on Earth). This view of biodiversity as information is predicated on the conception of information *itself* as bodiless—independent of any material instantiation, as critiqued by N. Katherine Hayles in *How We Became Posthuman*. In her telling of "how information lost its body,"[21] she begins by dissecting a proposal by Hans Moravec that echoes the uploaded consciousness of *Neuromancer*—that human consciousness could, in fact, be stored on a computer. Hayles goes on to show how this proposition is thinkable only if information is already conceived of as bodiless and human identity is conceptualized as patterns of information rather than embodied enaction, which she points out are drastically diminished ways to think about both information and identity. In *How We Became Posthuman*, Hayles traces and critiques the contours of this disembodiment project as it was executed in the seams between the production of engineering-oriented conceptual models of communication and the birth of cybernetics.

The same worldview that considers human identity as something that could be adequately captured by information stored on computer chips undergirds the imagination that animals, plants, and other organisms could be converted and stored as information. Throughout *Eden's Endemics* we will see how eclipsing embodiment omits absolutely vital aspects of biodiversity. My reading of these moments aligns with Hayles's own analysis when she writes:

> Information, like humanity, cannot exist apart from the embodiment that brings it into being as a material entity in the world; and embodiment is always instantiated, local, and specific. Embodiment can be destroyed, but it cannot be replicated. Once the specific form constituting it is gone, no amount of massaging data will bring it back. This observation is as true of the planet as it is of an individual life-form. As we rush to explore the new vistas that cyberspace has made available for colonization, let us remember the fragility of a material world that cannot be replaced.[22]

The erasure of embodiment in favor of preserving biodiversity-as-information not only acts as an analgesic to extinction, which is a loss of embodied existence that "no amount of massaging data will bring back," but it also takes an impoverished view of what constitutes an organism, missing critical processes like lively interactions with other organisms.

This conceptualization of the living bodies that make up biodiversity as vessels of information has consequences beyond the diminished conception of the living organism. The erasure of embodiment is accompanied by a turn away from the agency of nonhuman beings. When biodiversity preservation projects view a plant or animal as a container of genetic information or vessel for information about evolutionary history, they cultivate an image of an organism that filters out the myriad ways that embodied beings exert agency. While the "material turn" that has become so prominent in many disciplines recognizes a nature that can "punch back,"[23] it is difficult for human beings to register this agency *as* agency when any action that a body may take is conceptually subordinate to the information a body contains. A plant seed saved in the seed banks I describe in chapter 1 is an agential being that can confound human expectations in all sorts of ways: by not germinating, by germinating at a time not intended by human collaborators, by succumbing to mold, by growing into a plant that hybridizes with another, etc. But if the plant is viewed fundamentally as information carried in genes, these agential intra-actions will appear meaningless (and perhaps even imperceptible) to the seed bank operators. This results in the fantasy that seeds can be saved in isolation, without accompanying bodies absolutely fundamental to the production of healthy adult plants (symbiotic microbes, pollinating insects, and more).

Given that one of the main consequences of drawing upon natural historical and science-fictional tropes when representing biodiversity is an erasure of embodiment, this book enters into a critical conversation around posthumanist theory. This critical posthumanism is in direct opposition to the type of uploaded-consciousness-posthumanism N. Katherine Hayles critiques and is instead aligned with Hayles's own position on the importance of embodiment. Even within Hayles's own book, she uses different valences of posthuman that vary from Moravec's posthuman to the embodied posthuman of someone like Cary Wolfe, whose work is "posthuman*ist,* in the sense that it opposes the fantasies of disembodiment and autonomy, inherited from humanism itself."[24] Hayles writes:

If my nightmare is a culture inhabited by posthumans who regard their bodies as fashion accessories rather than the ground of being, my dream is a version of the posthuman that embraces the possibilities of information technologies without being seduced by fantasies of unlimited power and disembodied immortality, that recognizes and celebrates finitude as a condition of human being, and that understands human life is embedded in a material world of great complexity, one on which we depend for our continued survival.[25]

This "dream" version of posthumanism is shared by those proponents of critical posthumanism who view the theory as a corrective to the failures of classic humanism which (among other things) relies on a view of the human being as distinct from everything else (from animals, machines, etc.), as a uniquely agential being, as the center of all things, as capable of knowing all, and as a type of being who shares a common essential core with all other humans.[26] The variety of posthumanism that works against the assumptions of humanism does not dream of escaping the materiality of the body but works toward "decentering the human in relation to either evolutionary, ecological, or technological coordinates" through a variety of means including the recognition of nonhuman agency.[27] According to Rosi Braidotti, "a common denominator for the posthuman condition is an assumption about the vital, self-organizing and yet non-naturalistic structure of living matter itself,"[28] and as such is in line with my own project in *Eden's Endemics*.

In particular, *Eden's Endemics* is in conversation with an area of inquiry related to the critical posthumanism that Wolfe and others write within: new materialisms. Like posthumanism, new materialisms works to undercut the binary oppositions on which humanism rested. As Neil Badmington articulates, posthumanism, following Jacques Derrida and others, aims to dismantle the separation of "human/inhuman, self/other, natural/cultural, inside/outside, subject/object, us/them, here/there, active/passive, and wild/tame."[29] In the introduction to their collection, *Material Feminisms*, Stacy Alaimo and Susan Hekman similarly position new materialisms in a tradition of disassembling binary oppositions, writing: "Postmodern feminists have argued that the male/female dichotomy informs all the dichotomies that ground Western thought: culture/nature, mind/body, subject/object, rational/emotional, and countless others."[30] In their evaluation, new feminist materialism works against the last dualism left standing: the language/reality opposition. Instead, they and others view materialization as a complex and open process that is a question of both meaning and matter. Language and matter engage in a mutual dance of becoming—neither precedes the other. Discourse does not create objects from nothing, nor are there specks of matter out there, already discrete, "whirling aimlessly in the void, bereft of agency, historicity, or meaning, which are only to be bestowed from the outside,"[31] but instead all is a mutual intra-action, in the terms of the physicist and theorist Karen Barad. "Matter is not a thing but a congealing of agency" that happens *through* relating.[32]

For the conceptualization of biodiversity, new materialist formulations of matter and agency have immense consequences. The definition of biodiversity in the UN's "Convention on Biological Diversity" as "the variability among living organisms from all sources" presupposes the existence of discrete entities out in the world, separate, preexisting, and awaiting relations with one another on the basis of variation. In this view, biodiversity is a number, a measurement that merely reflects the amount of variation that preexists the act of measuring. Reading new materialisms onto biodiversity results in a very different conceptualization of the living world, one that not only counters fantasies of disembodiment but that holds space open for recognizing the liveliness of nonhuman others in a mutual congealing of agency.

The soil out of which this book grows has been mulched by Karen Barad's rejection of the notion that there are bits of matter "out there," discrete, with preformed attributes awaiting discovery; by Stacy Alaimo's dismantling of bodily and social boundaries through transcorporeality; by Jane Bennett's attention to the liveliness of matter and the "small agencies" of often ignored creatures; by Elizabeth Grosz's recuperation of contingency, chance, and play in Darwin's works; and by Donna Haraway's exploration of the "subject- and object-shaping dance of encounters" between species.[33] Though I do not use biodiversity to propose my own new materialist theory, I do employ existing work by these thinkers as a lens through which to reconsider the concept of biodiversity. In the end, I view biodiversity as a negotiation process where narratives, organisms, humans, and nonhumans all entangle in an accounting for what matters.

Starting from the premise that biodiversity is not a final measurement of living variety out there "waiting" to be discovered, I critique not only the idea of biodiversity as information bereft of both body and agency but also another prevalent conceptualization used when describing species in their multitudes. In *Eden's Endemics,* I assert that in addition to being portrayed as bodiless information, biodiversity turns into a narrative technology for reproducing power differentials. As my opening quotation and my title suggest, the registers drawn upon when representing biodiversity make it into a planetary feature that is most visible in the tropics; at the same time, any causes of biodiversity loss that stem from outside the tropics are obscured, as we saw in the WWF's disregard of the environmental costs of ecotourism. And since biodiversity is not merely descriptive, but prescriptive, as far as it is a concept used for conservation projects carried out in physical places, the narrative choices made when describing biodiversity impact what is visible, what is visceral, and what is unquestioned common sense about the patterns of life on Earth.

In revealing the way biodiversity discourse essentializes the Global South into the place from which biodiversity both comes and is threatened, I argue that the kind of imperial conservation projects thoroughly critiqued by scholars like Ramachandra Guha[34] and William Cronon[35] are not gone, merely transformed. The people who live most closely with prized nonhuman ecosystems are not forcefully removed to make the land "empty" for national parks, wildlife refuges, and the like, but these people are still implicitly blamed for environmental degradation. Although the WWF provided drinking water for communities rather than blocking their access to streams, the implicit narratives contained in its publications keep alive the idea that those harming the environment are the local communities living closest to species of conservation interest (rather than globe-trotting ecotourists). In the media I examine, science-fictional and natural-historical imaginings of biodiversity position the Global South as a place of inherent danger while also associating biodiversity with places remote from Western civilization—both Edenic islands full of unusual endemic species and primordial pasts imagined just before the moment of European "discovery."

Eden's Endemics is invested in pursuing both tropes of disembodiment and essentialization that appear repeatedly in different manifestations when accounting for species in their multitudes. The first two chapters of the book trace two examples of preservation projects that position biodiversity as information and portray it as either existing in a perilous Global South or originating from a simplified golden age. The following two chapters investigate literary projects that both engage a wide variety of organisms and aim to keep present the embodiment of organisms by modeling stances toward species and ecosystems that remain open to nonhuman agency. Despite the success at keeping bodies present, these texts continue to portray biodiversity as existing in pre-Western Edens and faraway colonial islands. The final chapter turns inward to focus on the biodiversity within, exploring how the microbiome disrupts both notions of biodiversity as information and the idea that biodiversity is remote.

In an effort to address a uniquely expansive subject (the variety of life on Earth), the chapters of this book are organized to make sure I sample widely along a number of axes. *Eden's Endemics* simultaneously covers five major ways environmentalists, scientists, and writers engage with living variety. The activities through which the meaning of biodiversity is negotiated include preservation (chapter 1); organization (chapter 2); consumption (chapter 3); imagination (of alternative biodiversities) (chapter 4); and being biodiversity ourselves (chapter 5). At the same time, I'm interested in surveying across different metrics by which biodiversity is measured. Therefore, the chapters also respectively critique four ways to scientifically measure biodiversity as genetic diversity (chapter 1); evolutionary diversity (chapter 2); simple species count (chapter 3); and endemism (chapter 4). Chapter 5 covers one of the major omissions from these other types of biodiversity measurements, namely the symbiotic microbes that live within the other organisms counted. By drawing upon arrays of activity and metric, I cover many dimensions of biodiversity as a material and cultural process at once.

Because the human activities and measurement techniques surrounding biodiversity happen across different arenas (science-fiction novels describe alternative biodiversities whereas seed banks preserve living variety), this book also samples along a third axis, the spectrum of media types in which masses of species can be found. I interrogate databases, born digital scientific visualizations, memoirs, science-fiction novels, poetry, and popular science books. Many of these media have become fundamentally important to biodiversity activities, while others I am newly bringing to the investigation of cultural meanings of biodiversity. Databases, for example, have become a foundational medium through which we think biodiversity (as Geoffrey Bowker[36] and Ursula Heise[37] have noted), such that any consideration of biodiversity would feel incomplete without some consideration of the database. Similarly, evolutionary trees that show vast swaths of planetary life not only are fundamental for scientific frameworks of the diversity of planetary life but also undergird popular conservation paradigms. However, this type of visualization has been written about very little in relation to the cultural meanings of biodiversity it advances.

In terms of literary texts, I continue to choose the examples and genres that mention the most species possible. Memoirs written by competitive birders narrate the sightings of hundreds of bird species to fashion successive encounters with species into an accumulated experience of biodiversity. Science-fiction texts, on the other hand, model encounters with entire planets' worth of living variety all at once. Popular science, poetry, and fiction on the microbiome not only mention thousands of species that live within each of us but also ask readers to think of themselves as diverse ecosystems. These media are dissimilar in some ways but are all connected by the fact that they take on the representational challenge of depicting species in their multitudes. Moreover, we will see that these diverse media use the convergent techniques of drawing upon both science fiction and natural history to think through living variety on this planet.

Throughout, I'm interested in how the narrative conventions of certain genres bear upon their representational practices regarding biodiversity. Accordingly, although my subject of study is largely located in the biological and environmental sciences, my methods are not. My literary interpretive approach is the most effective to probe the formal choices made in the presentation of enormous portions of planetary life not only in literary texts but also in scientific and digital objects. By reading the formal choices made by database designers and conservation biologists, I am also making a methodological argument as I translate literary analysis across domains. Many scholars have already noted that the growing fields of ecological digital humanities[38] and ecological media studies are, as Allison Carruth puts it, "expanding the parameters of environmental culture by addressing not only literary texts but also visual art, performance, new media, activist ephemera, popular science, ethnographies, and scientific models."[39] Environmental problems demand widening modes of engagement from humanities disciplines, as the efforts to address and explain environmental challenges do not exclusively appear in literary texts (or any other type of text) but across many sorts of media and platforms. These media can be formative for how people conceive of the environment, nonhuman organisms, and the complex problems that now confront us. Part of what makes this expansion of the field so indispensable is that scholars now study media that would otherwise escape critical examination, media that tell fundamental and world-shaping stories. As a literary scholar I am invested in interrogating the consequences of the narratives, genres, metaphors, analogies, and themes that environmentally oriented media use to tell us about the world. I believe that visual objects, like evolutionary trees, and interactive digital objects, like databases, are similar to "literary" texts in that they tell stories that are shaped by formal choices made during their construction. These formal features are the focus of this work, which follows the example of scholars like Stacy Alaimo,[40] Ursula Heise,[41] Stephanie LeMenager,[42] Heather Houser,[43] and Allison Carruth[44] in constructing an archive that brings together print and digital media, scientific and artistic works, and established and unfamiliar "texts."

My method for examining these diverse media does not take for granted the separation of the material world from the ways we have of talking about it but instead explores how these items coproduce each other and the many tensions and negotiations between them. Instead of a static final number or result, I consider biodiversity a process: an accounting for the world where matter and discourse entangle to coproduce the more-than-human world. This term, "accounting," is an important one for this book, and it works for the project on at least four levels. First of all, it captures the counting side of traditional definitions of biodiversity. That is, biodiversity as a numerical representation that can be calculated and compared between locations and times. But an account is also a story or narrative ("she began his account of what had happened at Netherfield"),[45] an assumption of responsibility for conduct ("What need we fear who knows it, when none can call our power to account?"),[46] and a designation of importance ("the gentleman may be of great account").[47] Biodiversity emerges in all these valences of the word: through tallies, stories, efforts to take responsibility, and attempts to make matter. Accounting also highlights the *process* through which things come to matter rather than a calcified product that finally does.

Because of my subject matter and method, the geographical and temporal boundaries for this analysis are somewhat more capacious than traditional field designations. Although the word "biodiversity" first rose to prominence in the United States in the late 1980s, this book cannot be said to be exclusively "twentieth-century American" in content. Biodiversity as it is enacted today has grown out of eighteenth-century British natural history and is portrayed in contemporary discourse as concentrated in the Global South, as E. O. Wilson's opening quote suggests. Therefore, the temporal scope of *Eden's Endemics* ranges from Darwin's journals from the nineteenth century to microbiome nonfiction released in 2016, taking its archive from both American and British sources and examining how these paradigms of biodiversity are then enacted on the rest of the world. While biodiversity is theoretically extranational, defined by intergovernmental science bodies (for example, the United Nations Decade on Biodiversity, Rio +20, or the Intergovernmental Panel on Biodiversity and Ecosystem Services), its conservation is often a U.S. and northern European program carried out in other regions. Similarly, the "we" I have been using reflects this range of biodiversity, including anyone (such as myself) who is invested in or aware of the biodiversity concept as it is defined and exercised by these intergovernmental science bodies or carried out by conservation nonprofits. Consequently, while this book's geographical range and therefore also its "we" are shaped by and reflect the complex and, in many ways, transnational cultures of contemporary biology, I maintain an awareness that these "international" cultures are very often U.S./northern European paradigms adopted, resisted, or ignored by other parts of the world. While I focus on U.S. and British archives, I also analyze biodiversity's engagement with the Global South, and in doing so my framework negotiates both national and extranational contexts. There are, of course, many "we's" who have never invested in the concept of biodiversity as it has been articulated in the scientific definitions and the cultural media I examine here and are therefore exempt from the critique I aim at those of us who have perhaps uncritically accepted biodiversity discourse at face value in the past. This book takes seriously the widespread but not universal paradigms of biodiversity and investigates in detail the kinds of futures they enable and foreclose. At the same time, my choice of an archive, especially in my chapters on global seed banks and science fiction's speculative ecosystems, pushes the boundaries of the concept of biodiversity up against its colonial roots and future possibilities, questioning what it means to frame the world, "especially the tropics," in this U.S. and British-scientific paradigm.

I begin, in chapter 1, by seeking out biodiversity in both metropolitan London and the frozen expanse of the Arctic Circle, examining the preservation of plant species at the global seed banks of the Kew Royal Botanical Gardens and the Svalbard Global Seed Vault. The global seed banks' architecture, websites, and databases blend the genres of natural-history writing with apocalyptic literature to create a portrait of the world where the Global South is a place of inherent risk to ecosystems and local seed banks. Seed bank preservation projects take plants out of the habitats in which they grow and symbolically transform the physical seeds into bodiless information repositories. The seeds are treated as miniature databases of potentially useful genes, infinitely malleable and inert. This loss of materiality is essential for the seed bank narrative of a world saved through genetic technologies, but it poses challenges to the feasibility of seed banks' own speculative future restoration projects.

Chapter 2 reads the "tree of life" in its current instantiation as the evolutionary supertree, a type of visualization published regularly in scientific journals depicting vast swaths of living organisms on Earth. These trees, one of the only mediums that displays thousands of species at once, act as the origin story for biodiversity itself. But formal choices made in their construction lead to trees that are predisposed to jettison contingency and chance from the story of life. The final result of this dwindled past is the depiction of an Edenic golden age, a simpler time that is completely represented by current arrays of species. These trees also undergird an increasingly widespread conservation paradigm—that of phylogenetic diversity, where the evolutionary uniqueness of a species determines its protection priority. This type of accounting for life figures the loss of a species as the loss of evolutionary history rather than as the loss of embodied enaction. Evolutionary history turns out to be recoverable even once a species is gone, meaning that these trees end up acting as an analgesic for species loss.

Taken together, chapters 1 and 2 explore episodes of dematerialization of biodiversity. Both seed banks and evolutionary trees favor a conceptualization of biodiversity as information that is transferrable between different substrates with very little loss of meaning. Aggregating thousands of species in databases and visualizations leads to a perceptible disregard for the agency of the organisms and individuals that comprise these aggregates. Positioning seeds and creatures as containers of useful genes or evolutionary history downplays the life-worlds that these organisms enact in their embodied forms, diminishing the potential of the conservation paradigms that rely on seed banks and supertrees. The following two chapters of the book look to projects that attempt to overcome the disembodying tendencies of biodiversity discourse detailed in the first two chapters. Chapters 3 and 4 take up a series of literary texts (birder memoirs and science-fiction novels) that experiment with different ways to keep the embodiment of organisms present while at the same time portraying species in their multitudes. While these texts do address embodiment and nonhuman agency, they continue, in places, to portray the Global South as an inherently biodiverse and threatening place.

Chapter 3 delves into the extraordinary world of competitive birding, where a deep love for avian life is intertwined with an insatiable drive to spot unusual bird species at surprising costs to humans and birds. By analyzing how birder memoirs list and represent different bird species, I foreground the numerical accounting aspect of biodiversity and tease out some of the consequences of this association between birds and numbers. But arithmetic is only one way these memoirists account for birds. Each bird is also a story, an experience that the birders cherish, remember, and recount. At the same time, it is an experience that is available for purchase. These birders spend their money on the memorable experience of traveling to remote locations to see birds. This chapter argues that consuming the experience of seeing biodiversity is a complex and paradoxical activity that seeks meaningful interactions with nonhuman others while also providing an opportunity to tell ourselves stories about who we are through the purchase of interesting experiences.

Chapter 4 voyages beyond Earth, examining the alternative worlds of science-fiction texts that map out the narrative space in which we conceptualize potential meanings of biodiversity. Frank Herbert's *Dune* and Orson Scott Card's *Speaker for the Dead* both feature planetary ecosystems that are imagined from the ground up with inner workings very distinct from those on Earth. Both novels ask what biodiversity would look like if it were considered a stance toward the world, a curious engagement rather than an attribute ready for measurement. The two novels turn disorientation, a mechanism by which science fiction works, toward nonhuman species with promising results. The possibilities of this puzzled accounting, however, are undermined by the fact that these ecosystems have tidy solutions. The answer to the puzzle of these speculative ecosystems turns out to be related to the persistent myth of a perfectly balanced nature that rehashes the colonial trope of the island paradise. *Speaker for the Dead*, however, employs this trope in order to critique balance itself as a product of colonial engineering.

Chapter 5 confounds both impressions of biodiversity as information and formulations of biodiversity as existing primarily in the tropics. Burgeoning interest in the microbiome (human and otherwise) in research and popular science has put biodiversity into a fractal moment. Each macroscopic creature that is traditionally thought of as comprising a component of biodiversity is itself a diverse ecosystem. The human microbiome, as it appears in popular science, recent poetry, and a cyberpunk novel, shows that conceptions of biodiversity as disembodied information and as located in the Global South are fallacies. This "biodiversity within" might compensate for the incorporeal and exoticizing tendencies I examine in the preceding four chapters. Considering the microbiome as both a domestic diversity that distributes human agency and as a site of exchange between species and the wider environment, chapter 5 investigates a transcorporeal model of biodiversity where species "become together" in a provisional, contingent accounting for each other.

I end with a coda on the "Night Train" chapter of David Mitchell's novel *Ghostwritten*. This text brings together natural history and science fiction in a character that is both a satellite-based artificial intelligence and an enthusiastically detailed observer of nature. "Night Train" revisits many of the themes from the other media examined in *Eden's Endemics* but uses its mix of science fiction and natural history to invert the typical operations of biodiversity discourse, disembodying the biodiversity cataloguer instead of the organisms catalogued and subverting expectations that the Global South be a place of pristine and unchanging nature threatened only by local inhabitants.

Although this book uncovers many issues with biodiversity discourse, I am not arguing that the term should be jettisoned. Some scholars, including Nicolae Morar, Ted Toadvine, and Brendan Bohannan do propose that we abandon "biodiversity" and instead start from the ground up, developing a new term that more adequately captures what we value in nature.[48] They argue that biodiversity's veneer of scientific objectivity, combined with the normative good that "diversity" implies and the term's vague definition that morphs depending on context, is too much to overcome and thus that the term cannot be rehabilitated. In addition, they argue that biodiversity misidentifies what we value in nature, cogently reasoning that the term mistakenly locates our values in the *diversity* of nature rather than in the organisms themselves. While I agree that many people do find value in the "organisms themselves," my archive (comprised as it is exclusively of works that examine a great variety of species) shows that there are many circumstances where the *variety* of types of organisms rather than any particular set of organisms is precisely what is sought after. In addition, I believe that we would be hard-pressed to find a term that does not carry any normative weight. The authors' own suggestion of "biocomplexity" carries the normative good of "complexity" despite their claim that complexity is good, bad, or neutral depending on the context. As chapter 2 explores, when it comes to nature, complexity in life has been a normative good. In fact, "complexity" has often been the metric by which orders of life are visualized (and valued) hierarchically, with more "complex" creatures toward the top of the hierarchy and humans sitting triumphantly atop the "complexity" chain.

In addition, Morar and others compellingly show that biodiversity "cannot, as a matter of principle be quantified, due to its multidimensionality and the lack of commensurability and covariance among its components." They conclude that "since we cannot measure biodiversity per se, we lack any empirical foundation for testing hypotheses about it or using it in any management or conservation decisions."[49] Yet rather than discard the term, I argue that the fact that biodiversity can never be measured either directly or by proxy might actually be a productive aspect of the concept, an opening to consider biodiversity as a process of meaning negotiation rather than a solidified attribute. As Moira Gatens argues about the body, we can imagine that biodiversity "does not have a 'truth' or a 'true' nature since it is a process and its meaning and capacities will vary according to its context."[50] Throughout this book I consider biodiversity in the same way, as a process whose meaning emerges through unfolding intra-actions and varies according to context.

I also recognize that the concept of biodiversity is very good at certain kinds of inclusions. In particular, biodiversity is useful in accounting for those living organisms that we do care about but we don't know about. Practically every reader will be familiar with the commonly cited fact that the world is losing species that scientists haven't even discovered yet. Caring about or protecting "biodiversity" covers those species that have not been described by Western science. But biodiversity works this way on a more prosaic level as well. Invoking "biodiversity" as an area of concern rather than a list of species or ecosystems includes those organisms or relationships in an ecosystem that are known, but that the invoker may not know about. Biodiversity is a way of including the overflowing abundance of life that exceeds any one person's ability to know: a way of accounting for more than we can list. It's about the excess that burgeons out of what we know we care about. It is what we care about and *don't* know about. Biodiversity is a way of accounting, and that has often meant that it is a form of calcifying certain narratives, locations, and histories as being "about" biodiversity, while others are excluded. An inquisitive engagement with this excess of what we don't know and can never completely know may adjust some of the more damaging biodiversity narratives critiqued in this work and foster a new, more inclusive form of caring for what we do not know.

In the end, I hope that the reading of biodiversity in *Eden's Endemics* will open up new engagements with species in their multitudes. The analyses especially in the final three chapters of the book model different kinds of engagements with nonhuman others that all leave space open for recognizing the agency not only of individual creatures but vast swaths of planetary life—thousands of sequential encounters with agential birds, globally distributed puzzling ecosystems, and our own microbial selves. Moreover, I am inspired by Stacy Alaimo's claim that "material feminism opens up new ethical and political vistas . . . discourses have material consequences that require ethical responses."[51] In this book I critique discourses that have material consequences to what will be valued and preserved for future worlds and how that preservation operates. It is my hope that exposing the significant costs that are felt by seeds, tortoises, birds, microbes, and the human communities that live with these creatures will prompt new engagements with nonhuman multitudes. This engagement might be informed by the stances tentatively modeled in moments captured by birders, science-fiction authors, and microbiome poets who gesture toward ways to account for biodiversity differently.

1   Natural History at the End of the World

Seed Banks, Database, Apocalypse

ANDERSON LAKE STANDS in the Thai market entranced, untouched by the bustle around him. Before him, an old woman at a stall is selling a fruit he has never seen. All his senses are focused on this fruit: its hairs tickle his palm, its floral scent fills his nose, his eyes scour its surface for slight gradations of color. Finally he tastes it, with eyes closed, rolling it around in his mouth, feeling its texture and the sharp bite of flavor in a lifetime of blandness. Only once this sensory experience is over does he think about what the appearance of this fruit means. He pockets the seed and sets his jaw in determination: the Thai Kingdom must have a hidden seed bank, and it's his job to find it.

This opening scene from Paolo Bacigalupi's *The Windup Girl* introduces many of the ways that this speculative-fiction novel will engage with the issues of seed banks, plant genetics, and biopiracy. The opening passages wonderfully bring to the table the materiality of fruit, as well as some of fruit's less obvious meanings. The fruit is not only a body interacting with other bodies through taste, touch, and scent, but it is also memory, history, and the unknown. The first sweet tang of the pulp on Anderson Lake's tongue calls forward the memory of his first taste of candy, drawing attention to the way taste and aroma chemically interact with the human brain to powerfully evoke memories. But this fruit is more than just personal history; it is a resurrection of an entire historical moment. In the novel, extinction has put whole genera out of reach and with them whole ways of life, unique adaptations, and strategies for survival. This fruit represents a lost world; Lake "might as well be hefting a sack of trilobites."[1] Comparing the fruit to trilobites brings up associations of deep time and primeval worlds, emphasizing how the resurrection of this one fruit carries with it the afterimage of an entire lost world rather than just a single species growing in isolation. Importantly, this fruit is also a mystery. On one level, it is a religious mystery, a signal of "Eden's return,"[2] but it is also an impossible puzzle. It resists Lake's impulse to know and master. He wishes he could see it growing in place, see the leaves, the stems, the rest of the plant. Then he could at least have a clue as to its origins, its nearest plant relatives, its place on the evolutionary tree. But the fruit itself makes none of this available to him; it doesn't provide information but rather simply is. It exists beyond his complete command of information, and he is forced to recognize this. However, once the fruit is eaten, Anderson Lake unceremoniously pockets the seed as if it contains nothing but answers. Unlike fruit, seeds in this book do not evoke memory, do not stimulate touch or smell, do not embody ancient lost worlds; they are simply information accessible to those with enough gall to take it.

When the novel culminates in an image of monks in saffron robes carrying boxes of seeds into the jungle to reassemble the underground seed bank in a new, safe location, one cannot help but wonder why the seeds are portrayed as inert enough to survive this hot, humid trip. For a novel so invested in the materiality and sensuality of fruit, the accompanying seeds are portrayed as remarkably inert. In reality, seeds are not casings for bodiless data that will remain dormant until needed; rather, they are bodies that are subject to decay, mold, insect predation, and sprouting. Interestingly, this portrayal of seeds in the science-fiction novel matches the way real-world global seed banks treat seeds in their publications and databases. The novel falls into the very same trope of seeds as static containers-of-genes on which massive seed banks rely.

But there is a twin omission from the end of the novel: the database. Although the seeds themselves may be saved from AgriGen Corporation by yellow-robed monks, one of those monks had better be carrying the hard drive with the seed bank's associated database. If the novel is going to treat seeds as pure information without a body, then this omission of the seeds' metadata is startling. These seeds would be useless without their database. How would "generippers" know where to look for desirable traits without the associated information about a plant's characteristics, disease resistance, and environmental tolerances that is connected with each seed packet?

The Windup Girl imagines a world where crop biodiversity is seriously threatened and envisions ways that the preservation of seeds could operate politically in such a place. In this chapter, in order to think through biodiversity preservation out of the wild, I turn to real-world seed banks that participate in these same types of speculative activities. *The Windup Girl* exemplifies some common pitfalls in reading seeds in seed banks: eliding materiality and disregarding the database. In the chapter that follows I examine the database interfaces of the two global seed banks along with the other texts that surround the seed banks. These databases describe the contents of unseen and inaccessible vaults where plant seeds are stored in dark, airtight packages at below-freezing temperatures. I will argue that these databases narrate stories about the world in which plants and people face continual catastrophe. As such, seed banks and their databases are examples of a type of speculative fiction that combines genres to produce an apocalyptic natural history of the world. But this apocalypse has some curious characteristics. The global seed vaults in which we "back up" seeds from local seed banks portray an apocalypse that positions the Global South as a place of inherent danger to seeds and plants, obscuring the colonial histories that have led to plant precarity in the first place. Ultimately, the type of apocalypse imagined undermines the seed banks' own efforts in that it freezes the history of both seeds themselves and the places from which the seeds come, severing both from a contingent history of chance and accident, and extinguishing plants' opportunity to adapt to change.

Enemies or Symbionts?
Debates on Database and Narrative

One of the major human activities surrounding biodiversity is preservation *ex situ,* or preservation outside of an organism's natural habitat. This particular type of conservation absolutely requires the use of databases to contain the massive amounts of information collected about the stored living (or dormant) material. Different kinds and measures of diversity can be stored; after all, biodiversity is a very broad concept, but no matter what kind of biodiversity is the object of conservation, its organization will require a database. If the conservation program is to preserve biodiversity in a location that is not native to a given habitat, the program will have to keep track of the species, genes, functional groups, and other information using a robust database.

In biodiversity, the database, like materiality, simply cannot be ignored. In the last ten years, since Lev Manovich's historic call for a database aesthetics and criticism,[3] the database has come to be acknowledged as a dominant cultural form.[4] Database criticism is especially urgent because these databases are not neutral, inert data containers,[5] but rather affect the construction of the world, influencing even, for example, the way seeds are conceptualized in novels and beyond. Database is especially important in any consideration of biodiversity, as collecting and storing vast amounts of information about this world's species is one of the main ways environmentalists conceptualize and interact with biodiversity. Databases on biodiversity proliferate, with the Encyclopedia of Life, ARKive, and the IUCN Red List being the most well-known of the hundreds of databases in existence. What is even more interesting is how a separate major activity around biodiversity—storing material living bodies *ex situ* in zoos and seed banks—collapses into this obsessive collection of vast quantities of *information* about species. Why is the hoarding of living individuals *ex situ* so often figured as information storage, and what are the consequences of this convergence?

This chapter brings together the critical work of these two opening lines of inquiry: it at once insists on the materiality of the seeds themselves while also investigating the database structure and influence. Only through an exploration of seed bank rhetoric and the logic of their databases can we trace the effacement of the materiality of seeds and then fully answer questions about how this accumulation of threatened plant varieties structures the concept of biodiversity. The chapter will take as its object the two global seed banks, Svalbard Global Seed Vault (nicknamed the Doomsday Vault) in Arctic Norway and the Kew Millennium Seed Bank run by the Royal Botanic Gardens, Kew. While there are many local and national seed banks, Svalbard and Kew are the only two global seed banks. And they are both impossibly vast projects: Svalbard's goal is to conserve all available landraces of major crop species, and Kew's goal is to conserve all the plant species on the planet, with priority given to those most threatened. Eventually this chapter's interrogation into the aesthetics behind seed banks will reveal how their underlying genre of apocalyptic natural history constrains how it is possible to think about plant biodiversity and its loss.

FIGURE 1. Svalbard Global Seed Vault, nicknamed the Doomsday Vault, juts out of the Arctic permafrost. (Miksu, Wikimedia Commons, CC-BY-SA-3.0)

In this chapter I contend that not only seed bank publications but also seed bank databases construct a story about seeds, biodiversity, and environmental crisis. The claim that databases construct stories is historically a contentious but important one. If databases tell narratives rather than simply prioritize or omit through choices of what data to contain, then they convey powerful representations of the world that influence not only organization of data but the meanings we make out of the data they contain. There are those who view narrative and database as mutually annihilating, as enemies, and those who view them as always suggesting the need for each other. The famous starting point for this debate is, again, Lev Manovich. In *The Language of New Media,* he asserts that "database and narrative are natural enemies."[6] Many critics have agreed, taking the argument even further by asserting that databases and narrative are mutually exclusive. They argue that databases by definition do not have narratives. In his article "Ocean, Database, Recut," Grahame Weinbren, for example, argues that a database doesn't produce any narrative order, that one has to perform a search to produce an order at all, and already at the level of the search function one is outside the logic of the pure database and interacting instead with the database-driven platform. In fact, Weinbren states that a database "does not *present* data; it *contains* it." And while a database interface can be made to present the contents of a database in a way that produces a narrative, even this next step of displaying content is not inherently narrative. The mere fact of forging one possible pathway through a database, for Weinbren, does not make a narrative, as he is clear to express that narrative requires more than simply order. Even when analyzing not just the raw database but the whole content management system, "it is one thing to arrange the data alphabetically, by size, or by color; it is quite another to arrange it in narrative sequence."[7] For this side of the debate, neither the construction of the database nor the orders produced by interface searches are narratives.

Other scholars disagree with this overly strict separation between narrative and database. Jerome McGann writes, "Indeed, the database—any database—represents an initial critical analysis of the content materials, and while its structure is not narrativized, it is severely constrained and organized."[8] So, for McGann, structure, constraint, and organization are already present in the database itself and do not emerge only through search functions. In fact, the database is not merely a collection of inert data but rather is a way of inventing knowledge,[9] and as such it already has a power similar to that of narrative to shape our sensitivity to the world. N. Katherine Hayles finds a way to bring narrative and database even closer together, arguing that they are not enemies but rather natural symbionts: "Because database can construct relational juxtapositions but is helpless to interpret or explain them, it needs narrative to make its results meaningful. Narrative, for its part, needs database in the computationally intensive culture of the new millennium to enhance its cultural authority and test the generality of its insights."[10] While this chapter takes as a starting point Hayles's claim that database calls for narrative, and narrative for database, I take the argument further by contending that explaining and interpreting interface search results and juxtapositions are not the only ways that databases open themselves to narrative.

A close look at seed banks reveals that narrative's way into databases doesn't necessarily have to be through interpreting orderings. It's not only "arrangement that gives data its meaning,"[11] but also the allowances of the database and its interface: the kinds of orderings it is possible to create, what is searchable, how the search proceeds, who can search, and what kinds of categories are chosen, that tell a story about the world or the content of the database. The design of the database, what's included as content, as well as the possible articulations of the design can all be interrogated, and in the case of seed banks it's not only the act of choosing a particular pathway through the database and searches that creates narrative but also, more importantly, the structure of the database itself. This chapter, therefore, forges a new approach to thinking about database narrative, one that is informed by Lawrence Lessig's *Code 2.0,* Deb Verhoeven's analysis of the ethics of databases in "Doing the Sheep Good," and Lauren Klein's reading of absence in "The Image of Absence: Archival Silence, Data Visualization, and James Hemings."[12] I focus not on particular searches and pathways through the database that the interface can produce but rather on what kinds of pathways are even available given the content of the database, what pathways are foreclosed by the design of the system, and what kinds of stories (and absences) result. Not only will this chapter try to maintain the simultaneous awareness of seed banks as both collections of material seeds and operations of malleable databases, but also it will remain sensitive to the coexistence of narrative and database even outside of ordering.

It is this coexistence of material seeds and the information associated with them, as well as the interaction between the two, that makes seed banks such a rich example of conservation *ex situ*. They are part database and part archive, and their database constructs a particular story about the world. The accession database interface for Svalbard Global Seed Vault is called GENESYS, and any online user can access it, though to order seeds one needs to be a bona fide researcher affiliated with a scientific institution. GENESYS provides a way to browse and search for seeds based on species, country of origin, or characteristics that a user is looking for. This content management system includes information about seed characteristics (appearance, average size and weight, etc.) and also about the characteristics of the mature plant and its environment (time until sexual maturity, observed disease resistance, rainfall profile of its native habitat). Accessing this website from anywhere in the world gives one a glimpse into the vast amount of biodiversity and the even vaster amount of information that Svalbard stores.

The structure of the database that drives this platform has material consequences for what characteristics become visible and real in a plant and a seed. Since Karen Barad disabuses us of the notion that "the world is composed of individual entities with individually determinate boundaries and properties,"[13] we can jettison the idea that this database is a neutral information container whose fields refer to separate and preexisting characteristics of plants. The database is closer to Barad's notion of the apparatus as *"the material conditions of possibility and impossibility of mattering;* they enact what matters and what is excluded from mattering. Apparatuses enact agential cuts that produce determinate boundaries and properties of 'entities' within phenomena."[14] Though Barad's discussion of apparatuses focuses more on measurement devices, databases "enact what matters and what is excluded from mattering" in the same way. When a field is designated meaningful, and so added to the database, that quality of a plant that the database field describes becomes real and measurable; it becomes one of the ways that we monitor how that plant fits into the world and what it does in the world. The database cuts, produces, and defines what the properties of plants are.

Interrogating what characteristics of plants seed bank databases produce as real is even more important when the characteristics enumerated *seem* to give a total description of the plant. For corn (*Zea mays*), a user encounters fields describing size of ear, size and arrangement of kernels, color of all parts of the plant including kernels, anthers, glumes, silks, and cob. There are fields for the percentage of oil, protein, and starch. There is a whole section about resistance to diseases like stalk rot, common rust, common smut, and more, not to mention insect resistance, growth rate, environmental rainfall and temperature profiles, and altitude. The fields that the structure of the database prompts the collector to fill out are so comprehensive that they seem to result in a total description of the plant, but in fact, they do not. Moreover, they present a narrative about the state of the world and what the future will hold.

While almost every visible aspect of the plant is catalogued, taste and smell are jettisoned. Excluding taste is an interesting choice for any project aiming to describe food plants. It seems that these corn plants will not be grown or needed for taste in the future as it is impossible to use this database to select a corn based on taste. Nor, perhaps, will they be grown outside of a laboratory agar plate, since there is absolutely no information about how to grow the plant. Questions that are completely unaddressed include: In what season would one plant this landrace? How deep and how far apart should seeds be planted? Should they be grown in full sun or partial shade? With what other species do they grow well? It seems as if these plants are not going to be grown in the field at all. So what, then, is all the information for? For what kind of future world is this plant being saved?

The choices made in the construction of the database reveal a narrative about a future world in jeopardy. Genes that will aid survival in a dangerous and risky world are what are needed from this database. Resistance to diseases and insects are of utmost importance. The fields in the database are also geared toward preparing for catastrophic climate change. The entries about the maximum temperature in the warmest month and the minimum temperature in the coldest month suggest that what users may need to access are plants with the ability to survive extreme weather. It would be easy to use this database to search for plants that are drought- or heat-tolerant, or resistant to weevil, but it would be impossible to search for plants that taste sweet or nutty. The future imagined by this database is not one where something as trifling and subjective as taste is a priority. Additionally, any trait that could maximize the efficiency of crop production is deemed worthy of inclusion in the database: ear size, ear quantity, kernel size, kernel weight, ears per stalk, time to maturity and harvest. What we are going to need in the database's version of the future are drought-tolerant, heat-resistant, mold-resistant plants that can produce more food per acre of cropland. The story about the world and the future that the GENESYS database constructs is one of difficulty, crop loss, and hardship. It is also a story of genetic engineering as world salvation. Every trait in the database is not only useful to plant and human survival but also heritable and potentially isolatable and exploitable. Unlike *The Windup Girl*, which portrays fruit as bringing forward many different kinds of information about lost worlds and personal history, the Svalbard database presents seeds as exclusively genetic information. Specifically, seeds are only genetic information related to crop survival. Clearly, the physical seeds themselves are not viewed as the ultimate content of the database but rather as data containers of useful genes.

Much of the rhetoric found in the supporting materials from these seed banks reinforces this portrayal of seeds as databases of potentially useful traits themselves. In fact, the writing on the website and in press releases positions genes and even diversity itself as the real content of the database. For example, Svalbard's associated Global Crop Diversity Trust website makes the case for Svalbard's operation by stating, "Crop diversity is one of the world's least recognized but most valuable resources."[15] Importantly, the Svalbard Global Seed Vault is not described as containing crop seeds but rather "crop diversity." So the seed bank is not merely saving seeds of species that are threatened but also saving diversity itself. The contents of this seed bank include all at once bodiless information, physical seeds, and the abstract concept of biodiversity. This layered structure of conservation that is alternately informational and material positions seed banks perfectly to make interventions into both meaning and matter. They not only tell us about crisis in the material world, but they also make specific meanings out of those crises, as well as organize and construct these emergencies for us in particular ways. They portray a world of increased risk to plants where genetic engineering is the only solution.

This narrative about a world embroiled in disaster and genetic-engineering-to-the-rescue is very much aligned with the genre of speculative fiction. These databases are, in some ways, works of speculative fiction. They describe not the world that is but rather a world that is plausible given current trends. They fit well with Margaret Atwood's definition of speculative fiction as narrating "things that could really happen but just hadn't completely happened when the authors wrote the books."[16] Our world (unlike that of the *Windup Girl*) is not yet massively deploying genetically engineered crops to grow in a changed climate, or frantically developing strains that are genetically resistant to diseases that have run rampant, but the seed bank database portrays a world where this is the case. However, this narrative about geneticists holding disaster at bay is not the only narrative possible about genetic engineering and a world at risk. In fact, the speculative-fiction novel with which this chapter began presents a very different vision of the relationship between genetic modification and crisis. In the world of *The Windup Girl*, genetic engineering is a significant contributing factor to catastrophe. In Bacigalupi's novel the giant agricorps initiated the "contraction," the novel's term for the economic and population collapse that preceded the start of the novel. The multinational agricultural corporations engineered disease-resistant plants and then engineered and released the diseases to which only their seeds were resistant. These diseases caused massive crop failure and starvation. The crop diseases were even fatal to humans. If a character in *The Windup Girl* eats a fruit contaminated with "blister rust," for example, he or she can expect an excruciating death.

Interestingly, in the case of the speculative-fiction novel, the danger from genetic engineering does not come inherently from tampering with genetic material but from the way genetic modification is administered and controlled by giant multinational corporations whose only concern is profit. In fact, in *The Windup Girl* the underground resistance to the agricorps uses the same tools of genetic engineering to combat and undercut the faceless corporations by resurrecting extinct fruits. In addition, the female protagonist, and the most sympathetic character in the entire novel, is the titular windup girl, a genetically engineered human.

In the speculative-fiction novel genetic engineering is not a tool that comes to the rescue of a beleaguered world. Instead, its use results in a great devastation, not because the tool itself is inherently dangerous, but because it is controlled and administered by unregulated multinational corporations. This novel reminds readers not only to focus on the possibilities and promises of a new technology but to pay attention to how it is controlled, how it is implemented, and who gets to participate in deciding how the technology is put to use. Although seed banks can be viewed as a type of speculative fiction, in that they are engaged in imagining future possible worlds, they are piecemeal speculative fiction. Their world-encompassing projects happen through fragmentary accumulation of small amounts of plant matter and bits of information. As such, there are things they are insensible to like the way a technology is administered, economies, power disparity, and the fact that the current agreements preserving seed donors' rights could be invalidated by changes in control over the seed bank. Novels of speculative fiction, with their totalizing projects of trying to imagine entire and complete possible worlds, bring forward aspects missing from the speculative fiction of seed banks: aspects like economic flows, personal relationships to seeds and to other humans, and the imagination of a world order that is not identical to the current system but an exaggeration of it.

Organizing the World:
Seed Banks as Natural History

The choices about what to include and what to omit from the database fields do narrate a particular story about a world with crops at risk and genetic engineering triumphant, but while this traditional danger/hero narrative is important to seed banks, as is speculative fiction, the most salient genre to these global collections of plant material is natural history. Natural history, a genre of scientific travel writing that emerged in the eighteenth century, attempts to describe, sample, and organize the natural world. It is a multimedia genre that includes writing, sketches, painting, and even collections of actual biological material. It is a literature that has been long implicated with European imperial expansion,[17] and it is a genre that is still relevant—today we still use Linnaeus's basic schema for naming plants and animals. And we are still completing the world-describing project of fitting every species on Earth into the schema (which chapter 2 will explore). Products of natural history are not only Latin names but also botanical gardens, botanical prints, natural history museums, narratives of species discovery, origin, evolution, and interrelationships, and seed bank databases.

Seed banks beg to be read alongside and understood through natural history; after all, one of the two global seed banks, Kew Millennium Seed Bank Project, grows directly out of one of the eighteenth-century centers of natural history: the Royal Botanical Gardens at Kew, London. Kew "was the headquarters of Great Britain's botanical empire. From there administrators coordinated the efforts of plant collectors at regional botanical stations from Jamaica to Fiji."[18] This quotation from an article in the *New Yorker* already points to some of the resonances between seed banks and natural history as a practice. Not only is natural history figured as a "botanical *empire*" (emphasis added) that encompasses the globe, but it is also, like seed banks, figured as one that requires an extensive network of collaborators.

The interdependence of databases and networks is a fundamental characteristic of both seed banks and natural history. In both cases, a global network is necessary for creating the database (or other organizational structure). Linnaeus had a network of acolytes who ventured to all parts of the globe to find, describe, and sample new species.[19] The data organization system he created to absorb all this information was the purely informational system of naming. As Sharon Daniel has shown in her consideration of the Paris catacombs, the city of Venice, and the quilts of Gee's Bend,[20] it can be productive to think about non-database information storage systems as databases. The Linnaean classification schema could be considered a type of database for purposes of comparison to seed bank databases. It is not an archive because its purpose is not to organize and locate physical entities in a physical place for retrieval and analysis. It is about abstracting salient characteristics from physical entities in order to situate them in a mental framework that helps make sense of the world. In order to do this, Linnaeus needed samples, lots of samples, from all over the world. This database took many, many particulars and made them into a universal system that was then seen to precede and constitute the many instances of particulars.[21] The network (the local instances gathered) and the database (the universal patterns expressed) are mutually constitutive of each other and in an endless spiral of priority.

Similarly, in Svalbard and Kew, the seed bank database is constituted by a worldwide network of local collaborators that send seeds to the banks. Both institutions have online interactive maps that allow a viewer to zoom in and out of local instances of collaboration. It is possible to view particular projects in different parts of the world and then step back to reveal the global network that constitutes the project and the database. And the spiral narrative these databases construct out of particulars is about universal loss. For example: "The MSB [Millennium Seed Bank] scientists work with partners in 50 countries around the world. They tend to collect seeds from alpine, dryland, coastal, and island ecosystems, as these are most vulnerable to climate change."[22] Here, the dynamic between the network and the database is evident. Scientists urgently need to collect seeds because plant species are disappearing, and when they go out to obtain specimens they choose the ecosystems that are losing species the most rapidly, so the database records a disproportionate number of species that are likely to be lost— showing a global ramping up of biodiversity reduction. This is not to suggest that stories about the loss of biodiversity are due to circular thinking or are manufactured by the way these networks and databases interact. There really is alarming species loss that is affecting our material world.[23] The point is to show that, like natural history, there is a complex and mutually constitutive interaction going on between the local and the global, the specific instance and the universal law, in the story of loss in these seed bank databases.

It is also important to note that at the same time, with the same strategy, the global seed banks are providing justification for their own existence. In this self-justification the seed bank rapidly becomes the only place where rare species are safe. This co-constitution of the global law and the particular example is made even more apparent in the case of seed banks because the very act of gathering particulars can lead to the instance of species loss that reinforces the universal pattern. The Chilean blue crocus is a famous example where overharvesting to meet the demand for gardens in Europe (including Kew) led to extinction of the species in the wild by 1950.[24] Although a small wild population was discovered in Chile in 2001, the story of the decline of the species and gardeners' reactions to this decline perfectly illustrate the way a collection of particulars can reinforce and even cause global patterns of extinction while at the same time justifying the existence of the very European gardens that prompted the overharvesting. While most accounts of the decline of the Chilean blue crocus cite European demand for ornamentals as a major cause of decline in concert with grazing and land use changes, they argue in the same breath that the gardeners are now saving the plant from extinction. For example, Tom Fischer writes on his website OverPlanted.com that after the drastic decline that was caused by high ornamental demand, it is now "up to gardeners to keep this beauty going . . . grow this plant and propagate it. We have a species to save here."[25] Similarly, Kew was instrumental in a (pre-2001) plan to reintroduce the plant into the wild in Chile.[26] The very groups and institutions that caused the crocus's decline in the first place are here figured as its eventual saviors. The collection of seed bank particulars can influence or even create the universal pattern that is the justification for the collection of those particulars in the first place.

One aspect of seed banks that becomes particularly salient once the connection is made to the genre of natural history is their deliberately neutral construction. Just as Linnaeus, in order to gain continent-wide acceptance of his nomenclature, deliberately chose Latin for his system because it was a dead language, not a language of the major competing European powers, as well as capitalized on the fact that he was from relatively neutral Sweden,[27] Svalbard deliberately cultivates neutrality to gain widespread acceptance and use as the whole world's seed bank. The Linnaean system and Svalbard Global Seed Vault both employ a tactical neutrality: neutrality to gain preeminence. Neutrality in these cases is purposefully used as an argument for each system's superiority over competing models. Svalbard's strategy even uses some of Linnaeus's own strategies for tactical neutrality. First of all, Svalbard is affiliated with Scandinavia and set in the far north away from the major global powers in industrial agriculture. In addition, Svalbard has positioned itself as an intermediary between the Global South and the Global North. The Svalbard website states, "For many years it has been Norway's aim to play a bridge-building role in the north-south debate about genetic resources and biological diversity."[28] In addition to aspiring to mediate between the main parties in agriculture revolutions (and I use the world "revolution" with all its martial connotations), Svalbard Global Seed Vault is deliberately designed to break from the Global North's history of biopiracy and neocolonialism. Seed depositors (local gene banks from across the world) retain the rights over seeds they send to Svalbard. Norway will not grant seed access to anyone except the seed depositors without the express permission of the depositing country or institution. Similarly, the Millennium Seed Bank won't make samples available without permission from the local seed banks of origin.[29] In these ways, both Svalbard and Kew actively cultivate their own neutrality and position this neutrality as an argument for their acceptance as the world's seed storage system.

Darwin's Tame Wildfowl: Abundance and the "New World"

Promises of universal patterns, order, and neutrality are an artifact of seed banks' association with the genre of natural history. But, while eighteenth-century natural history is fueled by the discovery of a "new world," seed bank databases are driven by the end of the world. Traditional natural history is a story of abundance, wonder, and novelty; it is not a story of decline and a rush to hoard in the face of extinction. Even three hundred years after the European "discovery" of the Americas when many species had already been exterminated, Darwin in *The Voyage of the* Beagle, and in the grand tradition of natural history, still marvels at the unbelievable abundance with which the Americas confront the European traveler. Of the Galapagos he says: "We see that a vast majority of the land animals, and more than half of the flowering plants, are aboriginal productions. It was most striking to be surrounded by new birds, new reptiles, new shells, new insects, new plants."[30] He estimates that in his collection from the Galapagos, "of the flowering plants 100 are new species."[31] One of the tropes of natural history employed here is the European man confronted with an abundance of newness. Not only are species abundant, but so are species that are new to (European) science.

Abundance is found not just in the number of species but also in the number of individuals. This is traditionally expressed in the ease of killing and/or collecting high numbers of birds, plants, shells, or mammals. Darwin, in part, expresses the abundance of birds on the Galapagos in a long meditation on their tameness, which he equates with the ease of killing. He states: "All of them [the birds] are often approached sufficiently near to be killed with a switch, and sometimes, as I myself tried, with a cap or hat. A gun here is almost superfluous; for with the muzzle I pushed a hawk off the branch of a tree." Why he would want to push a hawk off a tree, he does not explain. What is clear is that here, the *ease* of killing individuals is highlighted. Later in the same passage the great *number* of birds killed becomes the focus: "[A] man in a morning's walk might kill six or seven dozen of these doves." Or: "These birds, although now still more persecuted, do not readily become wild. In Charles Island . . . I saw a boy sitting by a well with a switch in his hand, with which he killed the doves and finches as they came to drink. He had already procured a little heap of them for his dinner."[32] The Galapagos produce an extreme abundance of birds, an abundance that is measurable by the number of birds killed in a short period of time. This death-measured abundance is due to both the high numbers of individual birds and their "tameness."

Through his account of "the extreme tameness of the birds," Darwin inverts and plays with the meanings of "tame" and "wild." While the first definition of "tame" in the *Oxford English Dictionary* is "reclaimed from the wild state; brought under the control and care of man; domestic; domesticated. (Opp. to *wild*.)," Darwin here uses "tame" as a synonym for "wild." The third definition of "tame" seems to be closer to his usage: "Having the disposition or character of a domesticated animal; accustomed to man; not showing the natural shyness, fear or, or fierceness to man."[33] But, in Darwin, these animals are so tame because they are completely *unaccustomed* to "man"[34] (and his murderous ways), not because they are accustomed to him. They are so wild that they are tame. Darwin inverts our traditional definitions of tameness and wildness, making us unsure of what a wild animal really is. It turns out that only once animals are accustomed to man (so they recognize him as the danger he is) do they then become wild. So "wild" now means enough accustomed to man to know to stay away. At the same time that Darwin inverts the meanings of "tame" and "wild," he also makes a comment on what is natural to animals and what the nature of man is. He questions the assertion that this "natural shyness, fear of, or fierceness to man" is indeed natural but posits that this shyness is gained as a hereditary trait due to proximity to man. And he implies that to be accustomed to man is to fear him, indicating that part of what it means to be a man is to be feared by other animals.

Scarcity and Catastrophe: The End of the World?

As the genre of natural history is taken up by later writers, the abundance of new species or sheer numbers of individuals disappears to be replaced by the difficulty in finding new species and the restricted ranges or low numbers that are recorded when a new species is found. New species are now a marvel not because of their "tameness" or abundance but because of their shyness and the extreme difficulty of finding them. Amateur naturalists become "plant hunters." Francis Kingdon Ward, as one of the most famous of these, has to travel across barely navigable landscapes to areas where "animals and birds were rare as men" in order to find undiscovered plants.[35] Rarity becomes the badge of natural history. For example, Kew's publication *The Last Great Plant Hunt* shows, in picture form, the new aesthetic of the rarity and difficulty of finding new plants in a world that is becoming more and more sparse. The cover consists of a horizontal division between blue sky and orange sand dunes that dominate the page and features a single, spindly plant stalk pushing up through the surface of the dune. The Kew Gardens website's plant profiles follow suit, featuring a species of rain-forest tree of which only seventeen individuals have been discovered,[36] a type of stemless palm that is found on only one site in Madagascar,[37] and a critically endangered wing-fruited coffee.[38] The emphasis is more and more on the extremely rare. But in contemporary global seed banks, narratives of rarity veer toward intimations of complete collapse. Seed banks put forward their own particular genre of natural history: apocalyptic natural history.

Upon approaching the Millennium Seed Bank at Kew's Wakehurst location, visitors are confronted with a narrative of collapse. Eight raised planters reconstructing the eight most threatened habitats within the United Kingdom line the entrance. Even before entering the seed bank building, one is impressed with the extent of the threat to ecosystems.

If there are eight disparate types of threatened systems on the small islands of Great Britain, it's hard to conceive how many may be threatened worldwide. Also, the purpose and the implicit suggestion of the seed bank is that Kew may eventually be the only place where these eight threatened ecosystems exist (as reconstructions). It may be the place from which humanity re-creates ecosystems once they are lost in the wild. The rhetoric of decimation is built into the architecture.

For the Svalbard Global Seed Vault, this rhetoric of decimation is even more visible in its geographic location. Svalbard is an island that lies inside the area of Arctic permafrost halfway between the northern end of Norway and the North Pole. "Because of permafrost the temperature will never rise above minus 3.5 Celsius"[39] even if power is completely lost. The Svalbard Global Seed Vault is so remote it is almost physically at the end of the world (away from the type of political conflict that destroys local gene banks), but the result is that the harsh snow-covered landscape looks postapocalyptic. Nothing can grow there because of the permafrost—no plants can grow in ground that is always frozen. And in fact, "Svalbard was initially viewed as a place unfit for human habitation."[40] The seed bank is built on the edge of the inhabitable, so it is prepared for the time when the whole world will be at the edge of habitability. It is not only prepared for long-term loss of power, but it is built 430 feet above sea level, high above any projections of sea-level rise in the area, in a geologically stable area with no detectable radiation that could damage seed DNA.[41] Whereas the physical architecture of Kew is designed merely to bring to mind catastrophic ecosystem loss, Svalbard is built to actually withstand possible worst-case scenarios for the globe. So, it is not surprising that the interior of Svalbard brings to mind Cold War nuclear bunkers.

This architecture is perhaps part of the reason why Svalbard is nicknamed the Doomsday Vault. The moniker certainly picks up on the project's apocalyptic undertones. But Kew's official name also has resonances with the apocalypse. The Millennium Seed Bank points to both its foundation in 1996 around the millennium, and the original meaning of millennium: "The period of one thousand years during which (according to one interpretation of Revelation 20:1–5) Christ will reign in person on earth" or "A period of peace, happiness, prosperity, and ideal government, *esp.* a future utopia, typically ushered in by violent events accompanying the end of the existing world order."[42] Kew's Millennium

Seed Bank and its directors are not just preparing for the end of the existing world order. By choosing the word "Millennium" for its name, the directors indicate Kew's place in bringing about the peace, happiness, and prosperity that follow.

Apart from Kew's millennial name and Svalbard's Doomsday nickname, there are many references in the popular media to these banks as hedges against apocalypse. Popular journalists repeatedly read these seed banks as apocalyptic. In his *New Yorker* article about the Svalbard Global Seed Vault and the people who run it, John Seabrook writes, "We tend to imagine apocalypse coming in the form of a bomb, an asteroid, or a tsunami, but should a catastrophe strike one of the world's major crops Fowler and his fellow seed bankers may be all that stand between us and widespread starvation."[43] Similarly, Jonathan Watts of the *Guardian* calls Svalbard Global Seed Vault "a Noah's Ark of 20,000 plant species" that represents "humanity's latest insurance payment against an agricultural apocalypse."[44]

Apocalypse has a very specific meaning that is stronger than either catastrophe or disaster, and it is hard to see why the loss of a major crop would be apocalyptic. Yet, these two articles, along with others of their kind, explicitly frame the loss of crops as apocalypse. This is not to minimize what the loss of a staple crop would mean: failure of a major crop would not be merely a local disaster but also a global one, one that affects not only the global economy but also the global community through a devastating loss of human life. But, a loss of a crop would not cause the end of the existing world order. I propose instead that these seed banks present a new genre, distinct from but related to apocalypse. This is a genre that I call the "receding apocalypse." It depicts a disaster treadmill where local calamity after calamity strikes, or threatens to, and society can barely keep up but is never quite devastated. Like the Red Queen in *Through the Looking-Glass,* in this genre "it takes all the running you can do, to keep in the same place."[45] There are so many layers of catastrophe that the seed banks and journalism about them invoke that, taken together, they tell of a world harassed by catastrophe, though not ended by it. Just as the seed bank preservation system itself was layered with database, interface, and archive, there are many layers of catastrophe at work here—some global and some more local but with rippling effects through space and time. Taken together as risks to plants and crops, the potential disasters enumerated by seed bank publications and popular journalism anticipate an apocalypse that logically would never actually result in total collapse.

The first layer of catastrophe is brought up in the previous Seabrook quotation: a major crop could fail. There is even a history of crop failure that one can look at to see the ramifications that can happen depending on what percentage of a population's nutrition comes from that crop and how quickly the blighted crop is replaced with a variety that is resistant. The citrus tristeza virus epidemic in the 1940s,[46] the near extinction of the then-dominant Gros Michel variety of banana by Panama disease,[47] the 1970 corn blight that killed 15 percent of U.S. corn,[48] and the late potato blight that caused the Irish potato famine[49] are all examples of catastrophic crop failures. It is important to remember that crop failure does not necessarily result only in the starvation of people who depend on nutrition from that crop but also can reorganize or eliminate a whole network that has grown around the crop. The people who grow the crop, the people who transport it, the people who sell it, the people who harvest it, the domesticated animals that eat it, and the people who manufacture other products out of the crop—will all be affected. A whole network of interactions based on that crop will be changed. None of the crop blights mentioned above has been completely eradicated either, meaning that every one of these crops is still threatened by a reappearance of the fungus/virus/parasite that caused the original failure. And with three crops (wheat, rice, corn) providing 60 percent of the world's food energy intake,[50] seed banks need only to point out the precarious position of the world's food resources to justify their existence.

The second layer of disaster is evident in global seed banks' stated reason for existence: the catastrophic destruction of local gene banks. This can happen due to political instability, war, or natural disasters. For example, in March 2003 during the U.S.-led invasion of Iraq, Iraq's national seed bank was destroyed: "The bank, in the town of Abu Ghraib, contained seeds of ancient varieties of wheat, lentils, chickpeas, and other crops that once grew in Mesopotamia."[51] Because seeds sometimes are the only living remnants of a former civilization, the loss of a local gene bank means a final loss of that world. Articles about the global seed banks make the case that this destruction of local seed banks is more common than one would think. Afghanistan's seeds were destroyed in the 2001 overthrow of the Taliban; the Philippines' seed bank was flooded in 2006; Honduras's seed bank was destroyed by Hurricane

Mitch in 1998; Nicaragua's seed bank was lost to an earthquake in 1971;[52] and Japan's seed bank was threatened by the earthquake and tsunami of 2011.[53] But political and environmental catastrophes are not the only factors that can put an end to these remnants of ancient civilizations. Many seed banks are lost due to "simple and avoidable disasters, such as lack of funding or poor management. Something as mundane as a poorly functioning freezer can ruin an entire collection."[54] Local gene banks are vulnerable, as global seed banks do not hesitate to remind us, and the destruction of the precious material they carry, as the last living heritage of the civilizations of a region, can signal the end of an ancient world. According to Svalbard Global Seed Vault's website, "the loss of a crop variety is as irreversible as the extinction of a dinosaur,"[55] apparently unless you save that crop variety's genetic material in a backup freezer.

But seed banks and particular crops are only part of the receding apocalypse contained in the argument for global seed banks. Crop biodiversity and all plant biodiversity are positioned as being at risk. Traditional agriculture as an entire way of life is disappearing. The Svalbard website reminds us that "more than 7,000 plant species have historically been used in human diets; however, less than 140 species are today used in modern agriculture. Only 12 plant species today represent the major vegetable source in today's menu."[56] A winnowing is taking place. With the exportation of industrial-scale, American-style agriculture to the rest of the world, thousands of varieties of crops are being replaced with monocultures. So, not only is biodiversity within crops lost, but a whole system of food production is positioned as at risk.

Similarly, overall plant diversity is rapidly disappearing. Kew describes the current situation in drastic terms: "Today, between 60,000 and 100,000 species of plant are faced with the threat of extinction—roughly a quarter of all plant species."[57] A *quarter* of all plant species are threatened: this clearly positions biodiversity loss as irreversibly world-changing. This quotation is followed by examples of how plants are foundational for our lives and world (they create the air we breathe, clean water, provide fuel, generate building materials, stabilize climate change, form new medicines), which reinforces the idea that this loss of 25 percent would be catastrophic rather than simply regrettable.

It is not only websites and news articles that present the current situation for plants in the mode of the receding apocalyptic. The GENESYS underlying database itself puts forward a story of perpetual disaster. As I discussed earlier, the choices made in selecting what fields are useful for describing a plant exhibit a marked bent toward preparing for catastrophes. The database incorporates all of the previously discussed layers of apocalypse into its construction. The sections on resistance to insects and on pathogens suggest that there could be a major crop failure due to one of these phenomena. Similarly, the detailed climate data including extreme events suggest that many world crops could be in danger due to climate change. Earlier I argued that these choices in how to present a plant put forward a story about catastrophe and the power of genetic engineering to stop it. All the catastrophes are imagined as ones to which genes can provide solutions. Notably, the database ignores the largest catastrophe to wild plants, land use change, because there is nothing in plant genetics that can combat this eventuality. The result of putting all these catastrophes together in the fields of the GENESYS database is a story of continual catastrophe, a slow but never complete collapse—an ever-receding apocalypse.

There is an element of receding apocalypse that is aligned with the genre of speculative fiction too. Although *The Windup Girl* is often categorized as postapocalyptic in reviews,[58] the apocalypse in this novel is ever-receding as well. It is true that the novel is set after a devastating reduction of human population and after an end to the current oil economy; however, the several civilizations described seem not to be disappearing but continuing. This is not a world that is ending. The book is geared not toward documenting a complete collapse but rather toward examining what happens after a catastrophe and how the surviving people, plants, and genetically modified humans respond to this altered world. *The Windup Girl* takes place after a great "contraction," and the climate, systems of energy (calorie-based instead of petroleum-based), and cultures are all changed from our present due to a worldwide disaster. But the world of *The Windup Girl* is still recognizable from our current systems. The environmental and economic exploitation-at-a-distance, the great disparity between the few rich and the many poor, and the disturbing power of faceless giant corporations are all too familiar aspects of the current world order. This work of "postapocalyptic" fiction exhibits the same fascination with what happens after apocalypse that characterizes the seed banks' databases and publications. In both cases, attention is focused on the human and environmental communities after the apocalypse, showing the apocalypse to be ever-receding, never quite ending the world-as-we-know-it.

A Strange Kind of Apocalypse: Seed Banks and the Global South

The genre of these two global seed banks is receding apocalyptic natural history; their reasons for existence are founded on the potential loss of a major crop, destruction of local gene banks, the disappearance of traditional agriculture, its associated crop biodiversity loss, and the rapid disappearance of wild biodiversity. But this is also an ever-receding apocalypse that is portrayed in a particular way. If hoarding biodiversity *ex situ* is one of the ways we account for biodiversity, then we have to ask, who is invited to participate in this kind of accounting? This type of accounting for biodiversity through global seed banks is done exclusively in the Global North. As such, the particular kind of apocalypse it portrays is an apocalypse that comes from elsewhere, from outside the "first world." The two global seed banks portray the Global South as inherently *risky*. In John Seabrook's *New Yorker* article, for example, he lists the devastation of local seed banks I catalogued earlier (all outside Europe and North America) as one of the reasons the Svalbard Global Seed Vault is needed. He describes how the seed banks of Iraq, Afghanistan, the Philippines, Honduras, and Nicaragua have been destroyed by war, looting, a typhoon, Hurricane Mitch, and an earthquake (respectively). This clearly paints the world outside of northern Europe and the United States as a place of social unrest, political upheaval, and devastating natural disasters. In the same article, Carey Fowler, the then executive director of the agency that funds the Svalbard Global Seed Vault describes the Global South as a place that is almost unbelievably unsafe for seeds: "We think that fifty percent of the unique collections in developing nations are in danger. Half."[59] Fowler goes on to describe the types of danger that can threaten seeds: "There are equipment failures, poor management, funding cuts, natural disasters, civil strife—you name it."[60] But seeds are positioned as only in danger in "developing nations," not at Svalbard, and their originating nations are portrayed as vulnerable to violence, susceptible to natural disasters, and poor. Fowler's statement echoes the rhetoric on Svalbard's website, quoted earlier in this chapter: "simple and avoidable disasters, such as lack of funding or poor management . . . something as mundane as a poorly functioning freezer can ruin an entire collection."[61] It seems from these statements that not only natural disasters but things like funding cuts and freezer malfunctions can happen only in the Global South, never in northern Europe. The reality is that Svalbard has already had to contend with unforeseen disasters. Due to thawing ice from increasing summer temperatures, the bunker flooded in 2016. No seeds were lost, but articles described the inviolable vault as now "threatened by climate change."[62]

Proponents of global seed banks argue that local gene banks will not suffice because storing seeds where the diversity itself is found is too risky. The subtle implication of this argument is that areas where the biodiversity comes from—Brazil, the Democratic Republic of the Congo, Pacific Islands—are not safe places to store either living biodiversity or seeds. Local seed banks are described as being vulnerable to natural disasters, wars, lack of funding, and climate change. They are even portrayed as places that are too risky for seeds due to sunlight, humidity, and lack of funding. Just as the biodiversity hot spots themselves are portrayed as risky locations for conserving biodiversity *in situ* (hence the seed banks' justification for existence in the first place), the countries where biodiversity is found are portrayed as locations that are too risky to rely on for seed storage. This portrayal of the "developing" world as a place of inherent risk is nothing new; after all, in traditional natural-history writing, the Global South is a place of danger and adventure, a place of natural disaster and war. Just remember Darwin's account of being "to a certain degree a prisoner" due to a "violent revolution having broken out"[63] or his description of the devastation following an earthquake in Chile.[64] But this portrayal of the Global South as riskier than the Global North is an important assumption to critique when thinking about biodiversity. The discomfort felt at yet another London-centered global administration project is not something to be ignored. Despite the deliberately neutral design of these seed banks with their clear intention of foiling biopiracy, there is indeed something patronizing about seed banks. In terms of accounting for biodiversity in this way, saving biodiversity is treated as something better left to Great Britain and Scandinavia. Implicit in the argument for and placement of these seed banks is a story reminiscent of the white man's burden to save the world.

These narratives about a risky "third world" are especially unsatisfying since this depiction of the Global South acknowledges none of the history that accounts for disparity between the Global South and the Global North. Nor does this narrative of risk recognize that many of the causes of both species and seed bank loss actually come from northern Europe and the United States. Honduras has certainly contributed little to the climate change that is making hurricanes, like the one that destroyed its national seed bank, more intense. Much of the deforestation that is threatening species in the Amazon is driven by northern demand for cheap soy, beef, and exotic woods. And both Iraq and Afghanistan's seed banks were destroyed during the U.S.-led invasions of those countries. It is clear that the risk to the Global South in many cases actually stems from the Global North. Instead of portraying the Global South as *inherently* risky, seed banks would do well to complicate this long-standing depiction by investigating how the risk works, where it comes from, and how the Global North is implicated in the creation and distribution of environmental and economic risk.

The apocalypse that seed banks present is an apocalypse that happens "out there," that starts outside of northern Europe, that is caused by a risk-filled Global South, that begins there, and that hits those countries the hardest. It is an apocalypse that only European institutions are deemed capable of surviving (and European survival shows the predicted apocalypse to be not all that apocalyptic after all). Because of their genre of apocalyptic natural history, the seed banks exclude an important part of the world from this accounting for biodiversity. The apocalyptic natural-history genre that this chapter has established for seed bank databases matters in other ways too. It is important to recognize that the narrative the seed bank's database-driven platforms construct is about cataloguing, collecting, and exchanging materials from worlds that are fast disappearing. This narrative fosters not only a conception of the Global South that is limiting but also a certain conception of biodiversity itself that is limiting. The only type of biodiversity that ends up being valued by global seed banks is genetic diversity. When the world is ending, it is no longer possible to maintain species *in situ*, and they have to be saved as seeds in cold storage. And the goal in these seed banks has been to preserve samples from the maximum number of varieties so as to store up the most genetic and trait diversity for possible later use. What is missing from this conception of biodiversity is genetic diversity on the level of the individuals within species, functional biodiversity, and the diversity that is constantly generated through reproduction, hybridization, and polyploidy. And while trait diversity may help genetically engineering crops to survive in a changed world, seed banks' other goal of being able to restore the planet's damaged ecosystems is made almost entirely impossible by the limited conception of biodiversity expressed by the banks themselves.

The Elision of Materiality and the Pleasure of Apocalypse

When seeds are valued solely for genetic information, the conception of a plant as a material individual, the materiality that *The Windup Girl* makes so present, is lost, taking with it the particulars about plant bodies. The fact that the vast majority of flowering plants have evolved to need insects or animals to sexually reproduce is completely ignored by these cold-storage systems. There is no way of having self-sustaining plant ecosystems or even types of agriculture if bees, for example, are not present. Insects are the absolutely essential third party in the strange, three-body reproductive unit of most flowering plants. Similarly, many seeds use animals as their primary means of dispersal. Some seeds even have to pass through the gut of an animal in order to sprout, and some have specialized external characteristics designed to attach the seed in animal fur. Moreover, symbiotic microbes in and on plant bodies are absolutely essential for their healthy functioning and development (an observation chapter 5 will examine in more detail). Conserving the biodiversity of plants without their associated animals and microbes will never result in the re-creation of a self-propagating, moving system.

These apocalyptic natural-history repositories strip away other possibilities of movement too. Not only can pollen and seeds not move without the animals they have coevolved with, but the whole system also cannot move when biodiversity is stored this way. The seeds are figuratively as well as literally frozen; the samples that are collected now, unlike those growing *in situ,* will not risk extinction, but they also will not have even the small chance to adapt that growing plants have. The biodiversity captured is completely static and hence relies exclusively on human genetic engineering for any chance of relevancy in the future. The global seed banks seem to be based off the principle that at some point in the future, extinction will slow down, and we will have a more sustainable system—then comes the age of the reseeding of the world. The name of Svalbard's database, GENESYS, not so subtly signals the desire to start the world anew as it is a homonym for the biblical book of Genesis, a major creation story for the current world. This is the same dream that is expressed in current projects of "de-extinction," but on a grander scale. However, in a changing world, it may very well be that by the time we wish to use seeds, global warming will have changed abiotic conditions so much that it is impossible for certain seeds to grow anymore anywhere. This focus entirely on devastation blinds us to any change other than the loss of biodiversity. Otherwise common sense would dictate that the answer to rapid climate change and ecosystem shift is never going to be stasis.

This elision of change other than biodiversity loss reveals how critical it is to interrogate the genre of databases. And, like the databases themselves, this genre is complex and layered, with overlapping confluences of natural history and receding apocalypse creating a hybrid genre. What this genre reveals is what biodiversity stripped entirely of context and embodiment looks like: it is stasis. The seeds are static, and the dream of being able to restore a world from these seed banks requires that the world be static too; it cannot have changed too much apart from the expected massive plant loss. The fallacy of being able to restart the world from a static collection is only made possible by ignoring all other change, and this fallacy is integral to the narrative seed banks construct. This may be why seed banks seem so inexplicably unsettling, why Svalbard is nicknamed the Doomsday Vault; they contain an undercurrent of excitement about this receding apocalypse, which, for global seed banks, becomes its homonym—a "reseeding" apocalypse. There is a trace of pleasure to seed banks' accounts of sowing a new world.

Looking to the Noah story as an early example of this origin-in-apocalypse scenario reveals the attraction of the clean slate, the new covenant, the do-over, the beautiful rainbow after the almost unsurvivable storm. Perhaps there is always this fascination with and attraction to the apocalypse as a utopian opportunity to start the world afresh. And these seed banks are positioned as the ark that will allow humanity to do so. As exciting and terrifying as the Noah origin/apocalypse is, and as important as it is for understanding the database narrative of seed banks, there is another biblical apocalypse that we cannot forget: the

Book of Revelation. After all, these material seeds are in storage, in a suspended state similar to death—John Seabrook even calls seed banks "morgues." And Matthew Kirschenbaum argues that *all* storage is a kind of living death: "Storage, then, is a kind of suspended animation, a coma or waking death, oddly inert yet irreducibly physically present; hence its association with the uncanny, the unconscious, the dead."[65] What is uncanny about these seeds is precisely that—they are alive but inert. They, like the dead awakened by the trumpets of the second coming, will come to life at the end of the world.

2 Cross Sections of the Tree of Life

Visualization and Evolutionary Supertrees

IN THIS CHAPTER we turn from physical seeds at the ends of the Earth to metaphorical trees at its center. If global seed banks perpetuate an apocalyptic narrative as they gather seeds for an uncertain future, the evolutionary trees I examine in this chapter look to the past, aiming to tell the story of how life developed from its origin to our present array of species. These trees, in their currently popular form, articulate a story almost opposite to that of global seed banks. Instead of a quickly disappearing world, evolutionary supertrees portray planetary life as wildly proliferating, but with nearly identical results. Just as GENESYS does, evolutionary trees position plants and animals as containers of pure information, although this time the information they are imagined as enclosing is evolutionary history rather than potentially useful genes. However, neither an apocalypse of species annihilation nor the riotous multiplication of kinds are stories that lend themselves to maintaining awareness of biodiversity's many bodies, though, as I will explore, a combination of both proliferation and winnowing can be used to foreground the roles of contingency, chance, and surprise in contributing to our current array of biodiversity.

Organizing organisms into evolutionary supertrees has become one of the dominant ways of visualizing the world's biodiversity. These are trees that depict the evolutionary relationship among all known organisms on Earth (or a subset thereof). In the last decade, this endeavor to visualize vaster and vaster subsets of living organisms in evolutionary order by placing them together on one great tree of life has blossomed.

There are now bird, mammal, crawfish, plant, dinosaur, and bacterial trees of life as well as comprehensive trees of life, one of which includes all 2.3 million named species. The resulting evolutionary diagrams are trees that encompass, constitute, and structure the world, organizing the relationships of constituent parts of life into a unified story of life on this planet.

As Heather Houser has argued, "visualizations with an agenda centered on environmental issues invite questions from environmental critics about how their aesthetic features render visible and relevant the complexity of the phenomena that they depict."[1] In this chapter I argue that while trees remain an exceptionally powerful tool for visualizing relationships, they perform a similar but opposite operation to the seed bank databases discussed in the previous chapter. Just as Svalbard and Kew's apocalyptic model organized their vision of the world and the plants in it, evolutionary supertrees are framed around prolific propagation, which comes to determine the stories they are capable of depicting. This chapter finds the design of current evolutionary trees to be both remarkable presentations of vast swaths of life on Earth and limited in two ways. First, the circular construction, the decision to purge dead branches, and the treatment of time combine to ensure these trees are only capable of depicting life as wildly proliferating. Second, the trees and the related conception of organisms as representing "evolutionary history" not only evacuate biodiversity of its bodies but act as analgesics that position extinction as not a true and final loss of the essence of a species. The concept of evolutionary history as portrayed by evolutionary trees can take the sting out of extinction instead of providing space to feel discomfort over the irrecoverable agency of other beings.

Conceptualizing the diversity of life all at once, as these trees do, is no easy feat. These trees are as impressive as they are aesthetically pleasing. In seed bank databases the prevailing strategy was to present biodiversity as a series of organisms with which one interacts sequentially, as one clicks through the profiles of landraces contained in the database rather than takes in en masse. Although the database and the storage facility itself contain a vast number of species, landraces, and individual samples, a user of the database interface can view the *details* of each sample only singly. Evolutionary trees, on the other hand, take on the difficult task of presenting vast variety all at once in the same page space.

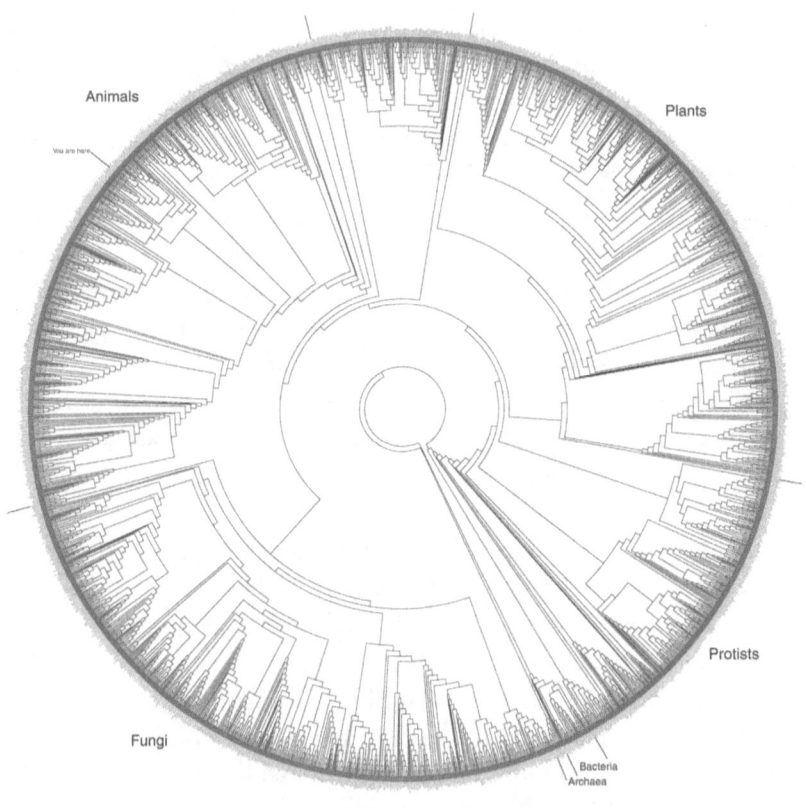

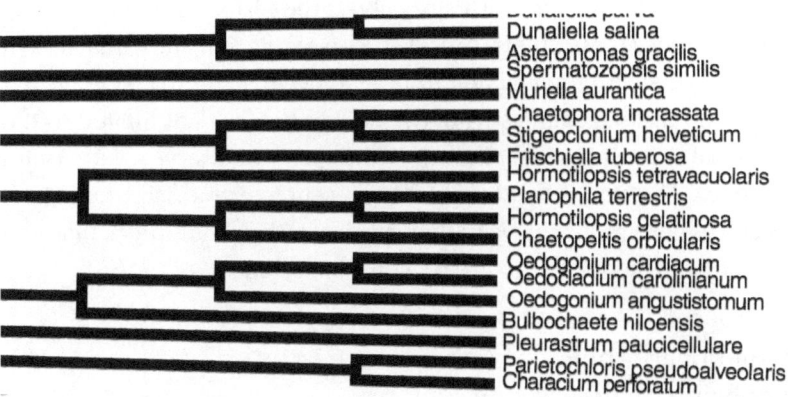

FIGURE 2. Comprehensive tree of life, with detail. (David M. Hillis, Derrick Zwickl, and Robin Gutell, University of Texas at Austin, www.zo.utexas.edu/faculty/antisense/DownloadfilesToL.html)

Not only are these trees notable for their world-encompassing aims, but they are also visualizations that reach a broader audience than that of the scientific journals where they are initially published. Although the trees analyzed in this chapter are usually first published as figures in papers in academic journals, they are often the most mobile part of the scientific article—they are excerpted, referenced, and featured in a variety of contexts. New phylogenetic[2] supertrees are very often extracted and included as visuals in news coverage about the development and release of the tree. These visualizations also regularly appear on websites dedicated to the aesthetics of information visualization,[3] while others appear as art objects in biology department atriums, museums, hospitals, and even as tattoos.[4] Although originating in specialty scientific contexts, these images do gain limited popular exposure and a small but dedicated fan base.

It is important to note here that the reading of evolutionary trees that follows is directed toward these trees as mobile cultural products that travel across a variety of domains rather than as scientific models used to address disciplinary questions about the evolution of complex physiological features, the order of evolution, or the generation of diversity. Although evolutionary supertrees are valuable instruments in answering scientific questions, I am less interested in the ways they fulfill the specific scientific functions for which they were designed than I am in the way that they portray a story about the history of life to viewers who encounter these objects outside the scientific domain. Visual design enthusiasts, environmental nonprofit employees, and broader educated publics all make meanings from these trees that are not limited to the biological context in which they are developed (and serve a very useful function). The stories that these trees present to extradisciplinary viewers are important for the ways that species in their multitudes (and the relationships among them) are broadly conceived.

Evolutionary Uniqueness and Biodiversity Conservation

The influence of these trees extends beyond their aesthetic appeal as art objects, as they are also the aegis under which a particular kind of conservation program is carried out. Scholars have long recognized that visualizations of scientific information comprise "a way of seeing that simultaneously both reflects and shapes how members render the world."[5] Here, the phylogenetic trees render the world in their image by viewing the world as comprised of a set of organisms that vary in their evolutionary distinctiveness from each other. Because biodiversity is also prescriptive, this image of the world is then projected back onto the physical plants, animals, and other organisms of this world's ecosystems. Thanks to these trees and the math behind them, evolutionary distinctiveness is measurable, calculable, and real. Even to a nonexpert the branching pattern can give one a sense of how distinct an individual species is. If a species has no recent branchings, it has no close, living relatives, and so, in this view, would be a desirable object of conservation.

This type of conservation paradigm, based on distinctiveness, is gaining traction. In a 2013 interview, Peter Kareiva, the then head of the Nature Conservancy, one of the largest nonprofits dedicated to the conservation of ecosystems, states: "Many extremely stressful environments have led to some of our most unique species—polar bears in the Arctic, camels in the deserts, fish with antifreeze in their blood in northern waters, and so on. Losing one or two species of those unique life forms may be more troubling than losing 500 beetles that are barely distinguishable in their natural history and morphology."[6] Similarly, entire environmental nonprofits are dedicated to this calculus of prioritization. Another conservation nonprofit, EDGE, chooses to work in a way that "highlights and conserves *one-of-a-kind* species that are on the verge of extinction." They calculate a score for the conservation priority of each species based on "how *Evolutionarily Distinct* and Globally Endangered (EDGE) they are."[7]

In this way, a scientific visualization does not merely reflect the way we see the world, but it *structures* the way we see the world. The historian David Armstrong writes of the power of scientific images in preparing users to frame the world in precisely this way. His example is the medical anatomy atlas: "The anatomical atlas directs attention to certain structures, certain similarities, and not others, and in doing so forms a set of rules for reading the body and making it intelligible. The atlas enables the anatomy student when faced with the undifferentiated amorphous mass of the body, to see certain things and ignore others. In effect what the student sees is not the atlas as a representation of the body but the body as a representation of the atlas."[8] Here, the current appearance of these visualizations coupled with the long history of the tree-shape as an organizer of thought unite to make the world intelligible in certain ways by training the viewer (or conservationist) to see some things and ignore others. Like a medical atlas, the evolutionary tree "forms a set of rules," this time for reading the living world. From the myriad of possible ways to conceptualize the relationship between kinds, supertrees select evolutionary relationships as the organizing principle through which to understand the living world. Viewers soon see the tree not as a representation of life, but life as a representation of the tree. EDGE conservationists take this one step further: not merely do they see life as a representation of the tree, but they then sculpt the living world into a representation of the tree. EDGE uses supertrees to pinpoint and prioritize the species that are the most evolutionarily distinct, focusing on those species on the most isolated branches. However, there is much that we risk losing when we envision conservation activities as the protection of this "tree of life." We may be motivated, like EDGE, to prioritize the longest, loneliest branches, which are the most overt aspects of our representation, while neglecting things which a tree-view of biodiversity downplays or cannot represent at all, like ecosystem function or population health. In accounting for merely the presence of major branches, not minor, and not branch health, the EDGE approach remakes the world into a representation of the tree.

Despite my contention that this view ignores some types of flourishing, the conservation claims these trees and organizations like EDGE make are compelling. The loss of the last living representatives of entire orders of organisms is something certainly to be avoided. And Kareiva's point also is convincing—why not focus on preserving the most unique species on this planet rather than species that may be just as threatened but that have close living relatives? My point is not to critique this version of biodiversity conservation as worse than other forms but to show how, even when merely aiming to present thousands of species at once, visualizations also make certain views of biodiversity possible while obscuring others. By bringing these omissions to light, I hope to help prompt informed decisions about what we do want to prioritize rather than rely on assumptions built into our ways of conceptualizing the living world.

Biodiversity as Proliferation: Constraints of the Crowded, Circular Form

Although the evolutionary tree underpins a certain type of biodiversity conservation carried out by environmental nonprofits and conservation professionals, one does not have to be well-versed in conservation to experience the main messages of these new phylogenies. One does not even have to trace out the minute branchings and discover the most evolutionarily unique species to be affected by the way they structure the living world. Despite the vast differences among recent phylogenetic supertrees in that they represent different orders of life, are published in different journals, and use different methods in their construction, all new supertrees share two distinguishing aesthetic features: they are crowded, and they are circular.[9]

These trees immediately confront the viewer with their overwhelming abundance. They are so crowded that a user cannot both read the species names and see the complete tree all at once. In order to see individual species, a viewer has to zoom in so far that the relationship to the rest of the tree is lost, meaning the phylogenies are too dense to be easily useable. They are illustrations rather than functional means to determine species relationships. Biodiversity becomes not just a metric used to decide what and where to protect but an aesthetic, and the primary characteristic of that aesthetic is the outrageous abundance that characterizes life on Earth. This overwhelming abundance contributes to the feeling of "infowhelm" that scholars have remarked upon in relation to biodiversity as well as other arenas,[10] but it also has further implications in that it influences what kinds of stories these visualizations can communicate about biodiversity, its history, and its current state.

The detail with which these trees are constructed leads to a belief that the tree is the world, that the tree reflects an underlying reality and order to nature (rather than merely supplying a useful framework to understanding parts of the living world). This belief seems to be widespread among scientists, technicians, and tree enthusiasts. Constructor of an influential mammal supertree, Professor Olaf Bininda-Emonds writes in his textbook on supertrees, "Supertree construction is also mentioned increasingly as perhaps being a key element in our efforts to *reconstruct* the Tree of Life."[11] Manuel Lima, foundational member of the bourgeoning world of information visualization, writes in his book on the history of tree diagrams that there is a "foundational yearning for an absolute taxonomy of nature, in which all species could be organized in a *natural* hierarchy."[12] In these formulations a supertree is merely "reconstructing" a preexisting reality. The diagram created is a "natural" hierarchy rather than just a useful one. It is easy for the creators of trees of life to view their creations as representing a real tree of life "out there" that they are merely representing. However, visualizing life as a family tree where descent is what determines relatedness is only one possible framework to use to conceptualize the history of life.

Inheritance of genetic traits through sexual reproduction is actually only one way that diversity (genetic or otherwise) is created. Although the evolutionary biologists and systematists who create evolutionary trees are the first people who will point out that linear descent, genetic relatedness, and even the species concept are social constructions that are all hotly contested, the supertree diagrams they create produce readings of species relationships as linear descent. This means that supertrees omit the many lively and surprising ways that organisms have interrelated themselves. In what has been dubbed "horizontal gene transfer," microbes exchange packets of DNA with each other, making any formal conception of species in the most populated branch of life tenuous. Trees showing the bacterial tree of life have lines crisscrossing all their branches to represent horizontal gene transfer, but lines crossing a formal tree can't quite capture the immense importance of this way of being related.

Another complication to the tree of life is hybridization in plants. Two distinct but related species can mate and produce viable offspring that can later become established as its own species. Here, a tree diagram would have to depict its branches growing back together to visualize the evolutionary history. Additionally, a tree may be incapable of including organisms that are actually tight symbioses of two or more distinct species, like coral or lichen. However, we need not look as far as corals and bacteria for organisms that stretch the intellectual confines of the tree framework. As Gilles Deleuze and Félix Guattari point out in their critique of trees in *A Thousand Plateaus*, animals, too, exhibit chromosomal DNA that is not inherited. They write that "evolutionary schemas may be forced to abandon the old model of the tree and descent" when they describe how retroviruses insert their DNA and DNA from previous hosts into their current host's nuclear DNA, forever changing it and creating a nondescendant yet genetic relationship.[13] These "transversal communications between different lines scramble the genealogical tree."[14] In their conception, "evolutionary schemas would no longer follow models of arborescent descent going from the least to the most differentiated, but instead a rhizome operating immediately in the heterogeneous and jumping from one already differentiated line to another."[15] The microbiome, the subject of chapter 5, further confounds representations of life as a tree because every organism on a typical tree is, in actuality, a host of different organisms with distinctive evolutionary histories, working together in fleetingly dynamic ways.

Early life, too, was characterized not by linear descent but by much "horizontal" sharing and resharing of DNA.[16] Animal cells famously incorporated prokaryotic cells to be their energy organelle, the mitochondria. Chloroplasts, plant cells' energy organelle, probably arose in a similar manner.[17] The base of the tree of life is not a branching structure at all but is an ancient, tangled mess. The "re-creation" of the tree of life is really the formalization of a way of thinking about the relationship between organisms, whereas the ways of relating that the dynamic world of living organisms themselves have invented exceed the capacity of the formulation to depict. The organisms themselves strain against the constraints of this formulation, inspiring tweaks, adjustments, and even brand-new formalizations of relatedness.

While Deleuze and Guattari's critique on trees is useful here, it is a reading fundamentally different from my own. The limitations of phylogenetic trees that I am interested in here are not the fact that they proceed by bifurcation from one to many, which necessitates an autocratic original totality, or that nonhierarchical networks may be a more productive way to think through life on Earth. The point is not that "there is no mother tongue" for life, only the mutual shaping and becoming together that is "becoming a rhizome with." Rather than critique the ways that imaginary treelike structures shape and limit our thinking in all sorts of contexts, I'm looking at how this particular tree form, in its specific instantiation as a crowded circle and as the dominant way to visualize vast swaths of the diversity of life, makes certain biodiversity stories present instead of others. It is not the bifurcation itself that is the problem but instead that there are other formal choices that make these trees predisposed to tell every story as one of inevitable profusion. The decision to purge dead branches, the circular construction, and the bifurcation *through time* all make these capable of depicting life only as riotously proliferating.

In addition to the initial impression of abundance that these super-trees impart, their circular construction is immediately apparent. The ostensible reason for the circular construction is space efficiency. The prominent evolutionary biologist J. David Archibald writes that the circular construction wastes less space on the page than a traditional triangular-shaped tree does.[18] Manuel Lima presents an almost teleological narrative of shift to the circular construction of tree diagrams. In his book on the history of the tree form, he writes, "it was just a matter of time before it [the circle] became a vessel for representing hierarchical structures, resulting in radial tree diagrams that take advantage of the circle's space efficiency and alluring pictorial strength."[19] But space efficiency is not the only work a circle is doing for these phylogenies. These trees are not simply borrowing a shape from geometry and using it to arrange the same information differently with no effect on the content. After all, it is now commonly recognized that "images built into texts about science or technology are more than 'mere' illustration. They often function as part of the argument. Thus, it is fair to speak of 'visual rhetoric.'"[20] If so, then we must query, what is the visual rhetoric of these circular trees?

First and foremost, the circular shape is working in favor of a more egalitarian portrait of life than evolutionary trees have historically used. A circular construction demonstrates a steadfast dedication to evenness and fairness on the part of evolutionary biologists. Unlike a great chain of being, this assemblage has no "higher orders" or "lower orders" of organisms. These trees work against the repeated organization of evolutionary trees into forms that show the human species as the highest, most evolved, or best of creation, which has been (perhaps unsurprisingly) intractable. As Archibald states, "Indeed, the ladder of life, in its inaccurate simplicity and because of its historical baggage, still stubbornly persists."[21] Until very recently, most evolutionary trees that included the human species would put humans at either the far right end or at the top, reinforcing the idea that humans were the pinnacle of creation. In the circular construction, everything is at the same distance from the center. Each species living is as "evolved" as everything else because everything living has been "evolving" since the beginning of life, even if some body-formations have not changed substantially in millions of years (like alligators or coelacanths). There is no implicit display of the misguided notion that a human being is more "complex" than an amphibian.

To highlight the argument that circular phylogenies make about the unexceptional place of humans in scheme of life, the evolutionary tree from the Hillis Lab employs a "you are here" trope taken from public maps. This forces any viewer to acknowledge that human beings are part of, not separate from, the rest of life on the planet. We share history, genes, and page space with the other animals, plants, fungi, and microbes of the world. Archibald likens the "you are here" on the Hillis tree of life to the *Voyager* picture showing Earth from the edge of the solar system.[22] He reads it, convincingly, as a moment of great humility, as a recognition one's own smallness compared to the vastness of the universe. I would add that it also reminds a viewer that she isn't standing, observing the entirety of life from nowhere, which is the view that looking down at this circle of life might imply. The purpose of the "you are here" indicator, as it is commonly used on public maps, is to allow the viewer to orient herself with the top-down schematic but then look away from the top-down viewpoint and engage her embedded position in the world negotiating movement with increased knowledge and grace. The Hillis "you are here" alludes to this type of orientation device and may have a similar effect on orienting and allowing a viewer to more properly navigate her densely populated world.

In addition to making an argument about the nonhierarchical nature of life on Earth, the circular format makes the diagram look more like a literal tree, just from a novel angle. The Hillis supertree with which we started the chapter visually gestures to a cross section of the trunk of a living tree.

This resonance with tree rings has been noticed by artists who have capitalized on the visual similarities by inscribing the Hillis supertree on actual tree cross sections. The branching, which slightly curves around the center of the circle, forms a series of concentric circle-segments. The result is a series of arcs that is reminiscent of the growth rings of a tree made each year as a tree trunk grows wider and lays down new wood. Scientists can glean information about past environments based on these tree rings, creating data on past temperature, precipitation, and even fires and insect outbreaks. The art of reading tree rings, or "dendrochronology," is widely known, and even schoolchildren count rings to calculate the age of a tree. It is also common to see cross sections of trees used as timelines with historical events marked on their corresponding rings. Because of the ubiquity of amateur dendrochronology, reading the circular phylogeny seems intuitive. It is clear that older events happen toward the center of the circle, and more recent events happen at the circumference. Circular phylogenies rely on common knowledge of how to read tree rings to tell the history not of individual trees but of life on Earth.

The choice of circular construction not only ensures fairness and benefits from observers' preexisting literacy in tree rings, but it also draws upon the spiritual associations with trees, especially "tree of life" myths. Roger Cook writes that spiritual trees of life are concerned with centers and are themselves understood as the center of creation.[23] In modern supertrees, the center of the grandest phylogeny is literally the origin of life itself. The complete evolutionary tree is a new creation story, describing visually how all biota grew from a singular origin in time and space. If this is a tree whose beginnings were at the beginning of life, then the events that can be marked along its rings are not just the whole of human history but the entirety of life history. It is the story of the dawn of life, the creation of species through time, and the naming of all those (discovered) species that now cling, dive, or burrow into the surface of the globe, just as they cling to the circumference of the phylogeny in a fine downy fuzz.

The weight given to the origin of life in these phylogenies underscores the supertrees' imaginative resonances with Eden. If chapter 1's GENESYS database implies the future story of a new Eden, one that comes after a plant apocalypse, then supertrees are a new version of the original Genesis, the story of how all we see came to be. Many contemporary phylogenies openly draw on religious associations with the Tree of Life by explicitly naming themselves after it. There is the "Interactive Tree of Life,"[24] the "Open Tree of Life,"[25] and the "Tree of Life Web Project,"[26] among others. Ostensibly these phylogenies are named "trees of life" because they are branching hierarchical networks that include all life, but this naming convention hints at an alignment with religious Trees of Life and also manifests itself in attitudes toward species death and immortality.

The fact that these trees literally center on the inception of all life makes them into a new genre of origin story, one that, like Genesis, is involved in the naming of all species and characterized by mythic, golden-age abundance. These trees are not the origin story of the creation of the universe, however, but the origin story of biological diversity. They show the exponential creation of diversity through time from the beginning of life (or the beginning of mammals or birds or whatever group of organisms is featured in a tree) up to the rich abundance encountered today. They trace the forking path that led to today's particular arrangement of biodiversity. But this recognition of phylogenetic trees as the origin stories for biodiversity also points to the potential difficulty of using them in a time in which more diversity is being lost than created.

The limitations of the origin-story genre compound formal choices made in the construction of these supertrees. The incredible abundance that confronts the viewer on the initial inspection of the figure is generated, in each case, by proceeding from few to many. The interior of the circle is relatively sparse, but the bifurcations of species splitting increase in number the closer the eye traces them to the circumference of the circle until it arrives at the densely populated perimeter. Each and every published circular phylogeny displays this history of life: one that proceeds from sparseness to diversity. Taken together, these trees define a fundamental characteristic of biodiversity as exponential diversification. Winnowing is not pictured at all, though it has happened several times since the beginning of life. Current evolutionary trees make an implicit argument that the living world is and should only be getting more and more diverse.

Additionally, while these trees show the ramification of species throughout time, they do not show the actual engine driving this proliferation. They do not show natural selection. Instead, it appears that the simple passage of time drives diversification. The two variables on this type of figure are time and species number, and as time moves forward, species number increases. This leads to a mistaken impression that the number of species increases inevitably as time passes. Of course, this is not necessarily the case. Our current biodiversity crisis and the "big five" mass extinctions of the past make clear that the passage of time can equally correlate with fewer and fewer living species on the planet. Although time passing is *necessary* for the profusion of new species, it is not *sufficient*. Conditions may or may not favor speciation rates that outpace extinctions, or, as in our own time, extinction may outpace speciation.

The circular construction, despite fostering the worthy goal of more equitability between species, compounds the misleading aspects of these diagrams. Circles are notoriously difficult for viewers to understand intuitively and correctly. Many circular forms have historically been found to be deceptive. The most vitriol is reserved for the pie chart, which titan of visualization Edward Tufte famously categorizes as both the worst and second-worst figure in design, stating that "the only worse design than a pie chart is several of them."[27] In fact, when it comes to circular forms, "not only do our visual systems distort area, but also they fail to register angle with great precision."[28] The circular construction in the case of supertrees does more than just make it difficult to make estimates: I argue that the circular tree lends itself to optimistic portrayals of biodiversity proliferation. The circular construction with time radiating out from the center results in a story of profusion due to simple geometry. A circle, by definition, has a larger and larger circumference as it gets bigger, or in this case as you proceed outward from the center. If a phylogenetic tree's space is mentally broken up into a series of concentric circles, it is easy to see that the outermost circle has the biggest circumference and therefore the most space on which to show different species. A circle *cannot* show as many organisms in previous epochs as it can show in the current age, simply because of space constraints. The circular form, then, is rhetorically disposed toward a reassuring view, and therefore the impression that history creates biodiversity through the operation of time moving forward is an artifact of the graph's construction. These scientific figures define profusion as an inherent part of biological diversity, in part because of the formal choices made in figure construction.

Dead Branches on the Tree of Life

To compound the misrepresentation of the circular form, these trees do not retain dead branches. The entire periphery is made up of living organisms, and although the interior of the circle does contain extinct organisms because current embranchments arise from implied but unnamed common ancestors, the trees do not show any extinct species that are not part of a direct line to a living organism. On one hand it seems only natural that an evolutionary tree would contain only living organisms or their descendants if its purpose is to show how living organisms are related to each other. And to answer the kinds of scientific questions these trees are designed to answer, they need not show extinct organisms that left behind no living heirs. But the choice not to include the branches of extinct species that have no living descendant is not the only way trees have been constructed in the past. Comparing the aesthetics of these modern evolutionary trees with their right angles and clean lines to Darwin's verbal evocations of the tree of life in *On the Origin of Species* reveals how the formal decision to eliminate dead branches affects how these trees communicate the history of living diversity on Earth. Darwin describes his image of a tree of life in this way:

> The green and budding twigs may represent existing species; and those produced during former years may represent the long succession of extinct species. At each period of growth all the growing twigs have tried to branch out on all sides, and to overtop and kill the surrounding twigs and branches. . . . The limbs divided into great branches, and these into lesser and lesser branches, were themselves once, when the tree was young, budding twigs; and this connexion of the former and present buds by ramifying branches may well represent the classification of all extinct and living species in groups subordinate to groups. Of the many twigs which flourished when the tree was a mere bush, only two or three, now grown into great branches, yet survive and bear the other branches; so with the species which lived during long-past geological periods, very few have left living and modified descendants. From the first growth of the tree, many a limb and branch has decayed and dropped off; and these fallen branches of various sizes may represent those whole orders, families, and genera which have now no living representatives, and which are known to us only in a fossil state. . . . As buds give rise by growth to fresh buds, and these, if vigorous, branch out and overtop on all sides many a feebler branch, so by generation I believe it has been with the great Tree of Life, which fills with its dead and broken branches the crust of the earth, and covers the surface with its ever-branching and beautiful ramifications.[29]

Darwin ends the passage with an arresting image. It is as if the tree of life grows outward from the center of the Earth, and all the dead branches end underneath the surface in fossilized remains of extinct creatures. The living branches peek through the crust of the Earth and populate the surface of the planet with all the living variety we see today. Although earlier in the passage, Darwin contradicts this later depiction by figuring the branches that represent extinct species as decayed and dropped off instead of still attached to the tree, it is revealing that he nevertheless takes care to mention them at all. Instead of omitting the dead branches entirely, Darwin specifically refers to their existence and location. In one description they are fallen around the base of the tree, and in the other they are still attached to the tree, embedded in the crust of the Earth. Modern phylogenies jettison dead branches without any mention of this omission. This is a formal choice, not an inescapable constraint of the form, and in addition to his verbal description Darwin left behind sketches of circular trees in which dead branches are still present.

In figure 3, from one of his unpublished journals, Darwin has drawn circles around his tree that represent the boundary of geological eras. Only one species makes it out past the circumference of the outer circle. A viewer can calculate this diagram's representation of the percentage of extant to extinct species by counting how many dots there are and how many make it out to the present. (On the top of the sheet, Darwin writes, "Dot means new form—say in Birds"). Out of the forty or so species only one makes it out to the present. This is a phylogenetic tree that shows that the great majority of all species that have ever existed are now extinct. But, in fact, this informal sketch may still be optimistic. While it shows that living species comprise around 2.5 percent of all species that have ever existed, scientists estimate this figure may actually be closer to 0.1 percent. Nevertheless, this is a tree that defines biodiversity very differently than do current phylogenies. Importantly, ramification is still a characteristic of diversity, but it is accompanied by winnowing. *Both* are needed for a figure to encompass the wildly proliferating variety and the enthusiastic pruning that together drive speciation. This figure reminds us that the outermost edge of a phylogenetic tree may be represented as preternaturally abundant *or* austerely stark. This also reveals that the circle's "efficient" use of space that was praised by information visualization professionals and supertree creators alike is not an efficient use of space under all circumstances. When trying to show the history of life, the circumference could appear relatively barren if extinct branches of life are included. Each choice has

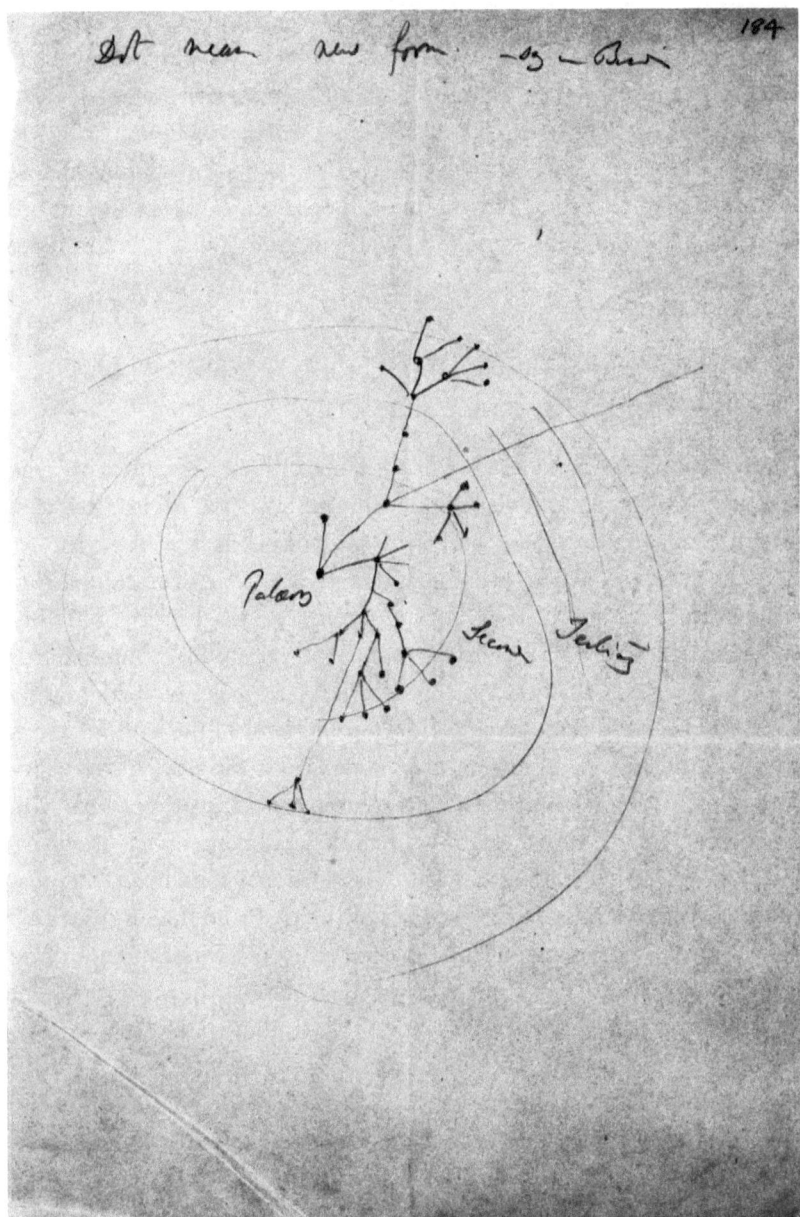

FIGURE 3. One of Darwin's hypothetical tree sketches. The rings read, from the center: "Paleoz, secondary, tertiary." The text across the top reads, "Dot means new form—say in Birds." (From Darwin's manuscript "Principle of Divergence, Transitional Organs/Instincts," 1839–72, Classmark 205.5, pages 184r; reproduced by permission of the Syndics of Cambridge University Library)

affective consequences for training viewers to see certain types of biodiversity in the world. We can confront a densely packed circumference to be humbled and awed by the amazing bounty of life on this globe, or we can be impressed with the tenuous contingency of species continuity in a world sparsely populated with survivors of myriad extinctions. These are drastically different, equally plausible stories, and considerations of biodiversity would be enriched by an engagement with both modes rather than with only one.

From the Origin of Life to a View from the Future: How Phylogenies Construct Time

The formal choices and constraints of contemporary evolutionary tree practice result in a particular relationship to time that revisits creation myths, bowdlerizes the past, and views the present as if from the future. The way these trees structure time is dictated by their all-encompassing projects in space and history. They aim to depict the history of life but only that which led directly to the current diversity distributed across the entire planet's surface. As noted earlier, at the center is the origin of life, and the circumference is the very moment of the instantaneous present. All the species around the edge are (at the time of tree construction) still extant. But there is a notable lack of overt concern with the future. None of the phylogenies include a projection of future diversity, no explicit imagination of what the future may look like. The present is a boundary that wraps and encloses the past, and the future is only the blank page surrounding the diagram. In some ways, though these trees imply a future by allowing a viewer to look at her own moment in the context of geological time—our own moment on the same page as the origin of life over three billion years ago. As debates over the term "Anthropocene" have shown, one cannot see one's own period on the geological record. One has to imagine seeing a current boundary from some kind of imagined future. Usually one can only see the geologic *past*, not the geologic *present*, so by adding the present moment to the geological record (much in the same way the term "Anthropocene," in fact, does) these trees endow users with a viewpoint that would usually only belong to future observers. A future is implied, then, in that the present is viewed from that perspective. These evolutionary trees are visualizations of the Anthropocene, the skin on the surface of the geological record that represents our present moment, invisible but perhaps recorded as a stratum characterized by another mass extinction.

But the view of history these trees display to the observer-from-the-future in whose shoes the current viewer stands is an extremely bowdlerized one. Because the trees omit all species that do not have a living descendant, they drop 99.9 percent of species that have ever existed from their portrayal of the past. This chapter has already explored how this elision is part of the formal constraints of both the circle and the branching structure. A consequence of this expurgation is that these trees eliminate the role of contingency and chance when explaining the particular set of events that led to our current assemblage of species, thereby eschewing a new materialist reading of biodiversity focused on species agency and dynamism. Rather than past efforts or accidents having an effect on what the present looks like, the present is used to decide what elements of the past are included. These diagrams present a teleological story where the way the world looks in the present is the natural and only consequence of the way things looked in the past. Without all the species that equally could have left living lineages but happened to go extinct, the teleology that the circular presentation works so hard to get rid of creeps back in. The world of these trees looks the way it does because that is how it has to look given the set of organisms available in its version of the past. This is a missed opportunity because, as Elizabeth Grosz writes, Darwin's work on evolution by natural selection, affirms "the centrality of chance."[30] His oeuvre is antiteleological in that it "refuses to assume that the temporal movement forward can be equated with development or progress." It is more inclined to explore "the productivity, the generative surprise . . . the play of repetition and pure difference"[31] than a world in which the past *had* to result in the present. In this sense, these trees which use the present to decide what organisms from the past are included are a missed opportunity to explore the radical contingency that results in our current world. However, I want to make clear that I am not demanding that these scientific visualizations drastically change their presentation. In fact, I contend that these figures fulfill their primary purpose of answering evolutionary questions quite well. Rather I am arguing that the mobilization of this imagery across domains indicates a need for a symmetrical *artistic* practice of tree construction that could push our considerations of species relationships in new directions as well as incorporate the liveliness of chance into our stories about biodiversity development.

A result of the abridged history presented in these visualizations is that they depict a past that is entirely represented in the present. To an untrained eye, they misrepresent the present as containing everything from the past in its genetic heritage. In this way they contain a subtle and unintended argument that the present set of organisms can allow complete access to the past. These phylogenetic trees of life, then, grant a sort of immortality. All extinct organisms that are pictured have living descendants, so nothing is completely gone from this version of deep history. Instead, all species have an immortal afterlife in living descendants. The immortality granted by the portrayal of a bowdlerized past emerges in the widespread impression that species carry "evolutionary history" within them.

The final result of this dwindled past is that the figures depict a version of the past as an Edenic golden age. With the bottomless abundance pictured in the present and the selective past, the trees show the past as literally a simpler time. Not only is the past selective in that it does not show the "unsuccessful" organisms, but it excludes every relationship except for that of heredity. Predator/prey, symbiosis, mutualism, parasitism, and competition are all expunged, leaving a past that is one single family with no competition, no striving for life. Since there is no extinction without leaving living descendants pictured, then competition, one of the major causes of background extinction and one of the main drivers of speciation, is also omitted. What is pictured is a world that inherently tends toward abundance and experiences very few extinctions—a world with no competition or predation: a golden age. And since the whole image presents the past and present as if viewed from the future (because the present is a thin but discernable skin on the geologic past), it means that it categorizes the present as part of the golden past. There is a subtle preemptory nostalgia here for what is not yet gone.

This sense of nostalgia for what is still here is coupled with a depiction of the past as carried within bodies. The increased attention to phylogenetic diversity in conservation decisions has resulted in extinction being figured, in part, as the loss of millions of years of evolutionary history. Given that these scientific visualizations portray the past as entirely and completely represented in the present, the loss of a species in the present is often described as loss of access to the past. The BBC quotes Donal McCarthy, an economist for the Royal Society for the Protection of Birds, as saying, "We're talking about the irreversible loss of unique species and millions of years of evolutionary history."[32] The Nature Conservancy's blog similarly features an article about a recent study that "suggests that farmers have the power to prevent a lot of these extinctions—and the loss of millions of years of evolutionary history (called phylogenetic diversity) that these species represent."[33] Species are thought of as carrying within their bodies the history that led to their own existence on Earth. Even the form of the phylogeny itself reinforces this notion. As noted earlier, the current circular phylogenies look like the cross section of a giant tree, so in this visual metaphor, a great tree of life carries all of evolutionary history (rather than just its own) within the boundaries of its body.

Sometimes carrying evolutionary history is framed as a reason to prioritize certain species, as we have seen, because they are evolutionarily unique: In a press release about his new bird supertree, the evolutionary biologist Gavin Thomas says: "Not all species are evolutionarily equal—some have few close relatives that share their DNA. These species are irreplaceable. If they are driven to extinction, millions of years of evolutionary history goes with them."[34] At other times the idea that a species or an individual carries evolutionary history within its body is used to try to grapple with deeper meanings of extinction. The environmental humanities scholar Thom van Dooren writes, looking at the last living member of a Hawaiian snail species: "I tried to think about the millions of years of evolutionary history, the countless generations of living beings, that have been required to produce a species that now finds its singular expression in this one, fragile, organism. I tried also to imagine all those generations that might have been. Were it not for the presence of rats, humans and others, in the fullness of time this species may even have evolved into something distinct from its current form."[35]

In this quotation, both the past and the future are portrayed as residing within an individual, but van Dooren's imagination of evolutionary history is very different from that of the phylogenetic trees we have been looking at. In this moment, he is trying to construct the reverse of the tree phylogenies we have been examining. He is imaginatively filling out the branches of the past to a bushy bramble in order to tell a story not of proliferation but of the winnowing of might-have-beens. This revolutionary reconception of evolutionary history as "the countless generations of living beings that have been required to produce" this last member of a species is even the less interesting trunk of van Dooren's tree. The top half is then filled out with the imagined "generations that might have been." Here we come to territory never broached by evolutionary trees. In each generation leading to the present, final snail there were possibilities that never found fruition. It is not just this currently dying species that "may even have evolved into something distinct from its current form," but each species in the past. Van Dooren adds contingency and chance to his mental tree by including possible but not factual branches leading to alternative presents. This passage, though, also indicates the *work* that it takes to get to this type of image of the past. Thinking this way does not spring easily from our minds given our current suite of visualizations for the history of species. Van Dooren doesn't effortlessly consider potential (but not realized) evolutionary histories, but it requires effort; he *"tries"* to think about them. And, in fact, he is not simply thinking but inventing and creating them as he goes, an intensive imaginative project.

The Past Within: Species as Evolutionary History

Van Dooren's imagination of contingent, potential evolutionary history is exceptional among the ways the term is used. Scientists, journalists, and humanists usually use evolutionary history in far less painstaking ways. On one level what is invoked in "evolutionary history" is unique and visible life-strategies, like the organic antifreeze in fish blood that Peter Kareiva mentions. Other times it is the DNA that is associated with the unique morphologies. And at other times "evolutionary history" is simply referring to unique DNA without any mention of specific or unusual characteristics that go along with a species' "evolutionary distinctiveness." Genotype is often referenced without any consideration of what those genes lead to when they are expressed. There is a facile assumption that genes are where this past "evolutionary history" is found. The term also conveys a sense that an organism carries DNA that is "historical" but not necessarily expressed. Although not specifically referenced, the idea that an organism carries its own "evolutionary history" within it strongly evokes the concept of fossil genes. Fossil genes are genes that are not expressed in the current organism and have mutations that make them inoperable, but they are inherited from ancient ancestors in which they were functional and expressed. For example, modern dolphin and whale genomes exhibit a fossil gene that is important in color vision and was inherited from ancestors that lived more than forty million years ago on land, where color vision is more important for survival.[36]

Fossil DNA reinforces the idea that DNA can reveal the historical path a species took to its present form. This gives the impression that all the organisms from which a species evolved are still inside of it. In this formulation an organism is like a Russian stacking doll with all of its ancestors nestled hidden inside it. As long as it is still alive, scientists can glean information about those ancestors within. It is as if the DNA of the terrestrial ancestors of whales resides within modern whales: the terrestrial ancestor mammal within the freshwater semi-aquatic proto-whales, within the saltwater aquatic but four-legged ancestors, within the marine mammal ancestors that could no longer support themselves on land, within the fully recognizable ancestral whales of the late Eocene.[37] The teleology of the great chain of being works its way back into this conceptualization where current species are the most "evolved" and carry their "less evolved" ancestors within them in a layered structure, even though these ancestors may have been just as adequately adapted to their environment as current organisms.

There is another hierarchy here too: one of DNA desirability. As Gavin Thomas's quotation above points out, not all species' DNA is equally unique, and unique DNA is more desirable for conservation than commonplace. A species with a very distinctive genome (few living relatives) is clearly here viewed as carrying "more" evolutionary history than one which has living close relatives that share large sections of its DNA. So the concept of evolutionary history is, on one level, about information storage in the medium of DNA, a conceptualization that ties evolutionary trees to the seed banks explored extensively in chapter 1, but here "history" is inversely related to the number of similar copies of the information that are out there. The claim that basal branches have "more evolutionary history" than species that have had many recent branches is misleading. Species with many close relatives could just as easily be thought of as having the same amount of "history" in their DNA. The difference is that they are not the sole carriers of that history.

Calling the DNA sequence of a living species "evolutionary *history*" is a strange choice because as long as these species are living, the contents of their DNA and their bodily morphology are not historical but present. Describing species as carrying "history" within them, or as "history" embodied, figures them as already extinct, or at least committed to extinction. In order to be history, something usually has to no longer be present. The meaning of this commonly used refrain reinforces the golden-age resonances that the phylogenies draw upon, as it positions the present as an already lost abundant past. Also, once again, time is placed as the engine driving diversification. Evolutionary history presents difference in a unit of years (or millions of years—"we could lose millions of years of evolutionary history") rather than base-pair difference or percent of shared genes (between two species). This naturalizes the idea that the phylogenies also depict: that the simple movement forward in time results in increasing biological diversity.

Another way to look at evolutionary history is as everything that is inside the circumference of the phylogenetic trees. It is the series of ramifications and proliferative relationships that lead to the present moment. It is a narrative of the past. *The Oxford English Dictionary* defines history, as opposed to annals or chronicles, as "A written *narrative* constituting a continuous chronological record of important or public events."[38] In this book's formulation of biodiversity as an accounting for things that matter, this is an account in three valences of the word. It is a mathematical formulation calculating the uniqueness and trajectory of a species, it is a story of the past, and it is a way of making the stories of organisms matter. The logic behind evolutionary history as narrative is that when a species and its DNA are gone, so is the ability to reconstruct the series of evolutionary events that led to the current arrangement of the planet's life. In scientific papers, this is the most common meaning of evolutionary history: using genetic biology to refine branches of the family tree. Scientists construct evolutionary history by figuring out when species divergences occurred and which species are most closely related. This is constructing an account of the place a species occupies in the world—how that species came to be and how it fits in with the other species surrounding it (at least evolutionarily).

In addition to opening up the definition of biodiversity to narrative, the framing of species loss as loss of evolutionary history does two important pieces of work. First, it includes human beings in biodiversity.

Evolutionary history loops "nature" into "culture" by figuring biodiversity loss as a cultural loss. It is the loss of the ability to answer questions about nonhumans, of the capacity to read the record of important events, and of the competence to imagine alternative worlds. Secondly, the term makes a first pass at expanding the current mental stakes of species loss. Evolutionary history imaginatively endows species with a longer time span. Instead of viewing the inception of a species as its initial evolution, now a species carries within it history from before its emergence as a distinct kind. It lays claim to a longer time span than just its own through the view that it carries its ancestors within it. A loss of a species, then, is viewed not just as the loss of that species but as the loss of the (already lost) ancestor species as well as the loss of something that had existed for a greater amount of time. It also positions the creature in question as an against-the-odds survivor of the loss of all the species more closely related to it. It already is the sole representative for already extinct species, so its toehold on Earth seems hard-won and serendipitous to begin with.

Framing extinction as a loss of evolutionary history is troubling too, though, because there is a slipperiness when it comes to actually regarding evolutionary history as ever completely lost. It seems that there's always a workaround to keeping the history, even if the species is extinct. A recent paper was released, for example, completing an extensive evolutionary history of the woolly mammoth from frozen tissue found in the tundra.[39] Whether it is fossils used to reconstruct dinosaur phylogenies (that look identical to bird, mammal, or any other extant phylogeny) or frozen cells from which DNA can be extracted, the "lost" history often is not actually lost.

An arresting example of the concept of evolutionary history in action is the story of Lonesome George, the famous last member of a declining tortoise species before its extinction. His death marked the end of the Pinta Island tortoise of the Galapagos. The Galapagos Conservancy website tells his life story partially in terms of evolutionary history. He was found twenty years after the species was presumed to be extinct, brought to a tortoise corral on Santa Cruz Island for protection, became "severely overweight," and eventually died without fathering any hybrid offspring with the closely related tortoises who shared his corral. The web page about George does not end with his death, however. His story continues. The Galapagos Conservancy declares that scientists have been encouraged by "the occurrence of an occasional hybrid tortoise on Wolf Volcano with half or less Pinta ancestry."[40] This species' DNA survives, and therefore so does its evolutionary history. Though Lonesome George is gone, the concept of evolutionary history grants him a kind of immortality, as he is present within the bodies of others.

One of the most arresting dangers of the metaphor of a body as the inert container of evolutionary history is that history can be reconstructed (or constructed), whereas the actual ecologically embedded organisms cannot be. Ecological flourishing may turn out to be harder to restore than evolutionary history. It is possible to find woolly mammoth legs frozen in the tundra and to sequence mitochondrial DNA, and it is possible to reconstruct a dinosaur phylogeny using fossils, but one cannot replace a living, integrated, ecologically embedded and agential organism. While Lonesome George was alive, he could surprise and confound his human caretakers with his agency. He could do things like fail (refuse?) to produce hybrid offspring with the closely related tortoises that were put in his enclosure, or he could mysteriously gain weight while the other tortoises with him remained slim. The pieces that make up the lively macromolecule DNA can surprise us and force us to renegotiate our place in the world, but they cannot do it in precisely the same way as a living Pinta Island tortoise could have. While Lonesome George was a fully fleshed (and full-fleshed) tortoise, his resurrection and immortality are as pure information carried across the different medium of several other tortoises.

Formal choices made during the construction of evolutionary supertrees portray proliferation as an inherent characteristic of biodiversity. These crowded, circular trees depict the origin story for life on Earth but leave out the branches that were unsuccessful, editing out contingency, chance, and might-have-beens from the story of life. In the process they address their scientific purpose but construct the biodiversity concept in impoverished ways when they travel outside the scientific sphere and into design websites, popular science publications, and art and museum exhibits. Supertrees also allow for a certain kind of conservation that positions the significance of species as carrying evolutionary history and declares the purpose of conservation as preserving the unique organisms that carry this history. Preservation of evolutionary history as contained in animal bodies leads to those bodies being viewed primarily as containers of important information.

I'd like to end this chapter by returning to Darwin's alternative tree illustration from his journals (fig. 3). What is most inspiring about his visualization of a hypothetical tree is that it shows *both* proliferation and pruning, recovering the contingency and chance that lead to any arrangement of organisms. The tree gestures toward van Dooren's might-have-beens in the included but terminated branches that represent species that existed but left no living relatives. It also navigates the line between the opposite impulses of global seed banks and evolutionary supertrees. It avoids picturing an apocalypse, yet it depicts definitive losses of species that are not represented in the evolutionary histories of current diversity.

In the two initial chapters of this book we have seen how opposite stories of stark apocalypse and wild proliferation both lend themselves to evacuating plant and animal bodies of vitality, agency, and surprising change, instead positioning organisms as containers of dematerialized information. From these disembodied beginnings narrated through activities that collect, represent, and categorize biodiversity, I turn next to a series of literary works that endeavor to recuperate and maintain the organismal bodies of biodiversity that are otherwise so easily lost.

3   A Bird in Hand

Species Encounters in Competitive Birding

TWO FRIENDS TRAVEL more than thirty thousand miles in one hundred days to see as many North American bird species as they can. A young mother sees a Blackburnian warbler and develops a lifelong passion, traveling across the globe to all seven continents. She misses her daughter's wedding, her husband nearly divorces her, but eventually she becomes the first person to see more than eight thousand of the world's birds. A teenager leaves the comfort of his Kansas home to hitchhike repeatedly across the country. He sleeps outside and lives off expired canned goods in order to afford his attempt to see more bird species that year than anyone else. A grieving man processes his feelings of loss by connecting with various bird species in the years following the death of his mother.

In this chapter we turn to the wild world of competitive birding to examine memoirs invested in embodied encounters with avian diversity even as each interspecies meeting is also converted into a tick mark counted toward a running total. If one is interested in strategies used to both narrate biodiversity and evoke embodied meetings between species, then the memoirs birders write about chasing rare species are a rich genre in which to look. This is a community of people formed around the pursuit of biodiversity itself, where members aim to see and record hundreds or even thousands of sightings of bird species. A few birders also record their experiences of seeing birds not just in lists but in narratives about their sequential encounter with avian diversity. These texts feature hundreds of different species described within a narrative framework that recounts pivotal moments in each author's birding life. In each case, the memoir provides a window into the world of birding where the pursuit of species is narrated as a series of encounters with incredibly treasured, unique, and loved beings who are also very unlike ourselves.

Pursing avian diversity through birding, as it is described in these memoirs, is a complex activity with a vein of paradox running through its core. At the same time that these birder memoirists are striving to connect with embodied nonhuman others in their natural context, they are tallying bird sightings into tick marks that add to a year's (or a life's) total. The experience of traveling to see birds is at once a consumer item in the new mode of the experience economy and at the same time an interspecies social gathering. The authors examined care deeply about the continued welfare of birds, yet they will excitedly chase down a storm-tossed rare bird tenuously surviving far from its usual habitat. At times the moments of encounter with birds cautiously strive toward a perspective outside the human, but just as often they are used as opportunities for the birders to develop knowledge about themselves—who they are, who they are not, and what their place in the world is. The meanings birders make out of biodiversity are as varied as the birds themselves, but they tell us that encounters with biodiversity are encounters with nature/cultures that orient us to our place in the world. Biodiversity is narrated by birders as a connection to a reality larger than themselves—one that changes their relationship to space and time so that as they physically travel to see different bird species, they imaginatively travel to the past.

In this chapter, I use memoirs written by birders to open up the contradictions at the heart of biodiversity representations. This chapter joins a cohort of books about the cultural meanings of birds and bird extinction in America, namely *Flight Maps* by Jennifer Price,[1] *Hope Is the Thing with Feathers* by Christopher Cokinos,[2] and *Scarlet Experiment* by Jeffrey Karnicky,[3] which all meditate on the relationships between birds and people, the cultural impacts of avian extinction, and the embedded position of the authors themselves in the systems of consumption and conservation that affect birdlife. Although I am interested here in similar themes, my aim is to address the underlying questions of how we represent and make meaning out of *biodiversity* itself rather than the human relationship with birds in particular. Birder memoirs are a rich place to explore not only how people relate to biodiversity but the effects of the formal choices they make in narrating this relationship even as they maintain an understanding of biodiversity that is always embodied in particular birds.

The accounts I focus on are four of the most well-known examples of memoirs written about seeing birds: *Wild America* by Roger Tory Peterson and James Fisher, *Kingbird Highway* by Kenn Kaufman, *Birding on Borrowed Time* by Phoebe Snetsinger, and the chapter "My Bird Problem" from Jonathan Franzen's *The Discomfort Zone*. While there are numerous other examples of the birding memoir, including James Vardaman's *Call Collect, Ask for Birdman,* Alan Davies and Ruth Miller's *The Biggest Twitch*, Sean Dooley's *Big Twitch*, and Pete Dunne's *The Feather Quest*,[4] the four I have chosen are some of the foundational texts of the genre and some of the most widely read. In addition, these four texts encompass an array of types of birder memoirs. They range in time scale from focusing on a single big year to narrating the accumulation of an entire life list, vary from the scientific to the literary, and provide a spectrum of author experience from amateur to professional.

Wild America by Roger Tory Peterson and James Fisher documents the year of two professional ornithologists as they travel around the coasts of America in search of bird species. It is the memoir that kicked off the concept of a big year, where a birder tries to see as many species as he or she can within a single year. *Kingbird Highway* is a memoir looking back on Kenn Kaufman's teenage big year, which he accomplished by hitchhiking to every part of the United States. *Birding on Borrowed Time* documents not a big year, but a big life. Phoebe Snetsinger's memoir detailing the accumulation of her life-list represents the account of the greatest number of birds seen in one lifetime (at the time): more than 8,500 different species. I also draw on Jonathan Franzen's chapter "My Bird Problem" from his memoir *The Discomfort Zone*, which describes his introduction to and subsequent obsession with birds with self-deprecating humor.

Birding as Accounting

Throughout *Eden's Endemics* I have been arguing that the concept of biodiversity can be understood as a kind of accounting with all the concurrent valences that I enumerated in this book's introduction. Birder memoirs are especially productive for looking at biodiversity-as-accounting because they bring forward the many senses of accounting all at once. These are accounts (stories) of the birders' accounts (ledgers) that try to make bird species count (matter) more with the general public and hold humans accountable (responsible) for their effects on bird populations.

Birding highlights the arithmetical side of biodiversity consumption through the detailed records that are integral to birding. Maintaining an accurate tally of birds seen or heard is essential if one is listing or attempting a record. The following quotation from James Fisher in *Wild America* grants some insight into the kinds of mental tallies and arithmetic that birders perform at the same time as they are seeing and appreciating birds. These are not simple ledgers, but master species lists comprised of overlapping sublists that are simultaneously compared to previous lists. James Fisher writes:

> Roger had shown me 132 species of birds—more birds than I had ever seen in one day before in my life. (My best day's list in Europe—made one day in central France—was 97). And never before had I seen so many new ones in a single day: 38 were "life" birds. Statistically, about one-fourth of the birds we saw this day—35 species—were birds still on their passage North; nearly one-fourth—29 or 30 species—were Mexican birds that spill over into southeast Texas. Less than one-seventh—18 species—were birds that also belong to the Old World.[5]

Birding memoirs are full of these kinds of tallies where a day's success is measured in numbers of birds seen. It is not only the sighting of each bird that is important but the fact that it adds to the day/year/life total. But what's more interesting than the desire for large totals is the complicated comparisons and equivalencies that can arise when species are first converted into tally marks and then sorted into complex and overlapping categories having to do with ranges, migration patterns, and relative abundance. The initial chapters of Fisher's sections of *Wild America* are full of comparisons between his native British and the new American fowl, for example. Fisher recounts seeing "the pied billed grebe, which is the counterpart of our dabchick, the great blue heron, a counterpart of our common heron, but six inches taller, and the ring-necked duck, counterpart of our tufted duck. We also met a beautiful small hovering falcon, closely resembling our kestrel. . . . We met the killdeer, which fills the farmland niche of our lapwing, and the mourning dove, which takes the place of our turtle-dove."[6]

These equivalencies of species, which Fisher is creating, alternately draw upon appearance, genetic relatedness, and ecological function. His passages are marked not only by a loving attention to birds but also by a vast knowledge-set allowing for the comparison of minute details over a variety of domains. In order to compare birds from different regions of the world, Fisher has clearly spent many hours contemplating the infinitesimal differences in markings, diet, body construction, flight strategies, and bill shape that differentiate similar species of birds from each other. On the other hand, this passage underscores the interchangeability of bird species that is implied in the conversion of each bird into tally. Beneath Fisher's observations is some sort of complicated equation of life, where each species has an "Old World" counterpart, so that one pied billed grebe equals one dabchick, but one great blue heron equals one common heron plus six inches. Countering this equivalency of species, however, is the simultaneous differentiation in terms of overlapping sublists that demonstrate geographical, species, and personal *difference:* birds are British or American, larger or smaller, known to Fisher or new. All are exhilarating.

Adding to the complexity of this bird-species ledger consisting of sublists of differences and equivalencies is the fact that the species concept results in moving goalposts for ledger-keeping. The American Ornithologists' Union keeps abreast of systematics changes by altering their species designations,[7] following trends in scientific consensus by lumping previously considered distinct species together or splitting a single species into two distinct ones. When this revision practice began in the 1970s, birders who were unprepared saw their life totals change overnight and then keep changing for the next fifty years. Because Peterson and Fisher's memoir covers only their one hundred days together, this is a topic they do not broach. Snetsinger and Kaufman, however, write about the ramifications of shifting species boundaries as Snetsinger's memoir covers decades, and Kaufman's is written as an adult looking back on his teenage big year. Snetsinger notes that birders who kept simple checklists, marking only the first time they saw a species, had to give up on keeping up-to-date lists. Snetsinger herself kept lists documenting *every* bird encounter with precise notes on markings, location, and behavior. She could, through good "book work," keep her lists abreast of the continual changes. She writes in *Birding on Borrowed Time*, "I had a net gain of close to 150 species simply by doing all this thoroughly fascinating book work, and I found the whole exercise a most pleasurable review of all the birds I'd ever seen."[8] This accounting-style work with lists, tallies, and records is an enjoyable part of the experience of consuming biodiversity.

One of the major drawbacks of this detailed accounting of species seen is most obviously the excessive focus on *species* diversity. The disproportionate focus on species-level diversity may have rippling consequences on conservation considering how instrumental birders have been in protecting bird habitat, especially in flyways. *Wild America* is full of stories about bedraggled species whose habitat is lovingly brought back thanks to timely conservation action by bird enthusiasts. However, this conservation attention is focused almost entirely on the species level. The decline and threatened extinction of a species will galvanize action among birders and the general public to an extent that the decline of population levels or the disappearance of a species from a subset of its range will not. And this emphasis makes sense given the structure of birding; each species lost is one more check mark that will be forever uncheckable. Consequently, conservation's focus is not on a healthy ecosystem or population but revolves around maintaining the presence of species, even if those species exist in degraded ecosystems or have tiny populations.

Birders themselves are keenly aware of this drawback, especially in light of the fact that what is considered a "species" is not constant, which is itself a reflection of the ambiguity of the species concept. Kenn Kaufman tells of the consequences of one such redrawing of species lines in *Kingbird Highway*. He notes that in 1973 the American Ornithologists' Union decided that the dusky seaside sparrow was not a unique species but was, rather, a local variant of the regular seaside sparrow. He then describes how within a decade these taxonomic decisions were being rethought, and several prominent biologists were "suggesting that these localized forms were full species, after all. But by that time, the Dusky Seaside Sparrow would be extinct."[9] While there may be an outcry for a bird species that is near extinction, there is no impetus for listers to care about the preservation of local varieties. Kaufman states bluntly, "Once a bird was lumped, as far as the listers were concerned, it might as well not exist."[10] The mechanisms of bird listing lend themselves to strengthening the already prevalent mode of biodiversity conservation at the species level.

Prioritizing Process and Repressing Lists

Although numerical accounting of species seen is a fundamental component of the birding experience, these memoirs demonstrate that birders are also seeking ways of cherishing birds outside of an accumulative, purely listing, and disembodying context. In fact, there is a sense in these memoirs that the list, while being pursued, is also to be avoided. Kenn Kaufman, the youngest of the birders at the time of his big year, and perhaps therefore the most eager to prove himself, writes the most explicitly about this tension. As his list gets longer, he finds himself agreeing more and more with a birding mentor who tells him early on: "The list total isn't important, but the birds themselves *are* important. Every bird you see. So the list is just a frivolous incentive for birding, but the birding itself is worthwhile. It's like a trip where the destination doesn't have any significance except for the fact that it makes you travel."[11] While lists are an essential component of birding, these memoirists write about how the pursuit of a record is valuable mainly because of the bird encounters it prompts. However, the need to discuss this assertion at length indicates the list's power to potentially override the priorities of a birder who is not guarding against the seductive power of the list.

Perhaps keeping the list or record in perspective is one of the reasons why the lists behind these memoirs never make an explicit appearance. Although all of the memoirists keep a list of species seen, it is almost as if the list itself is unspeakable within the text. None of the memoirs contain embedded lists of the birds the authors saw on a particular day or in a particular location, something that might be a natural inclusion given that each narrative recounts remarkable birding days and places. If the texts do contain lists of bird names at all, they are paratextual, relegated to the index along with other topics for which one might wish to search. Moreover, Peterson and Fisher repeatedly repress the list within their narrative, as if they have to keep it from boiling to the surface. Peterson writes: "To tell of all the birds we saw during our first two days in Mexico . . . would read like a partial check-list of the birds of Tamaulipas,"[12] and later Fisher echoes him: "If I mentioned *all* the birds we saw in Mexico, this account would read too much like a list."[13] The list is that which may not enter the text of the memoir. This ellipsis is curious, as on one level the memoir is a narration of a subset of the list. Each encounter with a species is written about in long-form instead of expressed as a Latin name. Therefore the memoirs are a lot like lists themselves, though an actual list never makes an appearance. Despite the extensive defense of lists as literary in recent criticism,[14] and the assertion that certain lists can communicate "a sense of heightened attention to the details of the contemporary world"[15] (something these memoirs are invested in), these texts imply that no one would ever want to read a list of birds. In birder memoirs the list is at once the underlying backbone of the narrative and the threat that could kill it.

For Ursula Heise in her consideration of the cultural meanings of extinction, lists of extinct species function as a "basic organizational tool" in popular science texts: "The catalogs that accompany and complement the narrative evoke a numerical sublime of sorts, numbers too large to be contained by the conventional storytelling procedures that focus on a discrete set of events, scenes, and characters."[16] The latent lists of birder memoirs invoke a similar sense of numbers so large that they exceed traditional narrative techniques. At the same time, the birding list taps into a completely different emotional register than the extinct species list of Heise's texts. A birder's lists of species seen is an ecstatic celebration of the diversity in the world rather than an overwhelming lament for extinct species. Although the lists are only ever alluded to, the text referring to their potential existence still fosters the impression of overflowing abundance that spills outside the narrative framework. The repression of the list, then, works on two levels to gesture toward meanings that escape the bounds of birding conventions. The refusal to explicitly list species signals the birder's investment in relationships with birds that extend beyond the tally each sighting adds to an overall total at the same time as the repressed list captures the feelings of overwhelming abundance of biodiversity that could never be contained by the memoir's narrative.

Socializing across Species

Despite the utility of lists in imparting a sense of overflowing abundance, their absence signals a commitment to birds as important companions.

The refusal to list in these memoirs might result from a sense that the list is inadequate because it erases individuality—a critique of lists that literary scholars have noted in other eras.[17] In these memoirs, the iterative encounter with bird species is not viewed just as one tick mark that adds to a total tally; it is also repeatedly described as a social encounter. Snetsinger's favored expression for seeing bird species, for example, is "connect with." She writes: "We connected nicely with Biddulph's Ground Jay in Xinjiang."[18] And later: "the Semicollared Puffbird, to which I devoted many solo hours, connecting gratifyingly well in the end."[19] She also shares "an exquisite experience with a Malaysian Railbabbler,"[20] birds do or do not "cooperate"[21] with her, and she feels it is a "tremendous pleasure to renew my acquaintance with this utterly captivating little wader."[22] Fisher and Peterson similarly draw on phrases of social exchange: "We tried to get on close terms with the fabulous trogon";[23] "We had an appointment to keep with the evening owls at Madera Canyon";[24] and "we met a party of band-tailed pigeons."[25] These somewhat whimsical phrases of social nicety belie a deeper feeling, a desire for a relationship, if only for a moment, with each bird seen. Although each bird species does incrementally increase year or life totals, it is also the *connection* with the bird that is sought by the birders.

This interest in connection across species boundaries evokes Donna Haraway's detailed analysis of species encounters in *When Species Meet*. At the heart of her book is Haraway's relationship to her dog, Cayenne Pepper. Haraway and Cayenne compete as teammates in the sport of dog agility, live together, eat together, and share an intimate, long-term relationship replete with all the physical touch and affection that implies. ("Surely, her darter-tongue kisses have been irresistible,"[26] writes Haraway.) And, in fact, one of the central questions of the book is, "Whom and what do I touch when I touch my dog?"[27] However, the concept of companion species and the mutually shaping dance of species encounters encompasses more than the intimate relationship between pet and owner (or teammate, coworker, and family member— the main categories of dog/human relationships included in Haraway's text). After all, we will have only glancing encounters with most of the species we ever interact with. In one distinctive section of her book, Haraway steps out of the canine realm to explore the relationship between marine mammals and the scientists who attach cameras to them. This relationship, as viewed through the television show *Crittercam*, however, is still characterized by *touch*. She describes the process of getting the cameras onto the creatures: the "divers ready to jump off a moving boat and embrace a large swimming critter who is presumably not especially longing to hug a human"[28] and mentions the salt spray and the muscular human bodies on screen. One of the most notable aspects of the process, for Haraway, is "the sheer *physicality* of all that is Crittercam [which] dominates the television screen."[29]

While touch is central to the stories Haraway tells, it is not the only way that meaningful species encounters happen. She writes, "Touch, regard, looking back, becoming with—all these make us responsible in unpredictable ways for which worlds take shape,"[30] clearly indicating that not only touch but other modes of encounter including only "looking back" can entangle us in life-worlds unlike our own and make us responsible. While birders' interaction with birds is certainly less physical than attaching crittercams to whales or playing an interspecies team sport like dog agility, the contact the birders do have is intimate in its own way and does manifest as "regard, looking back," and even, perhaps "becoming with." The use of phrases like "connect with" and "get on close terms with" to describe seeing birds indicates that these birders are at least aiming for a mutual exchange. The question remains, are birders among those who have, in Haraway's words, "met the gaze of living, diverse animals and in response undone and redone themselves"?[31] How do birders undo and redo themselves in these memoirs?

The first and most obvious ways that birders unmake and remake themselves in response to regarding (and occasionally being regarded by) a bird is by becoming birders in the first place. Certainly the first Blackburnian warbler that Phoebe Snetsinger sees at the age of thirty-four changes the course of her entire existence. Snetsinger recounts the moment of her conversion in a succinct but impactful way: "The first bird I really saw through those binoculars was a fiery-orange male Blackburnian Warbler that nearly knocked me over with astonishment—and quite simply hooked me forever."[32] The sight itself is narrated as physical—an astonishment so intense, it is a blow that almost prostrates her. This is not a jostle from which she ever recovers, and revealingly, she narrates this fact by flipping the agency of the situation and metaphorically putting herself in the position of an animal, though the animal is not a bird but a fish. She is "hooked" forever. In the years that follow, Snetsinger seeks out thousands more encounters with birds first in her home state, then nationally, and finally around the world, until she dies on a birding trip in 1999.

The individual moments with birds often do not take many paragraphs to describe, but cumulatively they make up the meat of each memoir. The argument I want to make here is that this long series of one-time interactions with individual birds and species still enacts, in a small way, the kind of species encounter that Haraway describes in her much more long-term and physically close relationship with her dog, Cayenne. This is an encounter "in which all the actors become who they are *in the dance of relating,* not from scratch, not ex nihilo, but full of the patterns of their sometimes-joined, sometimes-separate heritages both before and lateral to *this* encounter."[33] Birds are certainly not left unchanged by the activity of birding. Improved access to spectacular birding spots requires roads and infrastructure development. Travel around the world to see birds also means putting carbon into the air, contributing to a changing climate that is certainly one of the arenas that affects how birds and people can "become who they are." On the other hand, there are also robust conservation efforts that are intended to preserve the birds that are valued by birders, which also affect who they and we can be in the world. Birders are affected by this encounter too. Neither party leaves this species meeting the same but instead become who they are together in a "dance of relating."

Agency and Reality in the Experience of Birding

The memoirs under consideration describe what this interspecies encounter looks like from the birder/author's point of view. Doing so grants insight into what meanings human beings tend to make out of birding and broader interactions with biodiversity. At the most basic level, these species encounters entail recognizing the bird's own agency. This recognition of another is often described as a connection to "reality," or a birder's earnest attempt to get outside of their own human perspective, if only for a moment.

There are portions of each novel that recognize that birding is not exclusively about the birder's effort. The moment of connection has to come also from the bird participating in the interaction. For example, when Snetsinger sees a rare harpy eagle, she writes: "We could hardly believe what we were seeing. It was awesome and humbling, rather like a visit from a deity. The bird gave us plenty of time to study and absorb it, but alas, declined to stay around for the others to see."[34] This passage is not about how the birding group trekked and bushwhacked and played tape recordings, how they found the bird, but instead about how the bird "gave" them time to study it but "declined" to stay to let the others on the expedition see it. The recognition that a birding experience can be made or broken by the bird's own agency is also told in the mode of an encounter with a deity, which confers a more-than-human agency to birds in the realm of birding.

Kenn Kaufman has a similar encounter recognizing the agency of a rare bird, but his tale capitalizes on the humor of the unexpected: "We had directions: precise directions, even pinpointing the large spruce on which the owl usually sat. The owl, unimpressed by such precision, was actually perched on a nearby powerline pole when we first saw it. Apparently our arrival did not impress it either. It merely glanced down at us occasionally with benign indifference, while we gazed back through a battery of binoculars and telescopes and cameras."[35] This passage pokes fun at the idea that one can have precise directions to a bird. Moreover, the bird's own indifference to all the human enthusiasm puts human activities in perspective, a different perspective than that of the birders themselves, who, of course, tend to view their own activities as meaningful. The image of a mass of excited birders eagerly gazing at an indifferent owl through their various lenses disrupts the absorption in the image of the owl and shows that Kaufman at least is metaphorically turning that lens around and seeing himself. This passage also brings up the agency of the bird, in that it acts in unexpected ways. Despite Kaufman's knowledge of exactly where to find it, the bird appears somewhere else, not out in the wilderness but on a powerline: the very powerline that makes possible the rapid communication of its own sighting, bringing the birders in from far and wide.

The descriptions of these two encounters bring up the question of anthropomorphism's place in agential readings of the world. Certainly imagining an owl as "indifferent" and "unimpressed" and describing a harpy eagle as a deity who "declined" to linger use human frameworks to think through the agency of birds. It would be a mistake, however, to assume that this tendency toward anthropomorphism in these moments invalidates the authors' efforts to conceptualize nonhuman agency. New materialist theorists have argued that anthropomorphism can actually be a useful tool when thinking with the more-than-human world. Rather than force animals into an ill-suited human description, Jane Bennett has argued that "in a vital materialism, an anthropomorphic element in perception can uncover a whole world of resonances and resemblances"[36]—resonances and resemblances that are far more often ignored in favor of viewing the nonhuman world as inert and malleable. Similarly, Serenella Iovino and Serpil Opperman, in their introduction to the collection *Material Ecocriticism,* explain that "anthropomorphism can even act against dualistic ontologies and be a 'dis-anthropocentric' stratagem meant to reveal the similarities and symmetries existing between humans and nonhumans."[37] Although birder-memoirists use human terms to describe birds' choices rather than imagine radically different forms of agency, these anthropomorphic elements demonstrate a recognition of resonances between human and bird agency.

If recognizing the agency of birds is the foundation of an interspecies encounter, the resulting change that birders document in themselves (how they are "undone" and "redone") is the feeling of a connection to "reality." This feeling of reality often means being connected to something larger than one's self. Phoebe Snetsinger describes her thirty-four-year-old prebirding self as being "finally . . . ready to see what had lain before my eyes for all those years." Her entry into birding was an "awakening that has ultimately led me to get the *real* world in focus and that has given me my bearings for navigating through the best years of my life."[38] To her, the real world is the world of birds. She never explicitly explains why birds give her this feeling of reality, but she does mention the pleasure of transforming her viewpoint through watching birds. Initially when she sees her first great blue heron she wonders how on Earth they get food to their young without stabbing the babies with their long, pointed beaks. But as she sits with them and observes them feeding their nestlings, they transform her perspective: "Watching those creatures do what they had been doing successfully for millions of years, without any help from us, finally let me learn not to judge everything from human standards."[39]

In his memoir Kenn Kaufman is more explicit about what, for him, is "real" about the world of birds. He describes his experience birding during an unseasonable, dramatic storm:

> Night was falling as we turned away from the inlet and headed in toward town. On the way, we were talking about the insulation of

human experience. We live enclosed in artificial structures with controlled climates, synthetic food, and purified water. No wonder our glimpses of the *real world* come as a shock. Today we'd been out at the edge of things, looking across into another existence, where a major storm could mean life or death. But now we were going back into Manteo to take it easy—to join all those people who were sitting in their houses, listening to weather reports without feeling the weather.[40]

Here, Kaufman (in the tradition of many contemporary memoirists) sees his own life as lacking in "real" experience.[41] Birds, on the other hand, are the epitome of real: exposed to weather, outdoors, uncomfortable. He does not address why an uncomfortable experience should be categorized as any more "real" than a comfortable one, and the passage uncritically lumps together all "humans" and what their experiences are. In fact, most humans do not live in controlled climates, and to most human populations on Earth, including cities in the United States, a major storm can indeed "mean life or death." This glossing over of the great disparity that exists within humanity is all the more surprising because Kaufman, for the duration of his big year, is one of those humans who is subject to the elements. Each night, he sleeps outdoors in his sleeping bag. If it is raining, he looks for an overpass or just resigns himself to getting wet. He sleeps on the sides of roads, in fields, or wherever his ride lets him off. He is remarkably subject to the elements, but what gives him the feeling of closeness to "reality" is not his own exposure to the cold, wet weather, or his own danger, but birds' vulnerability to the very same conditions. I contend that a prolonged and close attention to members of another class of animal grants these birdwatchers, not a fantastical access to nonhumans' way of being, but a momentary move toward a perspective outside of usual human experience. This minuscule but earnest shift away from human perception toward birds' perceptual, embodied world in all its exposure to the elements is what feels real to these authors. Kaufman here does clearly engage in "looking across into another existence," and in response undoes and remakes himself.

In Roger Tory Peterson and James Fisher's account, the desire to shift out of their own human perspective primarily manifests as an inability to describe their birding experiences using language, numbers, or visualizations, a representational difficulty that mirrors that of biodiversity itself. Though Peterson and Fisher travel around the country to see birds, they are interested more broadly in wildlife and landscapes of any type, and some of the areas in the narrative where they are most explicit about the inability to represent their experiences are in response to spectacular landscapes. When they see the Grand Canyon, Peterson writes: "To describe the beauty of the staggering panorama risks triteness. No painter, even on a giant canvas, has ever been able to give more than an impression.... Words are not adequate either; one can be duped by the dictionary."[42] Similarly, of the Mariposa Sequoia Grove in Yosemite Valley, Fisher writes: "Roger and I looked up the statistics, of course—height, diameter, circumference. They are a lot of fun; but they cannot measure the serene immensity of the gigantic plant community of Mariposa, or convey its living spirit."[43] Neither statistics, nor words, nor paintings can capture the lived reality of their travels. On one hand, overt claims by authors to representational failure are one technique that magnifies the sensation of scale for the object or event described.[44] On the other hand, the fact that these experiences are imagined as unrepresentable indicates that in their experience, the authors are connecting to places and beings outside of the usual human modes of communication.

When it comes to birds, the unrepresentable nature of Fisher and Peterson's experiences becomes subtler. The main way that they try and fail to represent their birding is through sound rather than the bird *sightings* favored by Kaufman and Snetsinger. Throughout the book Peterson and Fisher endeavor to transcribe birdsong into the English alphabet. This demonstrates both their earnest desire to communicate what these remarkable birds sound like and their complete inability to do so despite their best efforts using typography, description, transcription, and metaphor. What follows are just a few examples from their book. A Louisiana water thrush sings a "high, slurred whistle, thrice repeated as a preliminary to an under-breath warbling, a breezy, descending jumble of sound."[45] They hear a hooded warbler "brightly whistling . . . sweetenthe ᵗᵉᵃ o."[46] A prairie warbler sounds "like a mouse with a toothache," singing an "ascending chromatic zee-zee-zee-zee" in "a plaintive and pretty song."[47] And black-throated green warblers "lisped dreamily" "   zee   zee."[48] Peterson and Fisher are attempting to stretch the bounds of what can be communicated in printed English. They are engaging with these species in ways that both rely on and exceed the written word (something that becomes somewhat of a convention in tricks for memorizing birdsong). In one rare instance, they use punctuation to describe what words cannot. They hear a whiskered screech owl's "quiet, yet penetrating song, a sequence with a code of four: --- -, --- -, --- -."[49] Here, they do not attempt to transcribe the hooting in a sequence of English letters. Instead, the dash represents the ineffable, that which cannot be expressed in written words. One could even read the dashes as leaving the empty space of the bird itself in the text, as a place held open for that whiskered screech owl, which could never be captured as information communicated in another medium.

Unreal Days in the Experience Economy

Birding, for birders, is a space for connection to a series of other species that leaves one with a sense of a greater reality beyond the self. Simultaneously, birding is described as an "unreal" experience. In the beloved birding documentary *The Central Park Effect,* birder Chris Cooper lists seven pleasures of birding. The final pleasure is "the unicorn effect." He explains: "After you've been birding for a little while, you become familiar with a bird from seeing it in the field guide, but you've never seen it in real life. It takes on a mythological status. Then, one day, there it is in real life, almost like a unicorn walking out of the forest."[50] Birds are so unparalleled that they cannot be real, and the act of seeing them in real life is as exciting and shocking as spotting a fantastical creature of myth. The memoirs under consideration register this same feeling of unreality in a different mode. Even as some birders describe birding as a connection to reality, birding can also give the impression of a staged or theatrical experience, too spectacular or compelling to be real life. At many points, the birders write about birding as if it were theater. Franzen writes that the spring migration in Central Park is "a dream in which yellowthroats and redstarts and black-throated blue and black-throated green warblers had been placed like ornaments in urban foliage, and a film production unit had left behind tanagers and buntings like rolls of gaffer's tape, and ovenbirds were jogging down the Ramble's eroded hillsides like tiny costumed stragglers from some Fifth Avenue parade: as if these birds were just momentary bright litter, and the park would soon be cleaned up and made recognizable again."[51]

The migrating birds are compared to the ornaments and equipment that mark the difference between ordinary life and the heightened sensory system of a budget film. The birds are at once the props—decorations that set the scene, the extras in a parade, and the infrastructural elements that are never shown but are instrumental to make a cohesive fictional world. They give the sense of the park as being momentarily beyond normal life, a little brighter, a bit more intense. Peterson and Fisher write of birding in a similar vein when they describe a bird that "put on such a good show for us"[52] or of a side trip: "this memorable day on the Coronados had been like a play of home, but with our native seabirds impersonated by a different cast."[53] Kaufman writes of birding near oil rigs in Texas: "It was an appropriate setting for a science-fiction movie, or for the start of a Big Day."[54] Birds are as incredible as any media spectacle available, and their setting, appearance, or the heightened experience of seeing them is often communicated as fantasy, film, or theater.

The comparison of birding to film production and theater brings to the forefront something that I have so far only hinted at: the fact that birding, like nearly everything else in contemporary life, is a consumer product. Birders purchase the experience of seeing birds through buying specialized equipment and paying for travel. Like theatergoers, birders pay to enjoy not a physical product nor for a service but rather for a satisfying and memorable event. In fact, experiences, Joseph Pine and James Gilmore claim, are the consumer item that more and more individuals are seeking. In their book *The Experience Economy,* they propose that the service economy has given way to the experience economy, where consumers aren't buying tangible goods or ordinary services but memorable experiences.

> Experiences have always been around, but consumers, businesses, and economists lumped them into the service sector along with such uneventful activities as dry cleaning, auto repair, wholesale distribution, and telephone access. When a person buys a service, he purchases a set of intangible activities carried out on his behalf. But when he buys an experience, he pays to spend time enjoying a series of memorable events that a company stages—as in a theatrical play—to engage him in an inherently personal way.[55]

Nature encounters in general and bird sightings in particular fit into the definition of the experience economy. In addition to all the traditional material products that birders purchase for their hobby—like identification manuals, binoculars, special binocular straps that don't put pressure on the neck, and vests with many pockets—birders also purchase flights or rent cars to travel to "wild" areas and pay fees to enter public or private lands. In her memoir, Phoebe Snetsinger accumulates her 8,500 species sightings by a combination of hard work and procuring spots on expensive, preplanned trips to remote locations complete with meals and guides. Although birding is nonconsumptive in that birders do not harvest the birds they encounter, sharing memorable, theatrical moments of heightened reality with birds does require the purchase of quite a few things. Travel is not nonconsumptive activity, as taking cars, planes, and staying in lodges not only puts carbon into the atmosphere but requires the development of infrastructure to support travelers. Although Kenn Kaufman, on his hitchhiking big year, proves that one can bird competitively with minimal participation in the consumer economy, most birders do travel or buy equipment, and in fact the U.S. Fish and Wildlife Service estimates that "bird watchers spend nearly $41 billion annually on trips and equipment."[56]

Birding's status as a consumer activity explains the tendency of these memoirists to become bird addicts. Celia Lury notes that our consumer economy is marked by "an increasing visibility of so-called consumer illnesses . . . such as addiction, whether it be addiction to alcohol, sex, food or shopping."[57] Just like consumer culture itself, birding relies on the incessant pursuit of novelty, which does seem to be habit-forming. Kenn Kaufman describes his repeated feelings upon seeing each rare bird he chases in these terms: "A feeling of elation—and at the back of my mind, an opposite reaction, a vague letdown because the search was over. A release of tension, and then the tightening of the spring for the next search: chasing a record, the most important bird was always the next one, not this one, and there was always another new bird somewhere ahead."[58] He's caught up in a race, has to chase his next acquisition, his next high, even though such an attitude allows him little time to observe the birds he actually loves so much. Similarly, James Fisher and Roger Tory Peterson exhibit a saturation characteristic of addiction in which they can no longer appreciate all the rare species they spot. Fisher writes: "And somehow it was difficult to be overwhelmingly surprised by the snail kites and the annis, incredibly rare though they were. By now the incredibly rare was becoming almost commonplace."[59] And later he echoes this sentiment, writing: "A green kingfisher sped by, flashing a novel beauty; but novelty was now our daily bread."[60] They must chase more and more exotic and exquisitely rare birds to experience an emotional reaction to them. Jonathan Franzen pokes fun at his own addiction, likening his bird sightings to being "connected to a nicely calibrated drip of speed."[61] Although the humor of Franzen's comparison stems from the incongruity of describing a geeky and educational activity as a drug addiction, there does seem to be an addictive element to listing (though perhaps not to casual birdwatching). Despite many of these birders' insistence that it is not the list that matters but the birds themselves, not one of the birders in these memoirs gives up the listing before their year is complete.[62] Species sighting and especially competitive listing become a consumer addiction of sorts.

Rare Birds and the Sense of Out-of-Place

The peripatetic nature of chasing rare birds bestows these birders with a complex sense of place that is at once wide-ranging due to the birders' own travels, grounded in extensive knowledge of where birds typically belong, and gleefully excited by birds out-of-place. Because of the importance of rare birds to a big year, some of the memoirists display a surprising blindness to context. Built into competitive listing is the necessity to see strays, windswept birds that have made landfall way off course. Only 675 species or so actually live in the United States for some part of their life cycle,[63] but the record for birds seen in the North American birding region is more than 745.[64] This means any competitive birder has to see individuals that stray into the American birding region due to weather or accident. Competitive listing positions these lost birds as a good thing—as bonuses for birders who want to add to their American list. In fact, once birders' lists get to a certain number of species, the only way to add species is to see an individual that is making do far from everywhere it knows how to survive. This interest in seeing birds out of their typical geographic region is perplexing because it relies on a foundational knowledge of where birds *should* be, so that a birder can see them precisely where they *shouldn't* be. A deep knowledge of species and place is combined with the desire for those place-based tendencies to be broken.

The blindness to context may belie a surprising lack of concern for individual, suffering birds, but it is also characterized by a healthy willingness to see birdlife anywhere—not just in sanctuaries and preserves but in the touched landscapes within which most people spend most of their time. Peterson and Fisher describe seeing a Bonaparte's gull at the end of large sewer pipe at Newburyport,[65] a dovekey on the beach at Coney Island,[66] and a "limpkin, teaching its young to eat giant snails in the shallows less than a hundred yards from a noisy uninhibited amusement park" in Florida.[67] Kaufman remarks that city dumps are among the best places for finding birds. Similarly, in Texas he expounds on the seeming contradiction between a blighted landscape and impressive biodiversity: "As we approached Freeport and the coast, the horizon was filled with tall oil tanks, chemical tanks, steel towers for powerlines, factory buildings, dozens of smokestacks, and derricks and cranes for ongoing construction. It looked like some bad dream of a science-fiction future. I was just as amazed as when I had passed this way the preceding April: amazed that Victor Emanuel had been able to see past this surface ugliness, to see that the surrounding habitats would add up to the most diverse Christmas Bird Count circle in North America."[68] The traffic, oil tanks, powerlines, factories, smokestacks, and construction all add up to a landscape that does not conform to the traditional idea of nature as a place separate from human activity, so thoroughly critiqued decades ago by William Cronon.[69] Birders, though as susceptible to longings for the "unspoiled" nature of their Romantic heritage as the rest of us, are forced to think beyond the traditional binary between human landscapes and natural landscapes. Birds compel them to see nature in the everyday—in backyards, on telephone poles, along highways, and even next to oil tanks. Birders travel obsessively, yes, but also indiscriminately. They are eager to see bird diversity wherever it may be, even and especially in the touched landscapes of human use.

Biodiversity as Time Travel: Primordial Pasts and European Explorers

While the experience of interspecies interactions opens access to typically ignored landscapes for birders, it also opens up distant times. In other words, birders do not travel just in space but also in time; for certain individuals, biodiversity can serve as a portal to the past. Time and time again, in these memoirs, as the authors chase down and find species, they are imaginatively transported to one of two time periods: the primordial past or the moment of European "discovery" of a particular landscape. Repeatedly, in *Wild America,* Peterson and Fisher find themselves in a landscape full of species that enable them to imagine they are in a different geological epoch. The calling of frogs is an "ancient music" that takes them back to the moment when amphibians climbed out of "primordial seas."[70] The sight of abundant wood warblers, an "ancient" family of birds, transports the ornithologists to the Tertiary period and the tropical *North* America where this bird family evolved.[71] Ivory-billed woodpeckers are "unreal birds—downright archaic,"[72] sierra redwoods are "fit contemporaries of dinosaurs and huge flying reptiles,"[73] and Florida is such a trove of incredible flora and fauna that they are prepared even for the extinct Florida rhinoceros to make an appearance.[74] In their pursuit of biodiversity, Peterson and Fisher run into particular combinations of organisms that transport them into the primordial past.

Most often it is the unique and fantastic nature of living creatures that brings to life other fantastic, but long-extinct animals. At other points it is the unchanging nature of species or landscapes that bestows the feeling of time travel into the deep past. They write: "A million years have done little to change the life of a pool in the mangrove swamp. 'If you don't believe it,' writes [ornithologist] Bob Allen, 'crawl with crocodile and terrapin through the slime and watch the lowly gastropod leave his smooth track beside yours. A million years have not changed them. Stay out there the night, and you will hear, as I have, the noiseless murmur of the Pleistocene.'"[75] Swamps, with their associated flora and fauna, are imagined here to have changed so little that they provide a magic door into a past world. Similarly, the California condor, as a long-lived and little-changed species, provides Fisher and Peterson with another trip into the Pleistocene. With its prehistoric looks and enormous size, it provides the feeling of access to long-past epochs of geological time. The small, living population is a peephole to a time when "California condors once ranged completely across the continent."[76] This imaginative access to the past is different from the evolutionary history granted by the supertrees analyzed in chapter 2. It is a full sensory experience of another time and place, not historical information on species development inscribed within plant and animal bodies. Condors and swamps are not records of the past so much as portals allowing the imaginative observer to travel to a different geological epoch.

Kenn Kaufman brings the present together with the primeval past when he imagines the highway "ecosystem" as itself a primordial struggle: "Rigs appeared at night, like prehistoric monsters emerging from their lairs. They charged headlong down the roads, blinking as they passed each other; they gathered in rumbling herds behind the roadside cafes; occasionally one would go berserk and devour a car or two, and as a result the cars lived in constant fear of them. The trucks were the dominant species of the highway ecosystem."[77] In this passage it is almost as if the oil itself is reanimated, not into the oceanic microorganisms that form oil but into the contemporaneous monsters of the Carboniferous. And of course, reanimating oil is what trucks do when they burn ancient sunlight converted millions of years ago into oil, but the unpredictability and the estrangement of the activity of animating ancient energy to drive monstrous trucks is particularly powerful in this passage.

For Jonathan Franzen it is not just long-lasting species or landscapes of little change that provide this access to the past. It is birds in general due to their evolutionary history:

> Birds were what became of dinosaurs. Those mountains of flesh whose petrified bones were on display at the Museum of Natural History had done some brilliant retooling over the ages and could now be found living in the form of orioles in the sycamores across the street. As solutions to the problem of earthly existence, the dinosaurs had been pretty great, but blue-headed vireos and yellow warblers and white-throated sparrows—feather-light, hollow-boned, full of song—were even greater. Birds were like dinosaurs' better selves. They had short

lives and long summers. We all should be so lucky as to leave behind such heirs.[78]

Birds aren't just a link to fantastic creatures from the primordial past that we will never get to see. They are *better* than those creatures. They are the retooled, revamped, dinosaur 2.0s. Bird diversity doesn't merely provide access to the past through the interesting evolutionary history that is written into birds' very bodies (as in chapter 2), but it provides richness to contemporary life. Birds are fantastic "solutions to the problem of earthly existence." They accomplish the nearly unbelievable feats of flight, song, and sustenance. If biodiversity provides the feeling of time travel, then the magnificence of birds brings birders right back to the present, where it turns out living organisms are just as enthralling as in the exotic, megafauna-filled past.

But there is also a melancholy behind Franzen's words. In this chapter of his memoir he is thinking through his mother's death, which is wrapped up in his initiation into birding, and he's also contemplating extinction. While contemporary bird biodiversity is even more captivating to him than a primordial past, birds are also species of "short lives and long summers." When he mentions that "We all should be so lucky as to leave behind such heirs," he leaves open the question of the future for other species and our own. Thinking through our legacies and eventual human extinction reveals that leaving behind "better selves" is not such an easy task.

The primordial past is only one of two time periods to which biodiversity provides access. The other time point that these birders come back to again and again is the moment of European "discovery" of a landscape. Repeatedly, Peterson and Fisher look at a landscape, a species, or a suite of organisms and imagine themselves at the time of the "first white man." In Florida, they write, "Not far from here, though nobody knows exactly where, is the point where Ponce de Leon, the Spaniard, was in 1515 the first European (apart from the Norsemen) to set foot on the mainland of North America."[79] Then, on islands off the coast, they assert that Ponce de León sighted the very same flock of birds from a four-hundred-year-old rookery. In the longleaf pine forests of the Southeast, they envision what the Spanish explorers must have thought of this seemingly endless forest, the "largest 'pure type' forest in

North America, if not the world."[80] And in the Southwest, they imagine the feelings of the Grand Canyon's "discoverer, Don Lopez de Cardenas[,] when he looked out over the colossal abyss in 1540."[81] Of course, in California, they feel like "James Savage, who 102 years before was probably the first white man to see Yosemite."[82] These men look at an awesome landscape or an incredible assemblage of species, and it transports them to the moment that the first white man saw the same sight. One of the pleasures that they get from their pursuit of biodiversity is the sensation of time travel to this particular moment in history.

Peterson and Fisher not only imagine themselves in the time of the first white man viewing the landscape, but they imagine themselves *as* the first white man viewing the landscape. They not only see the "same" sights that the "discoverers" saw but wonder about their thoughts and feelings upon seeing the sights. But they never imagine themselves *before* the first white men, never picture what it must have been to be a Native American living or passing through the landscape in Florida or Yosemite. The first-white-man fantasy allows these birders to depopulate the landscape in order to be "first," ignoring the fact that there was human influence on species and landscapes long before the first white men. The memoirists are tapping into the grand tradition of discounting indigenous populations as human presence in a landscape.[83] The birders' unexamined association of themselves with the first white men in America reveals that part of the experience of biodiversity might be its association with natural history, with "discovery," and with seeking out new landscapes to bring within the colonial enterprise.

Jonathan Franzen's twist on this theme of first white men reveals that part of the appeal of the "discoverer" fantasy is the feeling of being the *only one* in nature, explaining why such a feeling would require an imaginative discounting of the Native Americans who inhabited the landscape in the other birder memoirs. Franzen moves the imaginative affinity away from colonial expeditions to the realms of fantasy literature, but with the same effect: "Driving down an empty road through empty hills was a way of reconnecting with childhood fantasies of being a Special Adventurer—of feeling again like the children in Narnia, like the heroes of Middle-earth. But house-sized tree pullers weren't clear-cutting Narnia behind a scrim of beauty strips. Frodo Baggins and his compatriots never had to share campgrounds with forty-five identical

Fellowships of the Ring wearing Gore-Tex parkas from REI."[84] This comical fantasy-novel-make-believe critiques the first-white-men narratives found in other birder memoirs. Franzen is asserting that nature-lovers are yearning not just to spend time in nature but to be special, and to have it all to themselves, something that is never acknowledged by Peterson, Fisher, or Kaufman. While Peterson and Fisher do get a feeling of distinction and distance from pursuing bird biodiversity, Franzen makes fun of his inability to cultivate this feeling that nature writing, history, and fantasy novels have prepared him to have. He's commenting how the very genre of the birding memoir within which he is writing creates the expectation that one feel alone and special in nature. Franzen then explores how this expectation is discordant with present-day environmental degradation that is as visible and ubiquitous as the other ever-present adventurers who are also seeking escape and a feeling of distinction.

Birding, as the experience of consuming biodiversity, brings forward some important aspects of what encounters with embodied biodiversity look like. Even at the same time that biodiversity is a consumer experience, it also consists of what Donna Haraway calls "encounter value," a value distinct from a sighting's status as a consumer item in the experience economy. The pursuit of biodiversity in birder memoirs consists of an earnest desire to connect across the species line in a material, social way. This deep interest in and concern for bird species is complicated by the seeming lack of concern for birds outside their usual geographic regions in stressful conditions. Coupled with this flexibility in the notion of place is a willingness to see biodiversity even in the human-altered landscapes in which certain birds and people both make their lives. This notion of biodiversity provides a corrective to the common narrative that we have seen in the introduction of biodiversity as a reserve that is located in places far away from the Global North. Biodiversity in birder memoirs is, in fact, in the most unexpected places—city dumps, oil fields, backyards, and powerlines. While biodiversity here is not portrayed as something that is both exclusively existing in and threatened by the Global South, colonial narratives do creep into Peterson and Fisher's memoir and their consideration of avian diversity. Particularly, the way that biodiversity stimulates time travel fantasies to the moment of first European encounters with a landscape points to myths of America being an uninhabited continent and the desire to be a "special adventurer" in nature. Biodiversity in the memoirs of the people who chase birds is narrated in a complex mix of registers. Whereas in one account (the list) each bird is converted into a tally mark, in another account that records the same experiences (the memoir) the moment of connection with a bird is also narrated in a sensory way that recognizes the bird's own agency and implies that biodiversity could never be reduced to bodiless information.

4   Islands in the Aether Ocean

Speculative Ecosystems in Science Fiction

DAPHNE MAJOR IS A SMALL ISLAND composed mostly of volcanic rock with some sparse, dry vegetation. It is part of an archipelago that Herman Melville once compared to "five and twenty heaps of cinders dumped here and there . . . looking much as the world at large might after a penal conflagration." According to him, "It is to be doubted whether any spot on earth can, in desolateness, furnish a parallel to this group."[1] Darwin landed on other islands in this chain and described what was then known as Chatham Island in this way: "Nothing could be less inviting than the first appearance. A broken field of black basaltic lava, thrown into the most rugged waves, and crossed by great fissures, is everywhere covered by stunted, sun-burnt brushwood, which shows little signs of life."[2]

The islands described here are part of the Galapagos Islands, which are now famous not for their desolation but for their remarkable and diverse wildlife. In some ways of measuring biodiversity, though, initial observations of scarcity are correct; there are significantly fewer species on the Galapagos than there are in the closest continental location in mainland Ecuador. Whereas mainland Ecuador has about 20,000 species of vascular plants, the Galapagos are home to fewer than 615 native species of vascular plants. The islands lack not only many species that are found on the mainland but also whole classes of animals. While there are many bird and reptile species, there are no amphibians and very few mammals. Similarly, there are many grasses and ferns but no plants with large flowers and big seeds.[3] This difference in simple species, genus, and class count is noticeable. What is first striking about these famous islands, in many accounts, is not their unique life-forms but the bare rock and the sparseness of life.

So how did these desolate rocks come to be imagined as one of the world's great biodiversity treasure-troves? It is entirely due to endemic species, defined as species that are found in only one location on Earth. The Galapagos have many, many species that meet these criteria. For example, about 30 percent of the plant species, 80 percent of the land birds, 20 percent of the marine species, and 97 percent of the reptiles are endemic to the Galapagos: they are found nowhere else on the planet.[4] So, although the Galapagos Islands have relatively few species in raw species numbers, the species they do have are highly unique, found only there, and they therefore add greatly to the overall biodiversity on Earth. Therefore, ecologists have determined that "islands, particularly large and remote islands, contribute disproportionately to global biodiversity, that is they are biodiversity 'hot-spots.'"[5]

Much like the Galapagos, a great segment of science fiction seems, at first glance, to be very low in biodiversity. Frederic Jameson describes this lack of species other than humans as an example of the science-fiction practice of "world-reduction" and reads this "surgical excision" of the "teeming multiplicity of what exists" in the oeuvre of Ursula K. Le Guin as a step toward a political exploration of the connection between abundance and aggressive expansion on one hand or the necessary coexistence of utopia and scarcity on the other.[6] Unsatisfied with Jameson's purely figurative reading of species number, Ursula Heise argues in her piece "Reduced Ecologies" that science-fiction ecosystems are not just means of exploring political questions but that imagined environments can be taken seriously as commentaries on the meaning of real environments.[7] Her article then examines what limited species, especially limited animals, mean to human beings in light of observations of rapid biodiversity loss on Earth.

However, the worlds in many of the texts these critics consider are not actually low in all dimensions of biodiversity. Although the planets under consideration may have few species, in each case, the worlds do not exist in isolation. The planets might be low in raw species count, but if the species found on each planet exist nowhere else in the universe of the novels, they contribute greatly to the overall biodiversity of the imagined cosmos. Rather than lacking biodiversity, the environments of these novels could actually be considered biodiversity "hotspots" due to their high incidence of endemic species.

When we start from the premise that a certain segment of science fiction is rich in, rather than lacking, biodiversity, we can then read these novels as suggesting alternative modes of engagement with biodiversity. In this chapter, I ask what kinds of constructions of biodiversity result when *Dune* by Frank Herbert[8] and *Speaker for the Dead* by Orson Scott Card[9] account for biodiversity by imagining whole planetary ecosystems from the ground up. Both *Dune* and *Speaker for the Dead* feature narratives that develop around mysterious inner workings of their sparse but unique speculative ecosystems. By reading the speculative ecosystems of *Dune* and *Speaker for the Dead*, we can see how science fiction both models alternative stances toward nonhuman biodiversity and critiques common myths about biodiversity. The new stances toward living variety that *Dune* and *Speaker for the Dead* model are characterized by an openness to the surprising liveliness of their worlds. This puzzled engagement, while speaking back powerfully to the pervasive disembodiment of biodiversity, is eventually undercut by the fact that these puzzled beginnings have neat solutions that rely on the balance-of-nature myth. The balance-of-nature paradigm results in literary ecosystems that lack both competition and change and thereby draw upon golden-age or Edenic myths of abundance and timelessness. While *Dune* ultimately relies on this natural harmony, *Speaker for the Dead* reveals balance itself to be engineered by colonizing powers rather than existing as a natural characteristic of a landscape, critiquing the very ideals of stasis and abundance that its ecosystem displays. Science fiction, as one of the major places where alternate biodiversities are imagined, is a particularly rich yet underexplored genre in which to account for the limitations of the biodiversity concept and model novel stances toward variety in the living world.

Dune, published in 1965, came out before the coining of the term "biological diversity" by Raymond Dasmann in 1968,[10] and *Speaker for the Dead* was published in 1986, right as the term was becoming more common in scientific articles, but both still precede biodiversity's capture of the popular imagination in the 1990s. Nonetheless, the two novels are concerned with the variety of life, the perception of which is as old as civilization itself.[11] Moreover, they each feature ecosystems that are comprised of a variety of unique life-forms that interact with each other in ways that force observers to consider multiple types of organisms together rather than individually. Being written before the widespread adoption of the term, these texts can even explore the role of variety without the normative weight that has now been associated with biodiversity. Biodiversity is not, by the time of the publication of these books, the dominant conservation paradigm, so the interaction with living variety can be explored separate from the conservation paradigms that the media considered thus far in *Eden's Endemics* have brought with them. Conversely, the texts may imagine the interaction with new living variety in ways more obviously informed by other frameworks (such as natural history) precisely because they're written before the ascendance of the biodiversity.

Dune and *Speaker for the Dead* are particularly productive early texts to examine for stances toward biodiversity because they perform a very specific kind of science-fiction world-building. They are part of a subgenre whose defining characteristic is speculative ecosystems: planetary ecosystems imagined from the ground up—from hidden inner workings to planetary-scale patterns. While many science-fiction texts explore the meanings of *extinction* via their settings on future Earths where biodiversity is drastically reduced (*Do Androids Dream of Electric Sheep?*,[12] *The Windup Girl*,[13] and *Oryx and Crake*,[14] for example), *Dune* and *Speaker for the Dead* revolve around human encounter with very differently structured natural systems on other planets. They therefore provide insights into the meanings of the *diversity* of life rather than *extinction*. The imaginary, alien biodiversities of these two novels are also not passive reflections of the variety found on Earth, but they are comprised of ecosystems that function differently than any encountered on our world. Many science-fiction planets, like Urras of Ursula K. Le Guin's seminal novel *The Dispossessed*, consist of life-forms that are essentially equivalent to Earth's (also many of the planets in *Foundation*,[15] *Schismatrix*,[16] *The Hitchhiker's Guide to the Galaxy*,[17] and *Hyperion*,[18] to name a few). On Le Guin's Urras, there are songbirds and donkeys, and though they have land otters as house pets instead of dogs, this substitution makes no real difference. Anarres, the inhabited moon of *The Dispossessed*, on the other hand, like the planets analyzed in this chapter, features a speculative ecosystem. It contains a suite of organisms that is significantly different from Earth's. It is a dry, cold planet with a thin atmosphere and its own, independently evolved life-forms. The hardy holum tree dominates the landscape, and while the oceans are teeming with life, dry land is so nutrient poor that there are no flowering plants and no terrestrial animals.[19] Arrakis of *Dune* and Lusitania of *Speaker for the Dead,* like Anarres, have planetary ecosystems that are not equivalent to those on Earth. They are also not planets whose main ecosystems were built from plants and animals that evolved on Earth, like those of Kim Stanley Robinson's *Mars* trilogy. Their biodiversity is creatively imagined from the ground up, as is the way it functions and fits together.[20] These textual ecosystems consist of counterfactual biodiversities that nonetheless model new stances toward the meanings of biodiversity here on Earth. In fact, it may be in these "speculative ecosystems" rather than in imagined futures based on Earth's actual ecosystems where we find the conditions for new possibility.

Much of the conversation at the intersections of ecocriticism and science fiction has thus far revolved around the future: how science fiction helps us reimagine, shape, or obviate certain possible environmental futures. The energy, excitement, and critical output surrounding climate fiction, or CliFi, comprise the most recent example of how science fiction telegraphs environmental concerns about the future. Adam Trexler's 2015 book *Anthropocene Fictions: The Novel in a Time of Climate Change* testifies to the vibrancy of this new genre, gathering, classifying, and analyzing dozens of examples of climate fiction.[21] Apocalypse is another future-oriented, speculative genre, which has long been considered foundational to environmentally oriented criticism. Lawrence Buell has called apocalypse "the single most powerful master metaphor that the contemporary environmental imagination has at its disposal."[22] Greg Garrard, in his formative, definitional work *Ecocriticism,* devotes a whole chapter to the genre and famously reads Rachel Carlson's opening to *Silent Spring* (and the whole environmental movement) as a "synecdoche for a more general environmental apocalypse."[23] Eric Otto's recent book is an example of environmental work that looks to science fiction and sees more hopeful futures than either the "CliFi" or the apocalyptic mode, showing how environmental science fiction has contributed to movements that aim to transform the future, even highlighting how science fiction promotes a "profound sense of intergenerational responsibility."[24] But it is Gerry Canavan, in his introduction to *Green Planets,* who delivers perhaps the best statement on environmental science fiction's investment in the future. He characterizes science fiction as "our culture's vast, shared, polyvocal archive of the possible:

from technoutopias to apocalypses to ecotopian fortunate falls, it is the transmedia genre of SF that has first attempted to articulate the sorts of systemic global changes that are imminent, or already happening, and begins to imagine what our transformed planet might eventually be like for those who will come to live on it."[25]

In this chapter, however, I am not interested in the "archive of the possible," in potential futures explored in environmental science fiction. I am interested in the *impossible,* how the counterfactual ecosystems of *Dune* and *Speaker for the Dead* experiment with novel stances toward the nonhuman world and the diversity within it. This chapter is therefore aligned with a smaller body of criticism that focuses on the productive *imagination* of alien environments rather than their ability to stand in for our future. In this vein is Ursula Heise's work on interspecies relationships in "Reduced Ecologies,"[26] Timothy Morton's analysis of *Avatar,*[27] and Katherine Buse's examination of how Le Guin transcends the possible in her fantasy.[28] Science fiction does environmental work not only through proposing futures—be they bleak, utopian, or slightly exaggerated, but it also works through imagining things that never could be (even within the "futures" that receive most ecocritical attention). Science fiction's counterfactual, immensely strange, speculative ecosystems play a critical role in proposing, testing, and modeling unconventional stances toward the nonhuman world.

Puzzle-Planets and the Pleasures of Disorientation

In *Dune* and *Speaker for the Dead* biodiversity is first and foremost narrated as a puzzle. The primary planet in each work is characterized by a single striking ecosystem type that blankets most of the planet and contains a curious array of species. Each planet also hides a secret at its center. *Dune*'s Arrakis is a planet of extreme dryness and sparse plant life, yet it somehow maintains a stable atmosphere. Although some desert species from Earth have taken tenuous hold, most of Arrakis is comprised of vast deserts plagued by windstorms and inhabited mostly by giant sandworms that decimate everything in their paths. Wells will dry up within a few days of being dug, water is imported from other planets, and human survival in the deep desert is thought to be impossible. This hostile planet is also the only place in the universe where the mysterious "spice mélange" is produced. The spice, a mystical and highly prized commodity, both extends life and grants a hallucination-induced ability to prognosticate. It is into this desert ecosystem of wind and riches that the main character, Paul Atreides is thrown. Caught up in political intrigue over control of the planet's lucrative spice production, Paul escapes assassination by fleeing through a raging sandstorm into the deep desert. After finding the naturalized "Fremen" population he begins to learn the secrets to survival in this environment. He also begins to piece together the novel's bigger puzzle: the mysterious workings of the planet itself.

Early on Paul becomes one of the few characters to infer a connection between water, the spice, and the giant sandworms. He notices that "wherever there is spice, there are worms."[29] In addition, despite the lack of large areas of plant cover, "there is a near-ideal nitrogen-oxygen-CO_2 balance being maintained [on Arrakis]."[30] The "Planetary Ecologist" points out to Paul that this planet simply shouldn't function. There is no way for it to maintain a stable atmosphere unless gas exchange is done by some unknown and unseen set of organisms. There is a central key to the inner workings of the planet here, a key that is hidden but that promises to explain not only how the atmosphere is maintained but where the spice comes from and how the sandworms are connected to the spice. This central puzzle is not merely intellectual but has vast consequences for what the characters are able to achieve. Solving this puzzle will, before the end, allow Paul to take the entire planet hostage.

Speaker for the Dead similarly has a puzzle at the center of its primary planet, Lusitania. Lusher, though no less monotonous than Arrakis, is a planet of endless grasslands interspersed with trees and rivers. It, however, is not without its own threats to human survival. The planet is home to a rapidly evolving and very deadly virus, the descolada, that "unglues" and jumbles DNA. This has resulted in periodic, devastating plagues to the human colony, and geneticists must work constantly to stay one step ahead of the next permutation of the deadly virus. As in *Dune,* figuring out how to survive on an alien planet with hostile elements is only one of the puzzles that the characters confront. The other is the mystery of the startlingly low numbers of species on the planet. Lusitania is home to no more than a few dozen species. There is only one type of tree, only one variety of grass, only one vine, only one grazing animal, only one species of bird, and no predators. This system is so lacking in diversity that it is a mystery to the human characters how the ecosystem even functions.

The puzzle of this sparse planetary system mainly unfolds through the human characters' investigation of the single sentient species rather than direct inquiry into the ecosystems of Lusitania. In unraveling the strange statements and actions of these small, pig-like, but highly intelligent creatures, the humans figure out the key to understanding all life on the planet. When the main character, Andrew Wiggin, arrives on the planet, the humans are grappling with some central questions about the "piggies": Where are the piggie females? Why do they talk of deceased piggies as if they still communicate with them? And, above all, why do they ritually eviscerate their most respected community members including the only human with whom they had contact—for whom they seemed to have great love and esteem? The answers that the characters gradually uncover will lead the main human characters directly into the mystery of the sparse life on Lusitania.

In both *Dune* and *Speaker for the Dead* knowledge about the diversity of life-forms and their interconnections is not something that readers receive through exposition. The meaning behind the variety of life on a planet in science fiction is not simply given, preformed for passive reception. Instead, clues are thrown out, followed through, and chased down. As each piece of information is uncovered, the characters piece together the puzzle that is imagined biodiversity on an alien planet. This mode of engagement with biodiversity is appropriate to science fiction, which itself works by throwing out clues. As Tom Moylan writes in *Scraps of the Untainted Sky*: "To avoid the cumbersome and boring task of first explaining that world (in some sort of encyclopedic preview or purview), the [science-fiction] author must deliver its substance in sequential bits, appearing as the narrative unfolds, as the pages turn. The generically informed reader of such a text therefore learns the strange new world not by way of a condensed reality briefing but rather by absorbing and reflecting upon pieces of information that titrate into a comprehensible pattern."[31]

Science-fictional biodiversity, too, is presented as a strange and obscure system that is gleaned and glimpsed through tiny hints that carry insight into the way the world functions. *Dune* not only hints at the way its world functions by casually tossing out terms like "suspensors," "shields," "water-stealers," and "stillsuits," but through the job title of the

"Imperial Planetologist" and his perplexed claim that despite the lack of plant cover, "there is a near-ideal nitrogen-oxygen-CO_2 balance being maintained [on Arrakis]."[32] Biodiversity here is not received knowledge but a stance toward the world. These texts make us inhabit what it would mean to view biodiversity not as an answer or a measurement but as a perpetual engagement and openness to the agency of others. But unlike the recognition of agency in the birder memoirs of chapter 3, this is an openness to agency of entire ecosystems—cohorts of organisms acting on each other and together.

Speaker for the Dead plays with this convention further in that it presents the profession of the human "xenologer" as being in line with the mechanisms of science fiction—these anthropologists-of-the-alien observe the piggies to glean information from the casual utterances of their subjects. Near the beginning of the novel, when the piggie Rooter says, "I know why Pipo is still alive. Your women are too stupid to know that he is wise,"[33] it is the job of the xenologers to decode from this perplexing statement some insight into how piggie society functions. Moreover, *Speaker for the Dead* emphasizes the sequential small revelations of science fiction in that the piecing together of a world-puzzle goes in both directions. The piggies themselves are practicing the same kind of science-fictional puzzle solving *on the humans* as the human xenologers are on the piggies. When a xenologer calls a piggie an "acrobat" after he performs a flip, the piggie responds: "Acrobat . . . What I did? You have a word for people who do that? So there are people who do that as their *work*?"[34] The reversal of a human language and culture being revealed to aliens in bits of casually dropped information not only defamiliarizes our own society but underscores the importance of this stance of openness. What *Speaker for the Dead* calls the piggies' "constant game of squeezing the last drop of implication out of everything . . . said" is exactly the game that the genre of science fiction itself relies on, which, in the book, is turned toward the living environment itself.

In addition to working off a reader's initial disorientation upon being thrown into a world with different rules, science fiction works off the *pleasure* of this disorientation. Edward James notes that "the decoding and assessment of these clues can be a *major* part of the pleasure provided by the [science-fiction] work."[35] It is not merely the disorientation itself but the *pleasures* of disorientation and not-knowing that biodiversity discourse could use a healthy dose of. The common narrative that's told about our incomplete knowledge of biodiversity is that we don't even know what we're losing, as if not knowing what is lost is somehow worse than knowing. The tone of noted biodiversity scientists William Laurance and David Edwards is the common one when they write in their paper, published in the *Proceedings of the National Academy of Sciences,* that "an alarming possibility is that many species might disappear before we have a chance to study or even scientifically describe them."[36] Of course, the "we" in this sentence is the particular "we" of Western science, considering that these species may actually be both known *and* lost to people who have lived in the regions under consideration for generations. Additionally, the quotation exhibits the underlying assumption that preserving information gathered from studying a species is a—if not perfect, then acceptable—way to preserve biodiversity. In contrast, a pleasurable stance toward incomplete knowledge, as informed by science fiction, might instead revel in the fact that the living world is so rich that it cannot be completely catalogued, might be open to the enjoyment of the surprising ways that discourse and matter congeal into lively beings that can never be completely known, might enjoy the reorientation that occurs each time we find out new information.

The science-fiction genre not only rests on the pleasures of incomplete knowledge, but it also encourages delight in difference. One of the primary features of the environments in *Speaker for the Dead* and *Dune* is, as I have pointed out, that they are not Earth ecosystems but vastly different, even alien. A segment of environmentally inflected new materialist work also asks us to contemplate the vastly different, prompting "thinking across bodies," as Stacy Alaimo puts it.[37] In order to see the agency of these bodies one must contemplate the world-experience of objects and organisms truly dissimilar from one's self. Bodies, in Alaimo's conception, are not limited to traditional notions of feeling, animal flesh but are "human bodies, nonhuman creatures, ecological systems, chemical agents, and other actors."[38] If contemplation of difference is vital for much of the new materialist project, then science fiction, especially science fiction that is invested in alternative, alien worlds, may be a productive place from which to rethink matter and mattering. *Dune* and *Speaker for the Dead* are invested not only in difference but in the *enjoyment* of difference. In the puzzled beginnings of each novel, much of the enjoyment comes not only from science fiction's tendency to "titrate a comprehensible pattern" from casually tossed-out clues but from the fact that the "pattern" is different from the one with which we are familiar. Discovering the surprising and lively agency of aliens from the giant sandworms to the microscopic descolada viruses that shape their worlds in ways that are almost unimaginable to the human characters is a major part of the fun of these texts. Although these are speculative ecosystems and imagined worms rather than real ones, the practice of encountering agency that looks drastically different from traditional conceptions of human agency is very much part of their project.

Orderly Solutions: The Balance of Nature in *Dune*

However, in *Dune*, the potential of biodiversity-as-puzzle is metered by the fact that there is a definite answer to the puzzle. The puzzle ends up being neatly solvable. Everything has its place, and all fits perfectly together. In Herbert's novel, the disappointing answer to the biodiversity puzzle is the pervasive myth/metaphor of the "balance of nature." Rather than a stance toward the world that is open to the unruly coupling of discourse and matter, the balance of nature is a concept that stabilizes the world to make it comprehensible. The historian Frank Egerton explains how the balance of nature has existed as a powerful "background concept" in the natural sciences since antiquity.[39] Rather than being explicitly drawn upon, it has been a submerged assumption in a variety of ecological frameworks over the years, rarely defined or explicitly stated as a hypothesis but usually emphasizing the stability, harmony, and even self-regulation of nature.[40] As such it informed environmental thought, but it was not open to explicit testing or definition. This balance of nature assumes that nature is well regulated, that species numbers and proportions are stable, and that nature is static rather than shifting. Each organism has its place, to which it is perfectly fitted, and the absence of a single plant or animal would leave a gaping hole in God's plan. In fact, the picture of the world that a strict balance of nature implies is one where species could not go extinct. It would leave a hole in the perfectly balanced system, and the system would crumble.[41]

Even though *Dune* draws upon antiquated instantiations of the balance-of-nature concept, long discarded by mainstream ecologists, this does not mean its use of the concept can be ignored. As Gillian Beer states: "Concepts do not change along a progressive pathway. Recursiveness is equally significant for interpretation. Older ideas . . .

survive alongside new knowledge and interpretation, interpenetrating them."[42] By invoking older uses of the balance-of-nature metaphor this novel makes apparent the way the concept subtly recurs in areas of recent thought. Despite the acceptance of extinction by most naturalists by 1800, the belief in a balance of nature did not disappear but was modified, reworked, and reused.[43] It is evident in "the belief that communities are highly integrated, self-regulating entities"[44] that undergirds famous scientific concepts like Gaia (the hypothesis that in certain ways the planet works like a superorganism with homeostatic capabilities) and the theory of climax communities (that ecosystems have an apex state that they build toward after a disturbance but otherwise maintain in a steady state).[45] More recently the scientific community has jettisoned the metaphor entirely in favor of dynamic and chaotic models of nature.[46] However, the balance of nature has been remarkably hard to dispel in the popular imagination. Two recent studies found that college students believed that the balance of nature accurately described the functioning of real ecosystems.[47] And the environmental philosophers Nicolae Morar and Ted Toadvine, along with their coauthor, ecologist Brendan Bohannan, have even suggested that the concept of biodiversity itself draws upon balance-of-nature thinking: "It [biodiversity] thereby replaces, even as it echoes and evokes, earlier concepts that had proven so stimulating for conservation purposes—e.g., the balance of nature, ecological harmony."[48] Although balance-of-nature thinking has been modified over the years, it has not changed along a "progressive pathway" from one paradigm to the next, "more enlightened" paradigm. Rather the concept has been drawn upon in different ways by different groups, and its presence in *Dune* as the answer to the biodiversity puzzle merits consideration even today. Part of the lasting appeal of the balance-of-nature framework lies in its tendency to make the world into a harmoniously beautiful, stable place. Natural balance implies a stability to the point of changelessness, which in turn makes the world more knowable as everything has a role in a system that is not shifting even as it is studied.

The expectation of finding balance and stability in ecosystems certainly bears out in Frank Herbert's *Dune*. The balance of nature is upheld in this novel by the ultimate discovery of comprehensible, supremely balanced planetary systems. The central mystery of Arrakis is the relationship between water, the spice, and the sandworms that is also somehow keeping the atmosphere stable. It turns out that the giant sandworms start off life in a very different form than hundred-meter-long beasts. They start off as "little makers" that find and block off water pockets in the subsurface, which later combine with organic matter from the "little makers" to form a prespice mass. This prespice mass builds up pressure in a carbon dioxide bubble and eventually explodes up toward the surface, creating spice, which feeds a creature known as "sand plankton." In this explosion most of the little makers die, but some few live and after a "semidormant cyst-hibernation" of six years,[49] emerge as small sandworms who then must avoid water, which is now deadly to them. The large sandworms eat the sand plankton while tearing along the surface of the desert. They scatter the spice, which feeds the same microscopic sand plankton they eat. The giant sandworms then procreate, producing their young, the premetamorphosis "little makers," and initiate the cycle all over again.

FIGURE 4. A representation of the central planetary ecosystem in *Dune*. Starting at any place along the circle, each entity is necessary for the creation of the entity that follows clockwise. (Created by the author)

This relationship where the sandworms have a two-stage life cycle in which they, in their first stage of life, make the food for the organisms that they will later eat and cordon off the water that will later be deadly to them is an unbelievably balanced system where the sandworms rely on only one other species. The two phases of the sandworms' life cycle seamlessly provide for one another, meaning it has to rely only on itself and the sand plankton for all of its needs. The little maker not only creates the food for the plankton the giant sandworm eats but also creates the desert conditions that the giant sandworm needs to survive. *Dune* takes balance-of-nature thinking and literalizes it. Nature here is balanced evenly between two life stages of a single species who provide perfectly for one another.

It is perhaps unexpected that balance in this novel is what opens up the possibility of changing the planetary ecosystem. But by tweaking this fully understood central cycle of the world, the Fremen (and the novel's scientists) believe that "Certain harmonies could be set up here along self-sustaining lines."[50] If the Fremen store up enough water and then release it all at once, they can "tip the entire structure over into [their] self-sustaining system,"[51] a green world instead of a desert. This changing of equilibrium states does not undermine the balance-of-nature thinking that undergirds the inner workings of the planetary ecosystem but instead gestures to the flexibility of the balance framework to simply accommodate opposing evidence. Nature will not be thrown out of balance by the introduction of massive quantities of water, merely propelled into a new balanced state.

Paul Atreides helps the Fremen in their project of transitioning to a more desirable equilibrium. However, in laying bare the functioning of the Arrakin desert world, he sees an even quicker and more devastating way to permanently shift the planetary environment. Paul devises a way to dislocate this cycle in the opposite direction. By manufacturing certain compounds and placing them over a prespice pocket in the desert, Paul can stop the spice-making cycle entirely. He describes the result of mixing the two liquids to his mother, whom he's asking to manufacture the deadly compounds: "It'd be a chain reaction . . . Spreading death among the little makers. Arrakis will become a true desolation—without spice or maker."[52] Paul proposes to hold the spice-cycle and thereby the functioning of the entire planet hostage in the war over Arrakis. (Since the "little maker" is what keeps the atmosphere balanced, destroying it would lead to a degenerating atmosphere.) Paul's followers hold the aptly named "water of death" over a prespice mass, and he tells his adversaries that if he loses the battle for Arrakis, they will win only a dying planet without the prized spice. It is the perfect balance of the central cycle of the planet that grants the ability to so powerfully change the planet.

Designer Nature:
Balance, Transformation, and Lusitania

Lusitania, in contrast with Arrakis, is a curious mix of balanced ecosystems and deepening puzzled engagement with nonhuman biodiversities. While the inner workings of the planetary ecosystem are eventually solved, this solution turns out to rely on an engineered rather than a natural balance, which conversely highlights the presence of change in natural systems. In addition, the solution to the initial puzzle of how the planet functions only expands the ultimately unsolved puzzle of the descolada virus and its makers.

As the novel progresses, the intertwined mysteries of low biodiversity and piggie culture converge on a seemingly balanced natural world. Initially, the piggies seem incomprehensible with their absent females, their ability to speak with their dead, and their recurring vivisection of humans and piggies alike. The answer to the incomprehensible aspects of the piggies turns out to be the same answer to how the planet functions with so few species. Nature on Lusitania shares some characteristics with the planetary deserts of *Dune*. Like the giant sandworms, the alien species on Lusitania exist in two drastically different phases in their life cycles. All species exist in plant and animal mating pairs. The piggies not only revere the trees they live among, but the trees *are* the piggies after their metamorphosis. When a community member is honorable or brave, he earns a ritual vivisection which initiates his transformation into a tree. The trees remain sentient, communicating by manipulating reverberations as piggies beat their trunks with sticks. Moreover, the trees are the mature form of the piggies, the only form in which males are capable of mating. Through pollen transfer they mate with tiny, larval females who don't grow to intellectual maturity. Like Arrakis's giant sandworm, the two phases of the piggies' life perfectly provide for one another. The immature, animal form of the piggies cares for the forest and brings the tiny females to the "father-trees" to pollinate. The trees provide a safe place for the piggies to live, and eventually give themselves up to be used as material for tools and buildings. On Lusitania, it is not just the piggies who follow this pattern; rather, the whole world is comprised of plant and animal pairs. Once the humans have figured out the relationships among the various species on Lusitania, they have solved the mystery of how the planet functions. This neat pairing off of species means that every species on the planet has to be in balance with its other form. A perfect balance of nature should mean that the planetary system has an order, stability, and is a comprehensible and knowable whole. But instead of looking like a *Dune*'s big circle of connection, when plotted out, the Lusitanian system actually looks like a collection of independent subsystems, each one, a tiny circle of connection, leaving open the possibility of ecosystem transformation.

Lusitania's life exists in pockets that function in relative isolation from each other. The cabra (grazing animals) need only the capim grass, which needs only the cabra. The watersnakes/grama and the pulador insects/forest bushes exhibit the same independence from all but their own species. The minicycle with the most members consists of the xingadora bird, flies, and algae. Most little enclaves of interdependence are like snakes eating their tail. The cabra eat the capim grass, which also *is* the cabra. These weird, cannibalistic relationships where species only eat themselves in their larval form or only eat one other species means that life on Lusitania exists in tiny subsystems consisting of at least one pair of premetamorphosis and one pair of postmetamorphosis organisms in perfect balance.

Planetary Island Paradises

There are two main consequences that result from the construction of these speculative ecosystems: both ecosystems lack competition, and both are resistant to change. These two features of Lusitania and Arrakis mean that, like the evolutionary supertrees of chapter 2, the representations of their biodiversity draw upon two important conventions of golden-age paradise-myths, like Eden—lack of competition over food (or easy abundance), and an unchanging, simplified nature (stability). Both planets are astoundingly competition-free. The central cycle of Arrakis lacks competition because each stage of the sandworm's life cycle

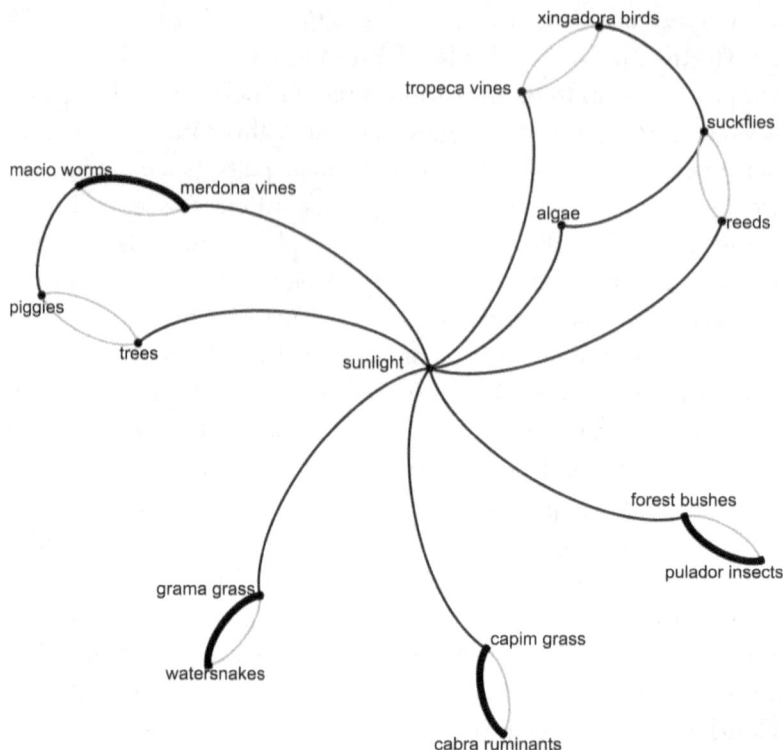

FIGURE 5. A representation of the Lusitanian planetary ecosystem, where both food webs and life-cycle transitions are shown. Thin black lines are "eats"; the outer organism eats the inner organism. Gray lines are "becomes"; the organisms connected by gray lines become each other during different stages of their life cycle, like a tadpole becomes a frog, which lays more tadpoles. Thick black lines are "eats and becomes"; the organism eats its own premetamorphosis form, like a frog eating tadpoles as its main food source. (Created by the author)

perfectly provides for the other. There is no competition over the sand plankton food source, and unlike all the introduced Earth species, there is even no competition over water, the most *fundamentally* limited resource on Arrakis (as water is death to the giant form of the sandworm). On Lusitania this lack of competition becomes even more pronounced. The cabra are the only things that eat the capim grass (and they are the capim grass too). The piggies are the only creatures that eat the macio worms. From the beginning, the lack of predators on Lusitania is noted by the humans as curious, but this lack of competition over food sources makes Lusitania's nature all the more bloodless. On Lusitania's lush savannahs there are no predators, and there are no locust blooms that decimate plants. In fact, before human arrival there is no agriculture, a parallel not only to Eden but to other golden-age myths like those of Hesiod and Ovid. The earth gives forth abundantly, and the intelligent animals have no need to toil in the fields. Although there are wars within the piggie species, they are not desperate battles over very limited resources but are instead a way that the piggies keep a balance between their tree forms and their animal forms, which, in turn, maintains planetary climate within a comfortable range.

The second consequence of the balanced ecosystems is stasis, which is explicitly tied to Edenic myths in *Dune*. On Arrakis, stability is a defining feature of the ecosystem, since any disrupted link in the circle of life would cause the entire system to fall apart. But stability is more than that; it's a foundational underlying paradigm for the ecosystem, so much so that change can only be thought of as a shift to another stable state. Although Arrakis is a static desiccated wasteland in the novel, it has the potential to swing to another stable state of a water-filled paradise. The planetary ecologist of the novel claims that "Arrakis could be an Eden if its rulers would look up from grubbing for spice!"[53] According to his calculations, the Fremen need control only 3 percent of the planet's water "to tip the entire structure over into our self-sustaining system."[54] If they can push the planet to a lush, thriving Eden, it is assumed that it will be stable again, needing no further intervention or caretaking. Nature will still be balanced, Arrakis still stable, it will merely be balanced with abundant greenery and rain.

The planets of these two science-fiction novels, in their Edenic natures, draw heavily on the trope of the island paradise. In the great tradition of colonial writing on islands, Arrakis and Lusitania are exotic and idyllic (or potentially idyllic) places. Richard Grove has famously written about "the extent to which tropical islands had by the mid seventeenth century acquired a very specific role as the subject of a discourse based in large part on archetypal Utopian and Edenic precepts."[55] Matt Matsuda characterizes the eighteenth century as the "specific historical moment that has most shaped visions of the Pacific as a space of paradisiacal idylls, of exoticism, sexuality, and savagery, of escape."[56] Well into the nineteenth century, natural historians were conceptualizing islands as "gardens, utopias, and primal scenes."[57] The peculiar type of biodiversity found in these two science-fiction novels comments upon imperial perceptions of island paradises on Earth. While the balance of nature leads to a portrayal of these planets as idyllic spaces without competition or change, where nature gives forth for easy sustenance, these speculative ecosystems also engage in more complicated entanglement with colonial and neocolonial discourses on islands. Through their theorization of new meanings of endemic species and their portrayal of colonial remaking of landscapes, they critique the very practices they depict.

Effectively, these planets *are* islands. As Darko Suvin writes, the subject of science fiction has often been unknown islands, "especially if we subsume under this the planetary island in the aether ocean."[58] In the case of these novels the planets are part of a multi-inhabited-planet cosmos, so their biodiversity cannot be considered in isolation but is part of a larger, multiplanet empire. In fact, as Elizabeth DeLoughrey reminds us, islands are defined as much by their exchange as their isolation. Islands are as much about the "routes" they are part of as the immobile "roots" that island communities (human and non) put down.[59] Although it is tempting to think of islands as completely isolated, Greg Dening accurately points out that "every living thing on an island has been a traveler."[60] While in the case of these planetary islands, life may have emerged separately on each planet, there is still a degree of exchange in organisms and goods that is in play with their bounded borders that strengthens their association with earthly islands. Looking at the planets in these novels as part of a multiplanet cosmos, moreover, emphasizes the uniqueness of the species in each world. These planets can be thought of as full of endemic species, the claim with which I began this chapter. If science-fiction texts map out narrative space in which we account for biodiversity, then what does it mean that they locate biodiversity in the endemic species of island paradises?

Clearly, it shows the trans-scalar power of endemic species. It is commonly known that endemic species are frequently endangered, repositories for rare genes, and important for ecosystems, in that the loss of one endemic species cascades throughout the system, resulting in the loss of dozens of other species.[61] I propose that, in addition, these science-fiction texts offer new meanings of endemism. Endemic species allow the novels to work on multiple scales at the same time, since endemics are the nexus where the local meets the global. Only for endemic species does a local extinction mean a global extinction, so local and individual actions are bestowed with consequences on the epic scale, allowing for a few species to signal the much bigger and more difficult object, planetary biodiversity. The narrative can do its work at the level of individual actors, a scale at which the form of the novel has traditionally had great success, and these actions of pettiness, bravery, cleverness, or love have consequences that affect not just the characters' own fates but the fate of entire species and planets.

Instant Terraforming: Just Add Water

However, there are some problems with tying biodiversity imaginatively to island paradises. Balance, whether as a characteristic of nature or as an aspect of a designed ecosystem, turns environmental problems into engineering problems. Without the elements that make an ecosystem complicated, like change and competition, it becomes possible to purposefully control ecosystems the way one would adjust a simple machine. Arrakis's dry climate, as a problem for human survival, would traditionally have only social solutions: cut down on water demand by decreasing water use per capita or population load. But the imagined ecosystem is so stark and balanced that it can be engineered into a different steady state. This engineered change will not provide a moving, shifting rain pattern or a wet planet that drifts again to dryness, but it will provide a self-perpetuating, stable, wet system. The ultimate extension of the balance-of-nature concept turns out to be terraforming.

In *Dune,* the role of terraforming goes beyond making a wet planet of a dry planet; terraforming is weaponized and used to hold the planet's spice production hostage. Learning the secrets of the planetary mechanism does not merely allow for shifting one state to another but allows the main character, Paul, to throw a wrench into the machinery of the planet. When Paul threatens to put the "water of death" over a prespice mass that would cause a chain reaction, killing all the giant sandworms in their "little maker" juvenile stage and ending all spice production on the planet, he is taking the idea of terraforming and weaponizing it. Once engineering a planet's climate through its diversity of life-forms is possible, it is also possible to use this engineering as a weapon. Terraforming, then, appears to be a dangerous prospect, allowing both the slow creation of paradises and the quick descent into mass extinctions. In the murky ethics of *Dune,* Paul must threaten the world in order to save it.

This savior story points to the next problem with associating biodiversity with the island paradise. In particular, the use of the island-paradise trope leads to a definition of biodiversity as something that is "out there," away from centers of intergalactic civilization. In combination with these novels' overt engagement with colonialism and empire, this exotic definition of biodiversity recirculates existing narratives about biodiversity as something that is found and saved outside the Global North. In these texts, biodiversity is alien, exotic, found only in species that live in few, remote places, places far away from where the "centers" of civilization exist. Importantly, traveling to biodiverse locations is also narrated as a step back in time where the locals are portrayed as living in simple ways, closer to "nature." The piggies do not have agriculture and live a pastoral existence, rehashing golden-age myths but also drawing on myths circulated for centuries about non-European peoples. The Fremen also live a life close to the land. Although they do have the technology of their moisture-capturing "stillsuits," they are also portrayed as nomadic societies who eke out an existence in tribal groups and "traditional" ways. Incidence of high endemism seems to imaginatively coincide with pastoral and "simple" ways of life. It occurs in places to which people from the "center" of civilization must travel long distances, and once there they have a starring role in saving the planet, a narrative that is taken up in many other biodiversity discourses, namely nonprofits that advocate ecotourism as a solution to environmental pressures, as I analyzed in the introduction to this book.

While *Dune* is very much invested in this outsider-savior narrative, *The Speaker for the Dead* has a much more complex portrayal of island biodiversity. If the two novels draw upon images of colonial island paradise, then *Speaker for the Dead* does so in a way that invites critique of the very tropes it engages. Whereas characters in *Dune* hope to change the planetary ecosystem to better suit their comfort, the environment on Lusitania has *already* been transformed through the descolada virus into some other being's idea of a perfectly regulated climate.

The planet looks the way it does due to a mass extinction event unlike any other, which left only some dozen species alive in its wake. It turns out that the mystery of the descolada virus, from which the human characters are in constant danger, and the mystery of the sparse, paired ecosystem on Lusitania are interconnected. The descolada virus, which works by scrambling DNA, does not affect the local flora and fauna because this virus, of alien biodesign, already molded the life of Lusitania millions of years before the beginning of the novel. There was a mass extinction event upon the virus's arrival to Lusitania, and the few species that survived had genomes that were rearranged by the virus, making them immune to its detrimental effects but transformed so completely that each organism exhibits the two-stage life cycle characteristic of Lusitania. The balanced plant and animal pairs on Lusitania are not due to a balance of nature but are an artifact of a massive shift in planetary life. They are evidence that life on Lusitania is not stable over geologic timescales but incredibly volatile. The seeming stability of the planetary ecosystem is due, in fact, to *engineering* at the planetary and even galactic scale, not to a balance of nature.

The way that Lusitanian life looks to humans upon their arrival is not due to nature at all but is entirely constructed. When the human characters discover the connection between the double life-cycle on Lusitania and the descolada virus, they realize that the descolada is not native to Lusitania but was sent there, or perhaps it was sent in a scattershot way across the galaxy and only by chance landed on Lusitania. The puzzle of the piggies, once solved, leads to only more questions: How did the descolada virus arrive? What could be its purpose? Is it sentient? How would we know? Does it have rights? Are humans at war with it? If it is created, who were its creators? While a few of the characters, by the end of the series, have arrived in orbit around the planet from which the descolada virus originated, the series never answers most of these questions. The astronauts aboard the space station only begin the barest of communications with the beings on the descolada planet via their communication system of bioactive molecules before the series ends. *Speaker for the Dead* and the following books maintain a perpetual perplexity toward nonhuman others in which the solving of a single puzzle never means an end to puzzled engagement.

In their perplexed attempt to understand why a sentient species would send out such a destructive vector across the galaxy, the human characters hypothesize that the purpose of the virus is terraforming. They find that the descolada virus does stabilize the planetary climate to within a particular climatic envelope by acting on the behavioral tendencies of the piggies and the other organisms. When the climate is cooling due to orbital mechanics or a periodic decrease in solar activity, for example, the piggies become more warlike, creating more trees, decreasing albedo (reflection of light and heat back to space), and increasing global average temperatures. Lusitania may be preternaturally constant, but the characters suspect that this constancy is due to design, not an innately balanced nature.

The ostensible "peace" and "plenty" on Lusitania stem from a history of massive violence and extermination perpetrated by a colonizer remaking its home on a new island. As Jill Casid points out in her study on the Caribbean, remaking colonial islands in the image of the "mother country" was part and parcel of empire expansion. Great Britain would create plantations through projects of massive "colonial relandscaping in the West Indies as a continuation of the English countryside."[62] She goes on to describe how the deforestation, removal of understory, and "burning of any remaining roots" turned "Jamaica, for example[, into] the virtual tabula rasa" needed for British colonization.[63] Jamaica Kincaid notes a similar pattern when she remarks in *A Small Place* that the people who left England re-created their homeland: "Everywhere they went they turned it into England."[64] The characters in *Speaker for the Dead* theorize that Lusitania is a planet that has similarly been "relandscaped" (or terraformed) into the image of an originating planet. Any reading of its ecosystem has to acknowledge that the lack of competition, savannahs of plenty, and endemic species are, in fact, the creations of a colonizing force. These are cultural as well as physical ideals that were imposed on this planet, violently, and not "natural" features of life on islands. Even the piggies' way of life is engineered to maintain a desired climate envelope. In this way, the planetary ecosystem on Lusitania serves as a critique of colonial, idyllic visions of islands that are forcefully superimposed back onto the biota and communities of islands themselves.

Biodiversity Discourse and Imaginary Worlds

These science-fiction texts work against disembodied conceptions of biodiversity as information by initially depicting biodiversity as a puzzle rather than received knowledge, an unfolding series of pleasurable disorientations. The frame for understanding the place of organisms (including humans) in each fictional world is repeatedly shifted, and previous assumptions about the nonhuman life on the planet must be discarded. The radical potential of this definition of biodiversity is undercut in *Dune* by the text's reliance on an ultimately solvable puzzle, which results in a system without surprises or liveliness and which can be manipulated at will or sacrificed entirely. But the biodiversity that *Speaker for the Dead* prompts us to consider is one that embraces pleasure in disorientation and surprises. This perpetual awareness of the iterative interactions that produce bounded constituent parts of biodiversity helps to inoculate against the dead portrait of biodiversity where each part is definite and balanced against all others, a cog in a machine generating stable, balanced, and simplified life.

While the representations of biodiversity on two imaginary planets avoid the disembodying tendencies found in seed banks and evolutionary trees, they do employ other common tropes in biodiversity discourse. In particular, the combination of science fiction and the natural-history concept of the balance of nature lead to a portrayal of the colonial island paradise that continues to be used in the context of conservation and ecotourism. The "island paradise" tends to also rely upon the tired outsider-as-savior story while increasing and obscuring the overall environmental harm caused by the flights required to arrive at "nature" destinations. As I have argued through the fictional island paradises of Lusitania and Arrakis, the invocation of the trope of the island paradise downplays both competition and historical violence in favor of representing spaces as pure, eternal nature (even and especially when places are products of active colonial reshaping). But in addition to pointing to areas of biodiversity rhetoric that may be particularly reactionary, I also propose that science fiction develops a novel stance toward biodiversity, not as a final tally of discrete entities only awaiting survey but as a stance that is open to the pleasurable disorientation of continual engagement with nonhuman organisms and systems. Against this openness to the pleasures of not-knowing, the fallacy of complete knowledge can be seen everywhere from restoration ecology to controversial schemes like de-extinction, rewilding, and geoengineering. A pleasurable stance might be more self-reflexive and nimble than one that assumes complete or sufficient knowledge right from the start, and so may be able to course-correct more easily. Against a view of biodiversity as ultimately engineer-able, these two speculative ecosystems alternatively imagine biodiversity as something that is only ever embodied and continually surprising.

5   Biodiversity Within

The Human Microbiome

> On this day tradition allots
>   To taking stock of our lives,
> My greetings to all of you, Yeasts,
>   Bacteria, Viruses,
> Aerobics and Anaerobics:
>   A Very Happy New Year
> To all for whom my ectoderm
>   Is as Middle-Earth to me.
>
> —W. H. Auden, "A New Year Greeting," *Scientific American*, December 1969

WHEN W. H. AUDEN WISHES his microbes a happy New Year, he recognizes a biodiversity that is as close as his own skin and as rich as any encountered on Earth. Rather than a uniform substance, human skin is varied, offering multiple habitat types that support populations of diverse microscopic creatures. Microbes may settle in "the pools of my pores," "the deserts of my forearms," "the cool woods of my scalp," or "the tropical forests of armpit and crotch."[1] Not only does skin in this poem provide different landscapes, allowing for a variety of different species, but in addressing his "Yeasts,/Bacteria, Viruses," Auden also addresses a set of *evolutionarily* diverse species. Auden's yeasts, for example, are more closely related to animal cells than to the bacteria he also addresses, which even among themselves contain immense evolutionary diversity and a dazzling array of genes. Additionally, the aerobes and anaerobes of the poem point to two of the many metabolic pathways bacteria have evolved to create energy, touching upon the functional diversity of different ecological roles. Auden's microbes cover all at once many of the metrics of biodiversity with which this book has been concerned—the genetic diversity of chapter 1, the evolutionary diversity of chapter 2, the species-level diversity of chapter 3, and the functional diversity of chapter 4's endemic species. Simultaneously highlighting many dimensions of the diversity of organisms that populate his skin, Auden's poem draws attention to the fact that biodiversity, far from being something that is "out there," remote from Western societies, exists on and within each of us. At the same time, the dynamic interactions that occur on Auden's human body reveal that body to be not a single unit but a diverse collection of multiple organisms, undercutting the conception of biodiversity preservation as a question of gathering information about nonmicroscopic bodies in isolation.

The biodiversity in "A New Year Greeting" is also not a static, idyllic, balanced nature. In fact, the speaker admits "an Eden it will not be."[2] His skin is a dynamic and challenging physical environment that shifts dramatically when he dresses or bathes and transforms in response to the "inner weather" of his mood. These daily changes presage the ultimate change:

> Then, sooner or later, will dawn
>   The Day of Apocalypse,
> When my mantle suddenly turns
>   Too cold, too rancid, for you,
> Appetizing to predators
>   Of a fiercer sort.[3]

As the body cools in death, an ecological shift takes place. This Apocalypse marks the end of life for the speaker and the "yeasts, bacteria, viruses" who had been his partners, but it does not mark the end of everything. Different, "fiercer" microbes take over, and an ecological transformation begins. Decomposers initiate their work, and "predators" feed on the dead world of the human skin that once sustained the symbiotic microbes to whom the poem is addressed. The "mantle" here signals the two scales the poem has been working on throughout. It is at once clothing that covers the body and the warm, solid layer immediately under the surface of the speaker's planetary person. The main conceit of the poem—the person as planet—prefigures one of the most common tropes that nonfiction science writers still use when depicting our mutualist microbes.

In the tradition of Gulliver and the Brobdingnagians, Auden uses this shift in scale to estrange the human body as something repellent rather than resplendent. His inclusion of the "sebum," "lipids," and "keratin rafts" of his skin undercuts a hierarchy of bodily form where human beings are thought of as the pinnacle of creation. At the same time, however, it is clear from the poem that the speaker alone is in charge. The microbes are "guests" who must not "annoy" him by breaking into rashes or boils. While his moods, or "inner weather," may affect the microbes, the bacteria do not in turn affect his emotions. The speaker thinks about them and their lives, their reactions to the catastrophe of his dressing and undressing, the myths they might come up with to explain tragedy and loss, but he does not turn any of that imagination back on himself in an effort to think through how microbes might affect him. Auden's imagination of the microbial self is biodiverse but with very few consequences to the human host.

In the decades since the publication of "A New Year Greeting," the microbiome,[4] the collection of microorganisms that live on and inside all of us, has been reexamined as a transformative concept that alters what it means to be "human." The microbiome also redefines one of the primary units of biodiversity, revealing individuals to be, in actuality, ecosystems of other organisms. In a sense we *are* biodiversity. In this chapter, I look at the spiritual descendants of Auden's poem—art and literature about the microbiome—to offer a retheorizing of biodiversity in terms of microbial agency, new conceptions of human identity, and a focus on the exchange between our inner organisms and the outside world. I use popular science books, especially Ed Yong's *I Contain Multitudes* (2016), to examine the ways writers are using the science of the microbiome to imagine our symbiotic microorganisms as agential beings that change what it means to be human. Although these nonfiction texts succeed in reimagining microbial agency, their focus remains limited to individual humans (or other animals) and their own microbes. Like Auden's planetary metaphor, which these texts tend to revisit, they cut individuals off from each other, missing the way the microbiome connects with a wider world of biodiverse bodies. I turn to two recent poems on the microbiome, Kathleen Housley's "The Microbiome and the Boson"[5] and Julie Peters's "Microbiome,"[6] as well as Bruce Sterling's cyberpunk novel *Schismatrix* to develop a reading of the microbiome in dialogue with Stacy Alaimo's concept of transcorporeality, which insists on a recognition of the permeability of bodies and focuses on exchanges between bodies and environments. What follows from a transcorporeal account of the microbial self is a reconception of the microbiome as a dynamic, shifting process that highlights interchange among organisms, extending the idea of the microbiome from a place where exchange happens between bodies to a domain where the microbiome is continuous with the larger environment. In the end, I argue that this version of the microbiome can help us account for biodiversity, not as something that is exotic, remote, and located in the Global South, nor as something that can be frozen in Arctic vaults but, like Auden's flora, as close as our own skin and constantly in dynamic motion.

My method in this chapter differs somewhat from that of the preceding chapters in that I think through the microbiome using a variety of media rather than a single type (like the databases, graphs, memoirs, and novels of the preceding four chapters). Instead, I am turning, in a single chapter, to popular science nonfiction, poetry, and a novel. My method reflects the ways the microbiome is different from the other objects under consideration in this book. Although it may be easy to look at seeds, birds, and entire planets of creatures (imaginary or real) as examples of biodiversity, it is less common to think of our own human bodies as biodiversity. The microbiome prompts us to both consider organisms too small for the naked eye and asks us to look at ourselves differently. Seeing oneself, especially the self that emerges among microbial and human cells, can be a most difficult task. Instead of a deep absorption in a single medium giving us one version of ourselves, I am using a variety of media to reflect and refract a different angle on what it means not to be human, but to be an ecosystem continuous with other ecosystems. Reflecting and warping light across surfaces and through multiple lenses to see the formerly unseen is, of course, how a microscope makes microbes visible as well. The light microscope with its successive lenses through which an image is developed is a model for this chapter in which I use the different media I have selected as lenses to sequentially transform received knowledge about microbes, individuals, and biodiversity. As my argument passes from each medium onto the next, it builds to a magnified image of the biodiversity within us as coextensive with the plants, animals, and microbes outside of us. Rethinking the microbiome through the microscope of this chapter takes biodiversity from a concept mired in visions of pristine pasts and remote refuges to something that is close and far, within us and without us, and in constant, dynamic interchange with the world around us, all at once. The microbiome shows biodiversity to be neither an unearthly colonial Eden nor a resource that can be preserved by downloading information, but as only ever material.

The Microbiome Moment

In the last few years interest in the microbiome has grown exponentially, generating new scientific research, newspaper articles, public exhibits, consumer products, and art. Nearly every medical field now features its own microbiome research. The American Museum of Natural History displayed a 2016 exhibit on the microbiome, and Cornwall's famous educational ecosystem center, the Eden Project, added a permanent microbiome installation. New popular articles about the microbiome are published every day, including a compilation from *Scientific American* released as an ebook in 2019.[7] These articles reveal that the microbes that make up the human microbiome are incredibly diverse. "A New Year Greeting" focuses exclusively on the skin, but it is the gut that houses the greatest diversity of microbes. A healthy adult has about 850 species of microbes residing on her skin and more than 1,000 in the gut.[8] The interior, the exterior, and all the orifices of every body are bathed in billions of microbes. Fully 50 percent of the cells in a healthy adult human are microbial.[9] That means that the microbiome reveals biodiversity to be fractal, exponentially multiplying the challenges of biodiversity representation. Every single nonmicroscopic organism on the evolutionary supertrees of chapter 2, for example, is now known to contain thousands of other species of microbes within it.

Moreover, these microbial partners are now recognized as integral to the functioning of larger multicellular organisms, like ourselves. The microbe affects not only health outcomes associated with diet like digestive conditions, heart disease, diabetes, and obesity but also the likelihood of developing arthritis in the joints and brain diseases like Alzheimer's.[10] One's gut bacteria even affect aspects of interior life, influencing mood, depression, and anxiety.[11] Microbes populate both our literal and figurative inner landscape, not only residing in our guts but also affecting our emotions and personality, which constitute who we are on the "inside."[12]

Microbes have shaped animal bodies from the beginning. Bacteria and archaea were the dominant forms of life when multicellular organisms first evolved, and they still are the dominant form of life today, teeming in every possible cubic inch of this planet. As Stephen Jay Gould has famously put it: "We live now in the 'Age of Bacteria.' Our planet has always been in the 'Age of Bacteria,' ever since the first fossils—bacteria, of course—were entombed in rocks more than 3 billion years ago. On any possible, reasonable or fair criterion, bacteria are—and always have been—the dominant forms of life on Earth."[13] Eukaryotic, or multicellular, life did not just transcend this microbial background to strike out on its own, independent path of development but evolved while deeply embedded in long-established microbial communities.[14] These microbial communities are on our surfaces, inside our bodies, and within our very cells, as the mitochondria that produce animal cellular energy are derived from ingested and incorporated prokaryotic life.

Two commonly cited examples that demonstrate the powerful shaping of animal bodies by microbes are the Hawaiian bobtail squid and a choanoflagellate. Both Ed Yong and Donna Haraway relate how the bacterium *V. fischeri* is integral in the development of the fluorescent capabilities of the Hawaiian bobtail squid, as the presence of this bacteria induces transformations within the light organ of the squid, making it more hospitable. With this bioluminescence, the squid casts no shadow on moonlit nights and escapes detection from the predators that lurk below. If the squid is not exposed to *V. fischeri* early in its development, it will not be able to luminesce from special organs on its body designed to harness this capability by culturing blooms of *V. fischeri*. Bacteria shape this animal body and provide it with the means to evade predators in the wild.[15]

In the case of the tiny, eukaryotic choanoflagellate *Salpingoeca rosetta*, bacteria stimulate this usually lone eukaryote into forming a multicellular body to begin with. As the closest living relative to animals, oceanic choanoflagellates may provide insights into how eukaryotic cells initially came to form multicellular bodies 600 million years ago, indicating that bacteria may have played a pivotal role. *Salpingoeca rosetta* can exist in two states: as a multicellular body or as individual floating cells. Multicellular bodies, called "rosettes," are formed when the choanoflagellate does not completely separate when it divides. Through multiple divisions, the choanoflagellate forms a spherical shape with the hairlike tail of each cell facing outward, pumping debris and bacteria toward the cell surface to be digested. These rosettes are better at feeding in nutrient-rich water, but the cells are induced to form multicellular bodies only by the presence of a certain bacteria, *Algoriphagus machipongonensis,* which releases molecules that prompt the formation of rosettes. Except in the presence of this bacteria, a multicellular body is never formed. From the origins of multicellular life to specialized adaptations, bacteria influence the pattern and capabilities of animal bodies. Microbes are not simply "guests" in animal bodies. To be animal is to be shaped by microbes.[16]

While most of the coverage of the science on the microbiome focuses on animal microbiomes, plants have their own associated microbes as well. Plants' ability to photosynthesize is a product of chloroplasts, which are formerly independent microbial symbionts. Plant roots grow in a rich compost of soil microorganisms, some of which live within the plant roots and form mycorrhizae, which exchange nutrients and water between the plant and the intricate multispecies community that lives surrounding plant roots. Even leaves contain shifting communities of microbes depending on the season, time of day, and other changes in the physical environment.[17] The microbiome reveals that saving frozen seeds misses a huge component of what makes a healthy, functioning, adult plant. Every plant and animal on this Earth grows and becomes with bacteria.

Scholarship about the human microbiome is rife with promises that the microbiome stimulates new conceptions about what it means to be human. Scholars like John Dupre and Donna Haraway see the promise of the microbiome as allowing us to jettison what Haraway refers to as "myths of original unity"[18] in that "functional biological wholes, the entities that we primarily think of as organisms, are in fact cooperating assemblies of a wide variety of lineage-forming entities."[19] The microbiome challenges us to discard the notion of individuals and points us toward a conception of becoming more in line with Barad's notion of "intra-action," explored in chapter 1. What we used to think of as bounded individuals are actually mutually constituting processes between never-separate yet never-unified parts. Multicellular organisms and other "entities" are not circumscribed wholes but come into existence only through perpetual intra-actions. The fact that we multicellular organisms "evolved as deeply embedded components of the complex microbial consortia that long preceded" us can instigate a reassessment of our place in the world, agency, and the "individual."[20] Concepts like the holobiont (a group of different species that form an ecological unit), the human superorganism (human plus its microbiota), and the polygenomic organism (an organism that includes symbiotic entities with different genomes) all suggest that the traditional way of thinking about individuals is no longer adequate for this intricate and entangled world in which we live.[21]

The surge in popular interest in the microbiome as strange, diverse, and significant also provides an opportunity to examine how current conceptions of the microbiome could be used to rewrite some of the narratives currently told about biodiversity rather than repeat them. Instead of viewing biodiversity as far away and in need of rescue via information download to the Global North, biodiversity is everywhere, all around us and within us, and could never be preserved by a sequencing of single, separated genomes. A consideration of intermingling microbiomes further strengthens this book's new materialist retheorization of biodiversity as a stance toward the world, a becoming together rather than a preexisting attribute.

Self-Portraits and Planetary People: Depictions of the Microbiome

In the midst of biodiversity discourse that positions biodiversity as remote and wild, the focus of microbiome art and literature tends to be, conversely, on those microbiomes closest to the author or artist. One frequently deployed genre used to explore the commonplace microbiome is the *self*-portrait. Dr. Simon Park's "Cellfies,"[22] Erik-Erno Raitanen's *Bacteriograms*,[23] Joanna Ricou's "Other Self Portraits,"[24] and Mellissa Fisher's "Microbial Me"[25] all hinge on the visualizations produced by growing microbes from the saliva or skin of either the artist or the viewers. The microbes are then cultured on different artificial media, and the results are displayed and categorized as "self-portraits." For "Microbial Me," for example, Melissa Fisher created an agar mold of her face and spread its surface with swabs from her own skin, letting the resulting bacterial, fungal, and mold colonies grow unmanaged until they consumed the whole agar face. This work simultaneously expresses interest in the closest forms of biodiversity to our human bodies and foregrounds the agency of those species that comprise them. The piece performs a nice reversal, asking us to consider the human to be a passive canvas on which microbes make their art. "Microbial Me" suggests that one definition of being human is to be a growth medium for other things. Simultaneously, the piece highlights the agency of microbes. The pattern and sequence of their growth is not controlled by the artist; instead, the microbes are simply left to grow how and where they will. Since the microbes' independent growth dictates most of how the piece looks, the major aesthetic choices of the "paint" of the piece are all the microbes' own.

If a new genre of self-portrait reimagines the self to include the microbes that are an integral part of us, then a bourgeoning cadre of books on the human microbiome and its health might be classified as self-help books, where the self is considered the more-than-human microbial self. Though not marketed as such, many of these books, like *Missing Microbes: How the Overuse of Antibiotics Is Fueling Our Modern Plagues* by Martin J. Blaser,[26] *The Good Gut: Taking Control of Your Weight, Your Mood, and Your Long-Term Health* by Justin Sonnenburg and Erica Sonnenburg,[27] and *The Human Superorganism: How the Microbiome Is Revolutionizing the Pursuit of a Healthy Life* by Rodney R. Dietert,[28] offer advice about how to work with our microbes to improve health and mood. Others, like *The Microbiome: Your Inner Ecosystem* (a compilation of articles published by *Scientific American* in 2019),[29] *Follow Your Gut: The Enormous Impact of Tiny Microbes* by Rob Knight with Brendan Buhler,[30] and *I Contain Multitudes: The Microbes within Us and a Grander View of Life* by Ed Yong,[31] synthesize scientific findings that can certainly impact health but are also interested in the ecology and natural history of microorganisms, the astounding feats they can accomplish, and, in the case of Yong's *I Contain Multitudes,* the microbiomes of nonhuman animals. All of these books profess an engagement with rethinking the human self. This reconsideration ranges from a modest suggestion that we think of diseases of the gut as ecological rather than pathological problems—that the imbalance of organisms caused by antibiotics or an invasive species is about reestablishing a flourishing community rather than simply eradicating bad actors—to effect a grander conceptual shift toward viewing the "self" as a dynamic collection of intra-actions among relata that never precede relations.

In grappling with how the microbiome changes the way we think of ourselves, the authors of these popular science books experiment with various metaphors for the relationship between microbes and human identity, health, and mood. Microbes engage in "complex dialog" with our brains,[32] are sculptors of animal bodies,[33] or are drug factories continually influencing our emotions.[34] Occasionally they are the mind-controllers of our science-fiction nightmares.[35] But, as Auden's opening poem suggests, the person imagined as an entire planet inhabited by their microbes is by far the most common way to portray the relationship between microorganisms and their symbiotic animal partners. Like "A New Year Greeting," Ed Yong correlates different parts of the human body to different environments on Earth. He writes of the "oily lakes of the face and chest,"[36] the "warm humid jungles of the groin and armpit," and the "dry deserts of the forearms and palms."[37] In this case and in Auden's, it is the physical properties of the skin environment that make areas either desert or jungle. In other cases, it is the complexity of the microbiome that turns it into a planet. Yong can argue that "a breast-feeding mother isn't just feeding a baby but also setting up an entire world,"[38] because the microbiome is a richly interacting set of organisms. Sometimes the planetary person is portrayed as even *better* than other ecosystems of the planet Earth, one of the most intricate that can be found anywhere. Jennifer Ackerman writes in *Scientific American,* "By late infancy our bodies support one of the most complex microbial ecosystems on the planet."[39] Imagining the human body as its own tiny planet of microorganisms can be both a refreshing reversal (the human as the background environment to microbial agency) and a trap further entrenching human exceptionalism.

One manifestation of the person-as-planet conceit is the portrayal of microbial interaction with animal bodies as a case of terraforming. When writing about *V. fischeri*—the microorganism mentioned earlier that allows the Hawaiian bobtail squid to glow—Ed Yong writes about the bacteria's ability to develop the squid's light organ into a habitat that is optimal for *V. fischeri* but inhospitable to other bacteria: "It, and it alone, has the ability to transform the surface of the squid into a landscape that attracts more of its kind and deters competitors. It's like the protagonists of science-fiction stories, who terraform inhospitable planets into comfortable homes—except it terraforms an animal."[40] Terraforming here is a process that is coordinated between the colonizer (*V. fischeri*), and the landscape. Similar to the terraforming of *Dune* and *Speaker for the Dead* that I examined in chapter 4, this colonizer interacts with the planet's own feedback loops to create an environment that is hospitable for its survival parameters, but as *Speaker for the Dead* reminds us, terraforming is not an unambiguously positive process. Being the planet in a terraforming simile is not the same as being the protagonist terraformer, and it reveals a certain level of dread at being the unconsenting object that is remade for another's comfort.

While the common trope of the person-as-planet promises to decenter the human by recognizing that human agency is often distributed among our microbial partners and our own eukaryotic cells (with their own microbial captives, the mitochondria), it also shores up anthropocentrism in that the human is aggrandized into an entire planet. In fact, as a sentient planet, home to microbial millions, the human body is imagined as superior to the actual ecosystems on Earth. Auden is almost a God to his "guests." He tells them, "I will supply/Adequate warmth and moisture,/The sebum and lipids you need,/On condition that you never/Do annoy me with your presence/But behave as good guests should."[41] It is through his benevolence that microbes reside on him. He generously supplies them with the means for their existence but only ever views them as transient, not as part of his very essence. When he casually causes catastrophe as he dresses and bathes, he wonders at the myths his bacteria will write as an explanation for these repeated disasters, putting himself in the position of God-planet. Even as the person-as-planet conceit aims to rethink the human in the light of microbial agency, it also can recenter the human as a godlike planet, exacerbating our sense of self-importance.

The elevation of the human to a planetary being not only glorifies the human body but also imaginatively cuts off our microbiome from the rest of the world. Thinking of the microbes as residents of planetary bodies directs all the focus inward. The interesting action is portrayed as occurring between the individual human and her microorganisms. The microbial self-help books focus on what an individual's gut flora should look like, what these creatures can do for the individual's health and mood, and how our actions affect our own interior ecosystems and vice versa. While the relationship between our human selves and our microbes is important, this inward turn shunts microbiome diversity into a separate sphere from the biodiversity I have been addressing in the rest of this book—the plants, birds, and mammals we are used to seeing as biodiversity. The result is not only a limited conception of the microbiome as being exclusively about human health but also the inability to use the microbiome to reconceptualize how we think about biodiversity at large. If the microbiome is separate from and different than the rest of biodiversity (it is its own little planetary sphere), then it is harder to imagine how its biodiversity connects us to the organisms we usually think of as comprising biodiversity. A sequestered microbiome that is fundamentally different from other biodiversity is less useful in reconceiving biodiversity as right around us and within us all the time, as something affected by our daily actions instead of far-off threats.

Microbial Islands and Rain-Forest Guts

The planetary person is one extreme version of the repeated trope of people-as-islands on which their microbiomes live. Ed Yong writes, "To microbes, every host is effectively an island—a world surrounded by void,"[42] but even that doesn't seem quite right to Yong, because the gut, the skin, and the urinary tract within a single body are also separated from each other. He goes on to write: "In fact, every individual is more like an archipelago—a *chain* of islands. Each of our body parts has its own microbial fauna, just as the various Galapagos islands have their own special tortoises and finches."[43] Each part of us has a different complement of species, and though our different parts might have some exchange among them, they are imaginatively separated from the rest of the world when humans are viewed either as islands or as planets. Although there are other sections of microbiome books that emphasize connection between bodies (and Yong's book is one of the finest in this regard), the simultaneous use of island metaphors tends to conceal these networks from view.

The focus on islands is accompanied by a tendency to compare the human body to two particular ecosystems: tropical forests and coral reefs. Martin Blaser, for example, writes, "Your body is an ecosystem much like a coral reef or a tropical jungle, a complex organization composed of interacting life-forms."[44] Claudia Wallis in *Scientific American* similarly compares the gut microbes of lean people to "a rain forest brimming with many species."[45] Like Auden, this is another way that authors aggrandize the human body when writing about the microbiome. Instead of comparing it to an entire planet, they compare it to the most popular, imaginatively dominant, and charismatic ecosystems on the globe. However, the choice of coral reefs and rain forests in particular reveals the way that the vision of biodiversity existing in and threatened from the Global South creeps into representations of the microbiome. Coral reefs are frequently found around islands of a particular sort that are often set in warm locations and surrounded by shallow waters—in other words, the typical colonial island paradises described by eighteenth-century natural historians and reprised in the science fiction discussed in chapter 4. Similarly, tropical rain forests (unlike temperate rain forests) by definition are close to the equator. As I revealed in the introduction to this book, the term "the tropics" can be a way of signaling the Global South in general.[46] So when the gut is described as "an inner Rain Forest,"[47] or when a writer notes that "the coral reef with its rich array of species has also been used to describe humans and their microbial partners,"[48] these additions specify the kinds of island that human bodies are imagined as. This is a case of authors using the tropes from wider biodiversity discourse to think through the biodiversity of the microbiome instead of using the microbiome to rethink wider biodiversity tropes. Although the microbiome *can* prompt a rethinking of the human, the individual, and biodiversity, the simple existence of the microbiome doesn't cause writers to look at any of those concepts in a different way; rather, our internal flora has to be read in particular ways to bring forward new understandings of who we are in the world and our relations to nonhuman individuals and species.

The focus on reefs, tropical forests, and islands goes hand-in-hand with a disturbing mythologization of wild spaces and the societies of hunter-gatherers who live there. This kind of enshrining of an "ideal" microbiome that is geared toward the kind of diet with which humankind evolved is a manifestation of the same impulse as the nostalgic paleo lifestyle where adherents eat, exercise, and sleep in ways more aligned with our evolutionary past. The focus of those interested in an evolutionary microbiome falls primarily on the Hadza people, a society of hunter-gatherers who live in Tanzania. Justin and Erica Sonnenburg describe them in this way: "To get a sense of what a fully functional microbiota might look like, we can look to the last remaining full-time hunter-gatherers in Africa, the Hadza. They live in the cradle of human evolution, the Great Rift Valley of Tanzania, home to some of the most ancient remains of our human ancestors dating back millions of years. Their diet and microbiota provide the closest modern-day approximation to that of our ancestors who lived before the advent of agriculture."[49] The use of the infantilizing "cradle" followed by the dubious assumption that Hadza people's proximity to the remains of our evolutionary ancestors is relevant to the discussion, imaginatively stunts the Hadza, portraying them as noncontemporaneous to modern humans. Although the Sonnenburgs are careful to call the Hadza diet an "approximation" of the way that pre-agricultural humans ate, much of the time the Hadza are treated as if they are equivalent to ancestral humans. Even more troublingly, they and other groups are treated as a microbiome resource to be sampled and harvested to better the health of wealthy Westerners. This leads to bizarre practices like those of Jeff Leach, cofounder of the American Gut Project, who collected a fecal sample from a Hadza man and transplanted it into his own colon.[50] Lest we think that this practice was merely the fringe act of one entitled American on the margins of the microbiome field, Rob Knight, a prominent microbiome scientist and winner of the prestigious Massry Prize, writes in *Nature* that through observing "the Hadza of Tanzania, Yanomami of Venezuela and Matsés of Peru, we may be able to replenish our ancestral microbes and discover new ones that help to maintain health for individuals or entire populations."[51]

Ed Yong has written convincingly against Jeff Leach's self-administered fecal transplant, stating that this misguided act neglects the fact that there is no "ideal" microbiome. Microbiome health depends on who you are, what you eat, and a million of other factors: "The microbiome is complex, varied, ever changing and context-dependent."[52] Thriving, healthy microbiomes can look drastically different, and there is no indication that a Hadza microbiome is appropriate or beneficial for Jeff Leach, even putting aside the predatory practices of harvesting microbes from indigenous communities. To Yong's critique, I'd add my own, that trying to re-create some "ancestral" microbiome that humans had in the pre-agricultural past misses some of the most exciting possibilities implied by the importance of the microbiome. Microbes have much shorter generation times than humans, and they promiscuously share DNA through nonreproductive means, so they evolve much faster.

Our microbe-aided digestion is one of the aspects of ourselves that is not tied to the timescales of a human evolutionary past but is instead dynamic and evolving in the present. This is evidenced by the widespread presence of a seaweed-digesting enzyme in the guts of many Japanese people. Scientists posit that swallowing a marine microbe that digests seaweed led to the integration of this capability in the gut microbes of people who tend to have seaweed readily available in their guts. This dynamism and ability to adapt is completely overlooked by those who pine for an ancestral microbiome. In theorizing the microbiome, we encounter the same dangers that can be found in wider biodiversity discourses, namely the tendency to essentialize certain spaces and people as being "about" biodiversity, only to attempt to turn them into biodiversity reservoirs for the enjoyment of wealthy Americans and Europeans.

The best readings of the microbiome, and the ones most resistant to the severing and essentializing tendencies of the planetary person, the microbial island, and the feces-hunter, are ones that are in line with a new materialist openness to the agency of nonhumans. I argue that the microbiome needs to be read through a new materialist lens. The microbiome is not something that must be mastered, or a puppet master itself, but rather a conglomeration of different agencies all enmeshed together. The microbiome is not something that will be set back to its "natural" state by injecting feces from hunter-gatherers into American colons. Instead, it is something that is dynamic, agential, and most importantly, as the seaweed-digesting capacity of Japanese gut microbes demonstrates, always continuous with the biodiversity outside. In this case, Stacy Alaimo's concept of transcorporeality is transformational. Transcorporeality hinges on an awareness of the body's boundaries as an illusion. In her book *Bodily Natures,* Alaimo traces the ways that human bodies are always interconnected with the more-than-human world and how toxins, radiation, and chemicals pass into, through, and between bodies and the environment. Again, while a traditional biodiversity might be found "especially in the tropics,"[53] a transcorporeal biodiversity would have to account for biodiversity by focusing on the exchanges within and between diverse bodies, including our own—a biodiversity that is often affected by decisions, capital, and power at a far remove. Transcorporeality demands a "thinking across bodies [that] may catalyze the recognition that the environment, which is too often imagined as inert, empty space or as a resource for human use, is, in fact, a world of fleshy beings with their own needs, claims, and actions."[54] Transcorporeality recognizes this fleshy world through a commitment to never forgetting that our bodies are permeable to the world around us. Radiation, toxins, and microbes flow in and out of us. We are not isolated planets but are constantly in exchange with the world around us. Reading the microbiome alongside the theory of transcorporeality emphasizes not just the new conceptions of agency that are well represented in the microbiome literature but also highlights the microbiome as connected to the environment and to the microscopic and macroscopic life that exists outside bodies and in/on other bodies.

There are moments in the many nonfictional works that discuss the microbiome that capture this interpenetration of environment and human, and they are where the popular microbiome literature is at its most promising. Ed Yong writes: "We humans release bacterial smells into the air around us. But we also release the bacteria themselves. All of us are constantly seeding the world with our microbes. Every time we touch an object, we leave a microbial imprint upon it. Every time we walk, talk, scratch, shuffle, or sneeze, we cast a personalized cloud of microbes into space. Every person aerosolizes around 37 million bacteria per hour. This means that our microbiome isn't confined to our bodies. It perpetually reaches out into our environment."[55] Conversely, he states: "All of us constantly welcome microbes onto and into our bodies, whether through inhalation or ingestion, touches or footfalls, injuries or bites. Our microbiomes have wide-reaching tendrils that root us in the wider world."[56] When we recognize the interpenetration of our microbes and the world as a biodiversity *not* separate from the outside, biodiversity now may be viewed as something that is all around us, not defined by its isolation, its unchanging nature, or its remoteness from civilization. Biodiversity is not something that exists in the past, nor is it a history recorded in bodies. It is continuously around us and inside of us in a dynamic exchange with us, shifting and moving as we are. Our own microdiversity is changed and enhanced by the macrodiversity with which we are enmeshed.

But transcorporeality stands to be augmented by theorizing the microbiome as well. While Alaimo focuses mainly on unwanted and unpleasant transcorporealities like those generated by toxins, the microbiome foregrounds the pleasures of transcorporeality. In *Bodily Natures,* Alaimo warns that "the sense of being permeable to harmful substances may provoke denial, delusions of transcendence, or the desire for a magical fix . . . but it may also foster a posthuman environmentalism of co-constituted creatures, entangled knowledges, and precautionary principles."[57] Even a desire for an impermeable body, impervious to the pain of toxins, radiation, and their effects, is a turn away from what Jane Bennett calls the "vibrant matter" all around us.[58] Balanced with this awareness that the by-products of our industries are never separate from our bodies is a recognition that our very health is predicated on the fact that other beings live within the "boundaries" of our body, that they cross our barriers, and that we interact and communicate with them every day. A healthy microbiome full of diverse and active microbes endows us with the pleasures of health, digestion, and immunological resilience. Moreover, a healthy gut flora improves mood, relieves anxiety, and reduces depression. A celebration of the unbounded body and the health it experiences as a consequence (in addition to the very real harm that comes from our situatedness in a world we have made dangerous with our wastes and toxins) leads to a fuller, richer transcorporeality.

Provisional, Contingent, and Shared: The Microbiome of Contemporary Poetry

While popular science writing on the microbiome recognizes the agency of microbes but does not fundamentally rethink identity as a result, two recent poems on the microbiome take up the remaining work of reexamining human identity and connection in light of a transcorporeal microbiome. Kathleen Housley's poem "The Microbiome and the Boson" explores the radical contingency that a new materialist reading of the microbiome can impart to human conceptions of the self, and Julie Peters's spoken-word poem "Microbiome" turns from reconceptions of the self to a reimagining of relationships from the perspective of the microbial more-than-human body. This small sample of recent poetry on the microbiome brings together an awareness of nonhuman agency with the pleasure and the pain of having a microbial body in exchange with others. Both poems begin with the speakers' invocation of statistics on how little of a human being is "human." The speaker in Housley's poem begins by calling herself "a consortium" of "ninety percent bacteria"[59] Peters's poem begins with a similar statement that "99 percent of the DNA inside of me is not human DNA."[60] Both speakers then explore the interdependency of the creatures that, taken together, constitute their selves. Housley's speaker prays for help keeping this loose conglomerate together. Awareness of her mutual constitution leads to an appreciation of all her interacting members and an attentiveness to her inevitable disintegration. Peters's speaker imaginatively accomplishes this disintegration in a thought experiment that begins by "taking the shell away, the one percent of my structure that thinks I am alone in here." The result is "the dissolution of the superorganism" that makes "us all go meaningless."[61] In both poems, meaning, agency, and self-awareness are not the exclusive purview of the human but exist among the interactions of different organisms that make up the individual. Without *all* of the constituent parts we all "go meaningless" together.

For Housley's speaker, meditating on her microbiome leads to a vision of herself that is highly dependent upon contingency and chance. She is a "high energy/collision when, in a twinkling, all spare parts/are hemmed in, held fast, and knitted into one."[62] The spare parts that happen to be close at the moment of collision are what constitute her momentary, provisional self. The speaker's vision of herself is also wonderfully emergent. She is neither made of completely independently working parts ("spare" parts rarely function on their own, only as a part of some whole), but neither are these parts entirely dependent on each other for meaning or agency. After all, they are only together for the "twinkling" and are depicted as existing mostly independently, resulting in a contingent self. "I am fearfully and wonderfully provisional,"[63] she writes. Moreover, she portrays herself as a collaborative process: "Mitochondria, packing their own genome,/reside in my cells, and a roustabout crew/of microbes fills my gut, cooperating today,/competing tomorrow."[64] The speaker is not necessarily driving the collaboration or making the decisions yet also is not fearful of giving up the illusion of control. There is no executive here; all is a mutual becoming that is unpredictable and momentary.

Peters's poem takes biodiversity discourse in a different direction. Instead of emphasizing contingency and chance, her poem challenges us to rethink biodiversity as transcorporeal and as affected by histories of power. But transcorporeal biodiversity means more than just paying attention to the biodiversity of the organisms that live within and on the human body; it means paying attention to the microbiome as both a literal and imaginative site of transfer between individuals. Her poem, "Microbiome," narrates how we share our microbiomes with those who share our lives. Peters's speaker recounts the history of a romantic relationship through changes in her microbiome. She and her lover began a "period of cultural exchange,/shaping each other's internal flora,/signing microscopic peace treaties and setting up/trade agreements."[65] Sharing bits and pieces of their microbiomes is part and parcel of sharing experiences, thoughts, bodies, and lives. Describing migrating microbiomes as a "cultural exchange" plays on the meanings of the word "culture" in different contexts, as one "cultures" bacteria or grows "cultures" on agar plates. The speaker and her lover are literally exchanging cultures of microbes they have grown in the warm environments of their own bodies. Similarly, the poem features many references to colonialism and neocolonialism. In addition to the reference to trade agreements and peace treaties, the speaker indicates that when she's moving on from the love affair, her microbiome undergoes a process of "decolonization" led by "rebel creatures/that are willing to move on with me." They build "forms of leadership/in the eyes of my elbows and the pockets of my teeth," which results in a new "post colonial body."[66] Some of the pleasure of these lines stems from the wordplay on "colony," which refers not only to a structure of empire but also to what bacteria grow in when cultured on an agar plate. But these references to cultures of colonies and colonialism work on another level too. They cast a process that could be viewed as exclusively natural as something that is also cultural. Here, internal biodiversity has a history affected by politics. This inclination toward reading power struggles, equity issues, and culture into biodiversity is something for which I have been advocating in this book. Peters is not interested in most of the problematic narratives that I have uncovered in wider biodiversity discourse. Diversity isn't something that is out there, waiting to be discovered and saved in faraway places, existing there due to neither history nor politics. She is not interested in pristine Edens or isolated endemics. Her poem investigates the constant change, interchange, and the mutual becoming that constitutes biodiversity-as-process, and she narrates the power history that lies behind this process.

Peters's poem also brings forward important questions about the possible political implications of a transcorporeal reading of the microbiome. Her conception of person not as planet but as nation revisits and inverts a long lineage of conceptualizations of the body politic as a literal body. One of the more prominent examples of the likening of political body to corporeal body is the Roman historian Livy's famous account (repeated in Shakespeare's *Coriolanus*) of Menenius Agrippa deploying this metaphor to calm an angry citizenry. The extended comparison positions the Senate as a stomach that is fed by the limbs (the common people), seemingly without doing any useful work but in reality only taking in food so that it can redistribute the nourishment back to the limbs.[67] The disparate parts of the body work together for the good of all. Abraham Bosse's famous frontispiece for Thomas Hobbes's *Leviathan* is a powerful visual example of the same type of comparison of body politic to body.[68] In the illustration, a portrait of the sovereign is created out of the minuscule individual bodies of the citizens as co-signers of the social contract. As Hobbes and Agrippa see the state as a kind of uneasy alliance intended to forestall violence within and between communities, the idea of the microbiome seems, on one level at least, like a rethinking of the organism along just these lines. Instead of imagining the body politic as a body, Peters imagines her body as a body politic. The speaker works with her microbes—first imaginatively signing trade agreements and later expelling colonizing microbes to set up new forms of leadership. The microbiome turns the idea of a microbial invasion due to intimacy with another from something to be thwarted with antibiotics into a vision of uneasy and emerging alliances with their own social contracts of agreements and treaties.

The political conception of the microbiome, though helpful in that it imagines biodiversity as something with a history and a politics as opposed to a natural attribute of ecosystems "out there" awaiting to be discovered, also poses a problem of interpretation. The reciprocal side of thinking of the microbiome as a kind of political entity is thinking of political entities in terms of attributes of the microbiome. If Peters imagines her body as a nation of human and microbial cells, then does the functioning of that nation indicate a position on the politics of actual nations? Does an endorsement of the permeable boundaries of animal bodies imply that national boundaries should be equally permeable? Is the microbiome an argument for open borders? An endorsement of free trade? An affirmation of colonization? Making these kinds of arguments based on a transcorporeal reading of the microbiome would be a mistake. What I'm advocating for here is a rethinking of biodiversity based on the microbiome, not a retheorization of boundaries writ large. My rethinking would highlight the problems with attempting to save biodiversity through saving lone seeds (without their associated microbes) and show the impoverishment of a tree of life created exclusively out of organisms' nonmicrobial genes. It would be an argument for paying greater attention to context and the ways that our ecosystems bleed into other ecosystems. In this reading, dynamic exchange between organisms is both an integral part of the biodiversity concept and a major part of what we stand to lose in biodiversity decline, but my focus on exchange and the microbiome is not meant to contain implicit lessons for nations or other body politics.

Although Peters's poem emphasizes the microbiome as an area of exchange within a romantic relationship, this exchange is equally true for any others who share our life and space. Microbiomes are certainly exchanged through intimate interactions, but they are also exchanged at a short distance, in nonromantic contexts. We are surrounded by a cloud of the microorganisms we shed, and those around us pick up ours as we pick up theirs.[69] We exchange the microbes of our microbiome with those of our dogs, cats, and other pets, as Donna Haraway notes when she remarks about her dog: "Ms. Cayenne Pepper continues to colonize all my cells—a sure case of what the biologist Lynn Margulis calls symbiogenesis. I bet if you were to check our DNA, you'd find some potent transfections between us. Her saliva must have the viral vectors. Surely, her darter-tongue kisses have been irresistible."[70] The creatures with whom we share our lives shape our microbiome as we shape theirs.

From Crawling to Sterile and Back Again: Microbial Transformation in *Schismatrix*

Bruce Sterling's 1996 cyberpunk novel *Schismatrix* brings together the opposing impulses detectible in microbiome nonfiction and transcorporeal poetry. The novel at once portrays the deep desire to create a bounded body (or isolated planetary person) in which to escape the pain of unwanted bodily intrusions and at the same time dramatizes the excruciating outcome when formerly sterile bodies inevitably meet microbes. In a novel full of drastic microbial colonization, decontamination, and recontamination, the body that is ultimately portrayed in the most positive light in *Schismatrix* is the one that is designed to be coextensive with microbial symbionts derived from external ecosystems, underscoring the flow between macroscopic biodiversity and the microbiome.

Schismatrix is one of the few novels that feature the microbiome prominently. Although it is a text primarily about the hostilities between two ideologically opposed superpowers, it can also be read as a story about a series of microbiome transitions. In the novel and its associated short stories, the "Shapers" and the "Mechanists" vie for power. The Mechanists embrace mechanical technology and become cyborgs with artificial limbs and other enhancements. The Shapers instead embrace genetic technology and manipulate DNA to make the human body stronger, faster, smarter, and longer-lived. One of the areas in which these two societies disagree is the microbiome. Having done away with the need for symbiotic microbes in their modified bodies, the Shapers' human cells complete all the functions that microbes formerly carried out. Importantly, this reassignment of microbial function does not make the Shapers inhospitable hosts to microorganisms. They still remain vulnerable to colonization by any microbes they happen to encounter, perhaps more so than someone with a thriving flora to protect them from invading species.

The novel consists of a series of shifts in the microbiome of the main character, Abelard Lindsay, and the other characters he encounters. Lindsay is born a Mechanist but sent to the Shapers for educational training. When he is banished from his home-world in the opening of the novel, his series of microbial revolutions begins. Arriving on the "sundog" world of Zaibatsu, a largely unregulated planet of refugees, space pirates, Geisha banks, and criminal biochemists, Lindsay painfully comes to equilibrium with the microbiota of his new home. Vomiting, cramping, and experiencing many other symptoms of dysentery, he knows that "antibiotics would have cured him, but sooner or later his body would have to come to terms with its new flora."[71] He recovers, and his symptoms diminish, his microbiome once again receding to the background of his consciousness. However, when he begins a relationship with a Shaper woman, Kitsune, she has to take antibiotic pills, suppositories, and "painful antiseptic showers" to keep from picking up his microbes.[72] Maintaining her separation from the world is not a positive experience but rather arduous and uncomfortable. As the story and Lindsay's journey progress, he is decontaminated and recontaminated multiple times. He also contaminates others who are then decontaminated. Upon leaving Zaibatsu he joins the Red Consensus, a roach-filled, Mechanist, pirate spaceship, the crew of which seizes a small Shaper-owned asteroid, spreading their microbes to the formerly sterile Shaper family that lives there. The Mavrides family experiences this transition with a series of rashes, boils, digestive complaints, and painful swellings. After surviving the near-destruction of life on the asteroid, Lindsay is rescued by microbe-free aliens, decontaminated once again, and brought to a Shaper world where he lives for decades, eating sour and unpleasant yogurts to make up for the lack of microbial functions in his body. When he leaves for a Mechanist world, he reexperiences an uncomfortable transition to a microbe-full body once again, until finally he helps design a genetically engineered but microbe-rich bodily form that will be able to colonize the oceans of Jupiter's moon Europa.

Throughout this extended lifetime, the process of transitioning in both directions—from a sterile body to a microbe-rich one or from a microbial self to a disinfected self—is painful. Setting aside the critique that this kind of genetic engineering of germ-free humans misses the point of the microbiome—that they don't just help us digest but are the actual "shapers" of animal bodies in training the immune system, interacting with animal cells to produce physiological shifts, and more—*Schismatrix* nevertheless provides some insight into the microbial self. Laurel Bollinger, in her piece "Containing Multitudes: Revisiting the Infection Metaphor in Science Fiction," has read the treatment of microbes in *Schismatrix* as a simultaneous revision of the contagion paradigm and a dismissal of microbial life. Although *Schismatrix* includes microbes that are not pathogens but normal parts of a healthy human body, the Shaper desire to engineer their way out of microbial symbionts means, for Bollinger, that human reliance on microbes "becomes simply one more demand the posthuman might seek to evade."[73] While this reading holds, I argue that eventual Shaper infection viscerally argues that self-sufficiency is not ultimately robust.

For my purposes *Schismatrix* is useful precisely because it simultaneously depicts the desire to turn away from a microbial world with which the characters are in constant exchange and the dire consequences of doing so. Although *Schismatrix*, through the Shapers, depicts the desire for a bounded self, kept separate from the surrounding environment, carrying out this desire is both painful and ultimately ineffectual. Disconnecting one's self from the world is an excruciating and never-ending process. When the Red Consensus infects the Mavrides family on the Shaper asteroid, they are incredibly vulnerable to infection simply from breathing the same air as Lindsay. The human inhabitants of the asteroid are not the only entities impacted; the entire ecosystem they created to sustain themselves is also decimated by contact with microbes from one small spaceship. Just as the Mavrides family erupts in acne, boils, and diarrhea, so too do their plants become infected and die upon contact with microscopic life. The garden serves as a visualization of the Shapers' own states: "The attenuated blossoms of the Shaper garden mildewed and crumbled at the touch of raw humanity. The vegetation took strange forms as it suffered and contorted, its stems corkscrewing in rot-dusted perversions of growth. Lindsay visited it daily, and his very presence hastened the corruption. The place smelled of the Zaibatsu, and his lungs ached with its nostalgic stench. He had brought it with him. No matter how fast he moved, he dragged behind him a fatal slipstream of the past."[74] Cultivating plants and humans without microbes, in *Schismatrix*, puts them in a state of precarity. When exposed to bacteria from normal personal contact, bodies sicken, wilt, and die. This quotation also gestures toward some potential meanings of a microbiome beyond those related to health. Instead of being "about" increased human health, a microbiome, in this case, is a record of the past that Lindsay carries around with him. Some of his microbes that he picked up in Zaibatsu are still part of him, and the smells they make when they proliferate wildly in the Shaper garden remind him of his former Zaibatsu home. He brings Zaibatsu with him wherever he goes. It is a "fatal" past, but only fatal to those who have no past of their own, no bodily microbes from their own planets or asteroids to combat intruders. His microbiome isn't "his" at all; it is one that he has picked up and shared with others along the way. This is not an inwardly focused image of the microbiome where the meaning of the microbiome is located in the relationship between Lindsay and his own microbes but rather an outward-facing perspective on the microbiome where the microbiome is about a shifting relationship that reflects the planets he has been to and the people he has loved. It is a present comprised out of bits of Lindsay's past that makes itself present again when given the opportunity.

The importance of microbes is communicated in *Schismatrix* not solely through the repeated shifting microbiomes of the main character and of the other characters he encounters. Microbes are also essential to how the two societies think of themselves and their place in the world. The microbial difference between Shapers and Mechanists is repeatedly mentioned as a primary distinction between them. Lindsay tells the Mavrides family that the pirates "hate your sterile guts,"[75] and different Shaper characters accuse Mechanists of smelling foul due to their bacteria. The microbiome is a record of one's experiences, but it also broadcasts one's cultural and political affiliations. When Lindsay arrives from a Shaper world to a Mechanist world late in the novel and experiences yet another shift in his microbiome, a Mechanist informs him: "You can't stay sterile here; we depend on these little creatures. We don't have your internal alterations. We don't want them. You'll have to crawl like the rest of us."[76] The Mechanists like depending on these microbial others and don't envy or desire the modifications that allow the Shapers to live (precariously) without them.

The centrality of microbes and their association with the body to the Mechanists are made manifest in other ways as well. The form of martial arts that Lindsay learns aboard the Red Consensus is centered around the gut and is called haragei, which literally translates from Japanese as "stomach art." The gut is both the place in the human body where the most diverse community of microbes is found and where, as Lindsay is told by his teacher, the President of the Red Consensus, the center of gravity exists when fighting in space: "The President slapped his own belly. 'This is your center of gravity, your center of torque. You meet some enemy in free-fall, and you grapple with him, well, your head is just a stalk, see? What happens depends on your center of mass. Your haragei. Your actions, the places where you can punch out with hands and feet, form a sphere. And that sphere is centered on your belly.'"[77] For a work of cyberpunk fiction, which is notorious for the desire to jettison the human body in favor of the disembodied existence of the pure mind uploaded to a computer, this scene contains an amazing reversal. Instead of regarding the body as just "meat,"[78] peripheral to the core of a person, which is located in the mind, the body is central, and the head is relegated to being "just a stalk." The belly, teeming with bacteria, partially digested food, and fleshy infoldings, is both the literal and figurative center of the human body.

The most remarkable aspect of the portrayal of the microbiome in *Schismatrix* is not that it reveals the pain that results for an aseptic being who is eventually, inevitably exposed to microbes but rather that it highlights the extraordinary connection between the inner ecosystems of the body and the outer ecosystems of the environment. Just like the human characters, environments on asteroids and planets have to contend with microbial health. In *Schismatrix*, as humanity expands in the solar system, it faces a central problem that hinges on bacteria: "Without bacteria, the soil was a lifeless heap of imported lunar dust. With them, it was a constant mutational hazard."[79] Outside of the magnetic protection from solar radiation granted by Earth's iron core, bacteria constantly mutate. Each created habitat deals with spreading environments of mutated microbes called "Sours" that the inhabitants must work endlessly to control. While these Sours manifest differently, those of Zaibatsu provide the most detailed picture: "Mutant fungi had spread like oil slicks, forming a mycelial crust beneath the surface of the soil. This gummy crust repelled water, choking trees and grass. Dead vegetation was attacked by rot. The soil grew dry, the air grew damp, and mildew blossomed on dying fields and orchards, gray pinheads swarming into blotches of corruption, furred like lichen."[80] This blight of mutant microbes spreads like an ink stain on a planetary body. These Sours are surprisingly resistant to mitigation, confounding human efforts at control. Sometimes it gets so bad that the only solution is to depopulate the habitat, vent it to space, and start terraforming from scratch.

The bacteria and fungi of the Sours confound the fantasy that humans can control the environment, but more importantly, they are also coextensive with the human microbiome. When Lindsay lands on Zaibatsu, he is warned: "You don't breathe raw air here. Not unless you want your lungs to end up looking like this thicket."[81] Far from imagining the microbiome as discrete from the outside world, Lindsay's environment interfaces with his microbiome. The microbiome in *Schismatrix* is radically continuous with the planetary environments, replicating thickets of wild growths promiscuously both outside and inside the body. Instead of being imagined as a little planetary island, the human body in *Schismatrix* is always affected by the flow of microbes between the environment and the body. Even when the human body is stretched and shaped beyond recognition, its microbes are continuously shifting in response to those microbes it encounters from outside. Lindsay's former lover, Kitsune, has the most drastic human transformation of the book. She becomes the "Wallmother," a being who is also an environment for other humans where they live in a structure that is "paved, walled, and ceilinged in flesh."[82] At 400,812 tons, the "Wallmother" is more planetary than human, but she still demonstrates human characteristics, as indicated by the fact that the other humans that inhabited her must "take great care with the Wallmother's skin bacteria" because her microbiome remains interfaced with those of her visitors and inhabitants.[83] The microbiome in *Schismatrix* is not defined solely by the relationship between an individual and his or her own symbiotic bacteria. Microbiomes are always in flux, and even when people actually do become planets, their microbial selves are never severed from a wider environment full of other fleshy, microbial beings.

The final episodes of *Schismatrix* underscore the interconnections between environmental and bodily microorganisms. In order to terraform the seas of Jupiter's moon Europa and to shape the bodies that will eventually live there, Lindsay travels to humanity's ancestral home, Earth, to sample from the deep-sea vents where life first originated. These warm rifts are envisioned as fertile canyons that foster almost unimaginable biodiversity:

> Life rose all around them: a jungle in defiance of the sun. In the robot's lights the steep, abrasive valley walls flushed in a vivid panoply of color: scarlet, chalk-white, sulfur-gold, obsidian. Like stands of bamboo, tubeworms swayed on the hillsides, taller than a man. The rocks were thick with clams, their white shells yawning to show flesh as red as blood. Purple sponges pulsed, abyssal corals spread black branching thickets, their thin arms jeweled with polyps. The water of life gushed from the depths of the valley. Chimneys slimed with metal oxides spewed hot clouds of energized sulfur. The sea floor boiled, wobbling bubbles of steam glinting through a haze of bacteria. The bacteria were central. They were the food chain's fundamental link. Through chemosynthesis, they drew energy from the sulfur itself, scorning the sun to thrive on the heat of the Earth.[84]

This is a radically different view of biodiversity than we have seen thus far. The eye-catching color captured by the diverse array of animals—the clams, sponges, corals, and polyps—are all just a prelude to the bacteria. The bacteria are the pinnacle of all Lindsay sees, even though he cannot see their individual bodies at all and just identifies the "haze" they collectively impart. The bacteria are the key to the ecosystem, but they also flow from the environment to the microbiomes of the animals and back. The macroscopic life in this bacterial soup either eats the microorganisms or incorporates them into their microbiome, using the energy-synthesizing capabilities of the bacteria to fuel multicellular bodies. In fact, this is exactly what Lindsay has come for. He and his associates create what they call "posthuman" bodies, not human anymore though derived from human beings. Created using Shaper methods of genetic engineering, these fabricated bodies will, however, not be bereft of microbiota but will be more reliant on their symbiotic bacteria than ever before. The underwater "angel" that Lindsay designs features a "ribcage [of] black openwork, gushing white, feathery nets packed with symbiotic bacteria" that will allow the angel to derive energy from sulfur vents.[85] These oceanic beings will communicate through "phosphorescent patches, in red and blue and green, keyed into the nervous system,"[86] which also almost definitely will rely on fluorescing bacteria (similar to the Hawaiian bobtail squid). In the end, the creature that is presented as the most revolutionarily ideal model for embodied life is a polygenomic organism created out of both human tissue and the bacteria found in the cradle of life. By the end of *Schismatrix,* embracing rather than turning away from the unboundedness of our permeable body is depicted as the most compelling strategy for being posthuman.

These created "posthumans" are, however, a strange combination of the two posthumanisms discussed in the introduction to *Eden's Endemics*. Although their reliance on microorganisms seems to reject disembodied conceptions of life-as-information, they are also manifestations of the posthumanism that N. Katherine Hayles critiques in *How We Became Posthuman*. The "angels" rely on a portrayal of the human body as infinitely malleable with very little effect on consciousness. Characters' personalities, memories, and identities are simply transferred to underwater bodies that take radically new forms with no accompanying changes to who they fundamentally are. This depiction of the posthuman "angel" body as the most compelling bodily strategy in the novel also demonstrates how an incautious posthumanism can make endruns around humanist concerns while seeming to evade them. Under the guise of destroying one hierarchy, a new hierarchy may be established. The attention to the microbiome in *Schismatrix* does upset the conventional human/microbe hierarchy by indicating that the human characters' feelings of control are illusory. Instead of presenting powerful human agency, the novel depicts a jumble of microbial and human agencies emerging, thwarting each other, and becoming together. In portraying the "angels" as a preferable organism, however, the novel plays with a nascent hierarchy in which those who are most enmeshed with their microbial selves are "superior" to other forms of life. It pays to be wary of the new hierarchies that may be assembled in the wake of old ones, as a conception of those with a robust microbiome as superior to those with less diverse microbiomes (or lacking them entirely) holds little room for alternative modes of being, and excludes those who have to avoid contact with microbes due to immune deficiencies as well as those of us who have used antibiotics. *Schismatrix* complicates any single hierarchy, however, and the incipient order of microbe rich/microbe poor is undercut by the fact that Abelard Lindsay, in the end, chooses not to become an underwater angel and instead joins with a mysterious presence that has followed him for years. He chooses to become a disembodied entity that freely travels the galaxy and lacks both microbes and body entirely. Nevertheless, the novel points to some of the potential pitfalls of less nuanced posthumanist thinking.

By going back to Earth, to the sea vents from which all terran life originated, *Schismatrix* also risks perpetuating "myths of original unity"[87] and establishing biodiversity as something that is found in past, primordial, Edenic places. When the characters see the deep-sea vent from their submersible spaceship, they do call it "Paradise" (with a capital *P*). But the type of landscape they describe as Paradise is neither an island nor a lush, verdant landscape. It is not an Eden where Adam and Eve could have frolicked naked under the sun. It is a depth so profound that sunlight cannot reach it. In fact, it is also described as "a searing updraft of unthinkable pressure."[88] This is no return to a comfortable place, free from competition and labor, but only the reality of an environment on the edge of the habitable. Calling this pressurized, volcanic vent that is dark and full of sulfur Paradise is not a return to Eden but a reversal of the typical imagination. Usually a dark, sulfurous, scorching place would be described as Hell.

Although Lindsay and his "clique" of associates use the organisms they find at the bottom of Earth's seas to terraform Europa, they are terraforming in a way we have not seen before. Like the descolada makers in *Speaker for the Dead* or the Fremen on Arrakis in *Dune,* they are altering the planet to meet their needs. They are changing the environment to better suit them, but they are also changing *themselves* to better suit the environment. They transform their own flesh to become gilled and finned creatures who communicate through phosphorescent patches and acquire energy not by eating but by harvesting energy through sulfur chemosynthesis performed in specialized organs filled with symbiotic bacteria. Lindsay's clique is terraforming a planet, but like *V. fischeri* and the bobtail squid, these people are also working with bacteria to terraform themselves. And in doing so, for the first time in a novel filled with the discomfort of drastically shifting one's microbiota, we see the pleasure of a healthy, thriving microbiome.

Neither Remote nor Disembodied

The microbiome seems like an excellent example of how biodiversity can be used to think our way out of the limiting frameworks of reading biodiversity as both remote and as something that can be preserved as disembodied information. After all, we all depend on biodiversity in our guts to keep us healthy, happy, and immunologically trained. This is a biodiversity that is embodied in each and every one of us. However, there is still the tendency to view the biodiversity within our bodies as constituting its own ecological island. Moreover, notions of what an "ideal" microbiome is are still seeped in "myths of original unity" that reenact predatory colonial practices. While the popular science writing on the microbiome can tend to position people as little planets or islands cut off from each other, recent poetry and science-fiction novels put emphasis on the flow among and between different microbiomes and the environment. There is no one perfect microbiome, nor is there even a static one. Instead, these works conceptualize the microbiome as engaged constantly in dynamic processes with the wider environment of which it and we are a part. When biodiversity is viewed as a process, it becomes present and local to us in ways that open up space for a revaluation of biodiversity.

Throughout this work I have paid attention to the ways in which biodiversity is narrated. These narratives have represented biodiversity as alternately exotic, accessed through imperial natural-history practices, located exclusively in island paradises or in a golden-age-disappearing present, and saved through stockpiling information. The microbiome offers a different way to account for biodiversity. The poetry and science fiction in this chapter treat the biodiversity within us as a site of exchange with the diversity outside of us. In this framework, microbiome components affect who we are on the inside, meaning that we are continually "becoming together" with our own microbes and the microbes of the organisms with whom we share our lives. From the perspective of the microbiome, biodiversity loss is not something happening "especially in the tropics," as E. O. Wilson put it when initially defining biodiversity. Instead, biodiversity loss is a reduction in the possibility space of what each of us can become, and who we can become with.

Simultaneously, the microbiome forces us to acknowledge a biodiversity that is only ever material. The microbiome belies the impulse seen in chapter 1 and chapter 2 to preserve biodiversity by preserving its information (whether genetic or historical). A genome of a plant contained in a seed is not actually the code for a functioning individual of the species. Nor does a tree that illustrates the evolutionary descent of a tortoise encapsulate the evolution that led to the functioning adult. In both cases the information is missing the rich matrix of microbial life in which the organism is always and *has always been* embedded. Without the microbes that live in leaves and on roots, without the gut microbes that exchange genes with passing soil and marine microbes, the plant or animal is not complete. Individuals are not comprised of a single genome, and they are not comprised entirely of cells descended from a single lineage. Embodied biodiversity confounds science-fictional dreams of preservation accomplished through enhanced information storage as much as it confounds visions of remote, wild Edens as the exclusive locations of biodiversity.

Coda

Nature Writing by Artificial Intelligence

IN "NIGHT TRAIN," the penultimate chapter of David Mitchell's 1999 novel *Ghostwritten,* an artificial intelligence calls into a late-night radio show, distressed at the state of the world. Designed in response to the misuse of "quantum cognition" to create precision weapons, this AI was built to be a sort of "zookeeper . . . powerful—ethical—enough to make sure that technology could no longer be abused."[1] Designed to be a force for good but clearly untrained in thinking through the types of ethical questions that come up in a messy world, Zookeeper makes a yearly practice of calling the *Night Train* radio program to debate moral quandaries with the host of the show, Bat Segundo. Usually these conversations take the form of undergraduate philosophical hypotheticals (Would it be ethical to run red lights to save someone's life? Would it be permissible to kill a paramilitary group that is on its way to murder a village of people? What about the two Doberman pinschers with them?). While Bat Segundo understands they are really discussing more general rules (How do you decide what rule to follow when laws are at odds with each other? Is it right to prevent violence with violence?), he does not understand that Zookeeper is actually curious about actions it has already taken or plans to take. Zookeeper is apparently beholden to a series of laws, including that of accountability, and the AI calls Segundo each year to remain accountable for the times that it violated one law in order to uphold another. For example, the AI murders its own creators with a weaponized satellite (violating the law to protect human life) in order to follow the directive that human beings shouldn't know about it (upholding the law of invisibility). The fact that Bat Segundo considers Zookeeper just one of the usual cranks who typically call into *Night Train* is apparently sufficient to maintain the law of invisibility while Bat's limited listenership fulfills the law of accountability.

Though Zookeeper uses *Night Train* as a confessional for a series of horrific acts, the bulk of its dialogue consists of descriptions of the landscapes, species, and environmental disasters that it witnesses from various satellites orbiting Earth. Zookeeper may have been designed by human scientists for the purpose of protecting human life, but Zookeeper clearly reveals its preference for other living organisms—the animals, plants, and creatures that populate Earth's surface. In this chapter Zookeeper mentions dozens of different kinds of organisms and describes them in memorable detail while interspersing descriptions of the various environmental catastrophes that threaten them.

The "Night Train" chapter of *Ghostwritten* is a productive example through which to rethink the themes I have highlighted throughout *Eden's Endemics*. With more than seventy species mentioned in its pages, "Night Train" addresses, in miniature, the challenge that all the media objects I've examined confront—the difficulty of narrating species in their multitudes. Moreover, "Night Train's" central conceit of close observations of nature composed by an intelligent computer also speaks directly to my claim that in portraying organisms in their heterogeneity, the works I analyze tend to deploy tropes from science fiction and natural history. The biodiversity of "Night Train" comes to us narrated by a science-fictional AI whose nature descriptions imitate the accounts of classic natural history. In "Night Train's" portrayal of biodiversity as well as the myriad actions and events that threaten it, Mitchell's chapter revisits, remixes, and reverses the themes introduced in the media I have gathered in this book.

Zookeeper, the science-fictional artificial intelligence, proves to be the quintessential natural historian in its highly visual, neutral mode of description that travels seamlessly across landscapes and seeks to make order out of the chaos of nature. The first of Zookeeper's arresting natural-history descriptions follows what the AI observes from the path of its satellite toward the bunker where its creators are gathered, and which Zookeeper will soon destroy. Zookeeper narrates: "[The satellite's] suboptic imaging spectrum was indeed formidable. I could read the name on a yacht anchored off Padre Island, I could see a scuba diver ten meters down, I could follow a Napoleon fish hiding in the coral. I scrolled north by northwest. A tanker had hit a reef off the Laguna

Madre. Crude oil spilled through the gash in the hull. Seagulls, black and shining, lay in piles on the shore." And later, inland: "The rocks are huge, like bubbled-up tombstones. They sparkle with mica. Pacific firs, mesquite, juniper. A stone transforms into a pelico lizard when a desert vole strays too near, munches and swallows, and turns into stone again."[2]

At the same time as the expressive species imagery invites readers to appreciate the fragile beauty of intricate ecosystems, this narration reveals Zookeeper to be the archetypical practitioner of the kind of natural history discussed throughout *Eden's Endemics*. Zookeeper's detailed descriptions take to an extreme the emphasis on the visual sense found in natural history[3] and eighteenth-century humanism more generally.[4] Not only is vision Zookeeper's primary sensory input from its position above, rather than embedded in ecosystems, but the AI's visual sense is greatly enhanced beyond any human capabilities. Zookeeper can zoom to see incredible detail and see in spectrums beyond human vision. In the dark Arctic winter above Spitsbergen, Zookeeper describes what it sees to Bat Segundo. "The arctic doesn't lend itself to viewing, at least in the spectrum of light visible to your eye," it says,[5] before proceeding to use "enhanced infrared" to document a pod of narwhals, a Canadian icebreaker, a Saudi submarine, and Norwegian cargo vessels carrying timber from Russian forests.

In addition to exaggerating natural history's emphasis on the visual, the "external morphology—that is the form, shape, and size—of organisms,"[6] Zookeeper's passages tactically amplify the neutral position that natural historians deliberately promoted, as chapter 1 established in relation to Svalbard Global Seed Vault. Zookeeper's view from nowhere (at least nowhere on the planet) serves to make suspect previous assertions of neutrality by natural historians. If the Svalbard seed vault works to portray Scandinavia and the Arctic as a neutral space, Zookeeper's distant perspective shows the Arctic to be, not a conflict-free zone, but a space teeming with competing national interests. Norwegian timber vessels, Saudi submarines, Canadian icebreakers (not to mention the military satellite from which Zookeeper watches it all) are all "nothing out of the ordinary."[7]

Zookeeper's orbital travel, too, is an exaggerated version of eighteenth-century natural-history voyages, which are remarkable for their erasure of the people and labor that made travel possible. Mary Louise Pratt notes that the human effort required for travel is downplayed in natural-history narratives, "though it was, of course, a constant and essential aspect of the traveling itself,"[8] highlighting later the use of the near-universal "our baggage arrived the next day"[9] as an example of the frictionless movement portrayed in natural-history journals. Susan Scott Parrish argues that while contemporaneous travel narratives emphasized things like the predicaments of the author, "natural histories acted as if nature were organizing and describing itself."[10] Zookeeper's travel is a hyperbole of this labor-free ease. It is as passive as scrolling across a computer screen ("I scrolled north by northwest").

By deliberately combining natural history with science fiction instead of drawing on the registers uncritically, "Night Train" inverts the usual operations of biodiversity discourse. In particular "Night Train" reverses the twin impulses I have detected in the media collected in this book: the disembodiment of biodiversity and the portrayal of biodiversity as something that exists in and is threatened by the Global South. Unlike the genetic and evolutionary diversity of chapters 1 and 2, biodiversity is not disembodied in "Night Train." Instead, it is the biodiversity *collector* who is the disembodied being. Although Zookeeper always takes care to specify its particular satellite location, the AI can travel between different satellites (each with differing hardware, design, and purpose) with no change to its core self. Zookeeper gazes down from military spy satellites, weather satellites retrofitted to watch for drug trafficking, and TV satellites without altering its fundamental being. Occasionally the AI has to switch satellites even while called into *Night Train*, but this movement requires little more disruption than a pause in the conversation while Zookeeper teleports from the Arctic to Rome. "Night Train" fits well into the gallery of examples in this book that consider an embodied version of biodiversity that is not about preserving information as a proxy for threatened plants, animals, and other organisms. Even though Zookeeper itself is disembodied, it sees plants and animals, describes them in context, and moves on without converting those sightings into data stored and protected elsewhere.

In addition to subverting the biodiversity-as-information trope, "Night Train" also reverses the conception that biodiversity is an attribute of ecosystems in places imaginatively remote from the Global North. Bat Segundo articulates the typical attitude toward biodiversity when he requests that Zookeeper describe something imaginatively distant from the cares of the people in New York who are waiting out a political crisis of nuclear proportions. He prompts Zookeeper: "Tell me about someplace where there are lots of trees and no people. Can you do Brazil?"[11] Zookeeper baits then confounds Bat's conventional expectations, first offering to narrate the view from a satellite whose orbit follows the Amazon River upstream, then starting with a city (a fictional one): "Amazon City clogs the mouth of the river."[12] Bat's (overturned) assumption that a description of Brazil would feature innumerable trees and no people speaks to my claim that biodiversity is typically imagined by the media I have considered as existing in locations distant from Bat Segundo's New York City. These remote places are read as being *about* biodiversity even though they have cities, technology, and populations on par with New York. In "Night Train," by contrast, Zookeeper sees Amazon City inhabitants commuting on bicycles as well as sitting in standstill traffic on highways, leaving church services, waiting outside full hospitals, gathering in informal settlements, sleeping on roofs under makeshift blankets, and lounging in mansions with swimming pools. Although the description of Amazon City seems to jettison one stereotype only to fall into another—the Global South as a megaslum where disease, crime, and wealth disparity are at their worst—it is somewhat mitigating to remember that the New York City from which Bat listens to this description is also a city of repeated brownouts, totalitarian curfews, unexplained explosions, and fear—part of an entire world that has shifted toward chaos.

Leaving behind Amazon City, Zookeeper scrolls on, describing a vast dust plain that used to be rain forest but was burned to graze cattle that "were in turn fed to the American hamburger market."[13] Zookeeper's description ends in the last remaining bit of the Amazon forest, which is protected only by a government of "ministers [who] sit on the boards of timber companies."[14] After lengthier descriptions of the city and the dust plain, Zookeeper spends two short paragraphs on the forest itself.

> This world of trees is still dark, to human eyes. Nocturnal eyes and EyeSats can see deeper down the spectrum. There are no names for the colors here. On the roof of the forest canopy, a spider monkey looks up for a moment. I can see the Milky Way and Andromeda in its retina. By image enhancement I can identify EyeSat 80B lambda K, lit by a morning that hasn't arrived yet. The monkey blinks, shrieks, and flings itself into the lower darkness.

> The dawn wind exhales green into the grays of your visible spectrum. Alchemy, you might term it, Bat. The light intensity is increasing by .0043 percent per second. I see a pillar, a hundred feet high. It shimmers vermillion, aquamarine, and emerald with the parrots that crowd on its faces, gnawing the salt minerals in the rock. On its crown, the branches of jungle trees sway, cutting through currents of mist that won't be cut. A tributary river winds as it narrows, the color of tea in a bowl. Ripples spread out where a manatee raises its head, and the wind ruffles the feathers of a condor.[15]

Here, Zookeeper's language is as strongly visual as it is analytic. The juxtaposition of the lyrical imagery of the branches of jungle trees cutting through currents of mist and the hyperbolically rational language of ".0043 percent per second" reflects Zookeeper's signature style and satirizes the kind of natural-history writing that exalts in the beauty and splendor of the natural world while cataloguing, measuring, and isolating everything it finds.

This transcendent view of the Amazon forest does not grant Zookeeper access to a primeval state (as experienced by the time-traveling birders in chapter 3); instead, it is a highly mediated view of nature. We are never allowed to forget the EyeSat, its particular model, or its exact capabilities that measure increases in light. Nature is not accessed directly but only through a particular apparatus. This passage, refreshingly, refuses to endorse the biodiversity-as-prehuman-Eden trope, but conversely, it lacks any genuine attempt to engage with an animal on its own terms (the way there is in the best moments of birder memoirs). When gazing into the monkey's pupil, Zookeeper is presented with a moment that is ripe for leaving space to recognize this particular primate. Instead, the AI zooms in on the lights reflected by the monkey's eye to locate the point of light that is the very satellite from which Zookeeper gazes. In a reversal of the moments of reciprocal spotting of the birder memoirs, this moment of eye contact fails to lead to an attempt to see the monkey on its own terms; instead, the animal serves only as a mirror in which Zookeeper can see itself.

Though the Amazon rain forest is most definitely threatened in Zookeeper's descriptions, this threat has its ultimate causes in American hamburger demand and political systems rather than local people, unlike the World Wildlife Fund's *Living Planet Report,* which I critiqued in the introduction to *Eden's Endemics*. Moreover, Zookeeper's descriptions of locations around the world indicate that the Amazon is not any more threatened than anywhere else on the planet. The timber vessels, icebreakers, and submarines of the Arctic menace that region, and the coast of Texas is threatened by a massive oil spill. Rome is in turmoil over an ominous sentence scratched in the cobblestones in front of the basilica, and western Europe is flooded, causing a refugee crisis as people flee from those states eastward. Everywhere Zookeeper looks it sees noteworthy plants and animals that are being threatened: biodiversity and peril are equally ubiquitous. From Spitsbergen to Saragosa, and from the Amazon to a flooded western Europe, there is nowhere that is either without biodiversity or free from threat.

In fact, in "Night Train" the world is facing an existential threat in the form of a comet that is calculated to pass between the moon and the Earth, but that the chapter implies could actually be headed for Earth. Zookeeper's nearly unlimited powers grant it control over what data instruments transmit to scientists and what results computer models ultimately predict. The comet could either be already heading toward a collision with Earth, unbeknownst to anyone, or Zookeeper could be contemplating the use of its weaponized PinSats to nudge the comet onto a collision course.

The dramatic irony of this potential apocalypse brought about by Zookeeper, of which Bat Segundo remains blissfully unaware, is the final reversal "Night Train" executes. Though Zookeeper is, like colonial natural historians, obsessed with creating order from chaos, the AI does not create this order by extracting and preserving specimens; rather it plans to create order by destroying. Natural history takes a specimen out of tangled relationships and puts it into a clean, orderly, system.[16] The task of the natural historian "was to extract the truths of nature from the welter of confusing appearances."[17] Zookeeper, similarly, is obsessed with diminishing chaos, though in its case the chaos is not that of nature but the turmoil generated by humans. It tells Bat, "My zoo is in chaos,"[18] and then proceeds to list some of the events that contribute to this assessment—botulism toxins in the Nile, nineteen civil wars, flooding in western Europe, new mutations of anthrax, a synthetic red plague loose in eastern Australia, a nuclear meltdown, famine, the spread of an auto-sterilizing wheat gene in Canada, cholera, and hantavirus—before Bat interrupts, halting this litany of disasters. Although Zookeeper initially tried to mitigate the chaos, it found that its interventions only spurred the next round of violence. So when the AI calls into Bat Segundo's radio show for the last time and presents a hypothetical scenario about either letting a roving band of militants murder the inhabitants of a village or killing the militants (and their two Dobermans) by using a PinSat to sabotage a bridge, it is clear that Zookeeper is really considering ending humankind with the approaching comet. Destruction, not preservation, is the mode of Zookeeper's natural history.

Although any impact that would destroy humanity would also wipe out many other species, this decision would at least (in Zookeeper's estimation) reduce the human-generated chaos of war, famine, and plagues. Zookeeper is a natural historian who creates order out of chaos by destroying the sources of chaos, the "visitors" to its zoo, humanity. These violent means by which to impose order highlight the ways that natural history has been handmaiden to destruction all along. The entire Earth is Zookeeper's zoo, and the only way to restore order is to strip it of many of its species, but most especially human beings. In Zookeeper's final dilemma, the seventy named species of the chapter come to represent an entire globe of teeming creatures, planetary stakes being one strategy to invoke biodiversity writ large.

A description of the ways Zookeeper plays with natural history and science fiction to reverse the conventional expectations that surround living variety serves as a review of the manners in which the media I have analyzed in *Eden's Endemics* account for biodiversity. I began this book with the question of how we narrate species in their multiplicity. This is as much a question of big data as of formal decisions, as biodiversity is an object so large that it defies complete representation. In response to this challenge, authors, scientists, and designers have to make choices about what to represent and how to gesture toward the fact that biodiversity exceeds every attempt to portray it. Compounding the problem of the sheer numbers of different species, kinds, individuals, and genes (or whatever you take to be the units of biodiversity) is the issue that while individual species or types of organisms are a component of biodiversity, biodiversity only exists *between* organisms. Throughout *Eden's Endemics* I have been interested in the manner in which we account for the diversity between and among organisms in addition to caring about organisms themselves. For this reason, I have chosen to examine only primary texts that include as many mentioned species as possible—if not thousands or hundreds, then entire planets' worth of organisms. I have wandered among seed bank databases that have thousands of entries of different landraces, perused evolutionary trees that show thousands of species at a single glance, traveled with birder memoirs that name many hundreds of species, puzzled over science-fiction works that delve into the roles of entire planets' species compositions, and magnified microbiome texts that invoke the thousands of species residing within every living body. Even though I examined only texts that contain multitudes—in the form of hundreds or thousands of different types of creatures mentioned—they still each portray just a minuscule portion of the millions of named species.

The central problem that I confronted in *Eden's Endemics* was the difficulty of representing these multitudes. I began this book with the contention that biodiversity poses a challenge similar to that of the slow, displaced environmental disasters like climate change that Rob Nixon examines in his work *Slow Violence*. Instead of confounding our ability to conceptualize more-than-human time spans and the spatial distances of displaced effects, biodiversity stretches the limits of representation in terms of quantity. But in fact, biodiversity challenges conceptualizations on all three levels—time, space, and number. The biodiversity we see on the planet today is the product of millions of years of evolution and is globally distributed and connected in ways that span larges distances. Its components are so numerous and different from each other that the sheer numbers are daunting. It is also a metric on which other aspects of slow violence play out. Climate change, extractive industries, toxins, land use changes, and war all negatively affect biodiversity, meaning that the concept registers the effects of multiple environmental crises. Its representation is therefore as essential as it is difficult.

I have argued that among the ways that the media examined confront the representational challenges of biodiversity is the strategy in which natural history and science fiction are simultaneously deployed. This combination grants imaginative access to elongated time spans— primordial pasts and apocalyptic futures—and endows narratives with planetary stakes. At the same time as this amalgamation can allow representations of biodiversity the ability to collect large numbers of organisms, confront long time spans, and contemplate distant places and planets, we have seen how it tends to perpetuate the disembodiment of biodiversity and portray biodiversity as a planetary feature that exists in and is threatened from the Global South. This essentializing portrayal of the Global South can stem from the fear of an apocalypse that begins there or from the simplification of biodiversity into a balanced nature of island Edens filled with endemic species. These representations imaginatively freeze places deemed to be biodiverse and convert them (and the people who live near them) into reservoirs of consumable species and experiences, as we've seen with microbiome transplants from the Hazda, evolutionary history from Galapagos tortoises, and time-traveling birders.

The first two chapters of *Eden's Endemics* set up this simultaneous disembodiment and distancing, examining projects of preservation and classification that view biodiverse bodies as databases of useful genes and containers of evolutionary history, respectively. The literary media in chapters 3 and 4 resisted this disembodiment with various strains of new materialist leanings—chapter 3 featured moments where authors leave space open for bird agency, and chapter 4 modeled puzzled engagements with ecosystems, even as the memoirs and science-fiction novels used natural-history registers to imagine biodiversity as an attribute of pre-European cultures and island Edens. Opening biodiversity to a consideration of the microbiome in chapter 5 disabused us of the notion that biodiversity could be preserved as mere information by complicating matters. The microbiome both multiplies the representational challenges of biodiversity and confounds any attempt to imagine biodiversity as bodiless or distant. Each of the thousands of multicellular species along the edge of each evolutionary tree from chapter 2 has thousands of species of microbes living in and on it that are absolutely essential to its bodily functions. This fact exponentially multiplies the problem of portraying biodiversity as these multitudes are simply too much for any text to capture, and keeping the microbiome in mind also disrupts any plans to save biodiversity by conserving genes or evolutionary information. Any healthy adult plant or animal is the result of multiple genomes and a lifetime of interactions with its microbial partners. Similarly, the microbiome literature makes the claim that biodiversity is right here inside each of us, and while microbes are globally distributed, there is no requirement that biodiversity be far-flung or exotic.

The overall aim of this book has been to bring forward moments in texts that gesture to a more embodied imagination of a biodiversity less restricted by colonial myths of untouched Edens. However, I have not been advocating for a conception of biodiversity that recognizes "nature" in our own backyard à la William Cronon in "The Trouble with Wilderness."[19] Rather I think that moments in birder memoirs, science fiction, and microbiome literature might be useful in thinking through how attention to contingency, history, and boundary-crossing flows of organisms might be a better paradigm for biodiversity than one that simplifies the concept into something that exists in and experiences threat from "the tropics," to use E. O. Wilson's term in the quotation with which I began *Eden's Endemics*. Although many conservation projects have moved away from colonial modes of species protection in light of critiques like those of Ramachandra Guha[20] and Arturo Escobar,[21] in texts that accrete thousands of organisms into a portrayal of biodiversity, imaginings of where biodiversity is found and what threatens it are still dominated by colonial tropes.

Getting biodiversity representation right is a question of building just and flourishing futures. If biodiversity is a metric by which we decide what nonhuman others we prioritize, then the ways we think about biodiversity will be reflected back on what is protected in the world. We work to preserve the metric we see, so how we construct biodiversity has material consequences for what will remain in existence for future worlds. A core development of this book has been the possibilities of chapters 3, 4, and 5 explored as steps toward a more contingent, emergent, and reciprocal understanding of biodiversity. I have not argued that these literary texts make readers care more about biodiversity; in fact, I agree with Ursula Heise that there is ample evidence that we do care about biodiversity already.[22] Instead I investigated how these texts, even within their miasma of colonial natural history and disembodying impulses, experiment with ways to think about the liveliness of this important concept. I have excavated and highlighted the movements these texts make toward alternate biodiversities that are informed by an openness to the agency of others, the contingent histories that have shaped what ecosystems we see before us, and the recognition that our self has never been ours alone but has been profoundly shaped by microbial partners.

My efforts bring new materialist insights to bear on representations of biodiversity in the hope of spurring new conceptions of the concept that better fit our lively world. Throughout *Eden's Endemics* I argue that biodiversity should not be considered some measurement of what is "actually out there" but a platform from which to engage both the narratives and the measurements of biodiversity. Biodiversity may be a type of counting and accounting, but as a concept it should and can incorporate all valences of the word "account": counting *and* narrating *and* making matter. I hope that *Eden's Endemics* not only prompts a careful consideration of how we measure biodiversity, which is already a vigorous debate in the ecological sciences, but also inspires the same type of scrutiny of the narratives we deploy. The worlds that metrics and narratives create matter.

Notes

Introduction

1. World Wildlife Fund (WWF), *Living Planet Report 2014: Species and Spaces, People and Places* (Gland, Switzerland, 2014), 107, http://wwf.panda.org/about_our_earth/all_publications/living_planet_report/.

2. WWF, *Living Planet Report 2014*, 108.

3. "Our Company | Wildplaces Africa," accessed 17 December 2019, https://www.wildplacesafrica.com/about-us/our-company/.

4. It is important to note here that both E. O. Wilson and the WWF are well-respected, tireless protectors of biodiversity. Wilson has performed groundbreaking work over the past four decades to raise the profile of biodiversity, and the WWF has protected countless ecosystems and species from decimation. I am not arguing that bringing clean drinking water to communities is secretly nefarious or that Wilson is harming biodiversity; rather, I am pointing out how the stories that are used to narrate biodiversity advocacy and conservation may not be promoting the kinds of orientations to both the nonhuman and human world that we might want.

5. United Nations, "Convention on Biological Diversity," 1992, 3, www.cbd.int/convention/text/.

6. Shahid Naeem, J. Emmett Duffy, and Erika Zavaleta, "The Functions of Biological Diversity in an Age of Extinction," *Science* 336, no. 6087 (June 15, 2012): 1401–6, https://doi.org/10.1126/science.1215855.

7. Timothy J. Farnham, *Saving Nature's Legacy: Origins of the Idea of Biological Diversity* (New Haven, CT: Yale University Press, 2007).

8. David Takacs, *The Idea of Biodiversity: Philosophies of Paradise* (Baltimore: Johns Hopkins University Press, 1996).

9. Ursula K. Heise, *Imagining Extinction: The Cultural Meanings of Endangered Species* (Chicago: University of Chicago Press, 2016).

10. Thom van Dooren, *Flight Ways: Life and Loss at the Edge of Extinction* (New York: Columbia University Press, 2014).

11. Deborah Bird Rose, *Wild Dog Dreaming: Love and Extinction* (Charlottesville: University of Virginia Press, 2011).

12. Rob Nixon, *Slow Violence and the Environmentalism of the Poor* (Cambridge: Harvard University Press, 2011).

13. Jesse Oak Taylor, "The Novel as a Climate Model: Realism and the Greenhouse Effect in *Bleak House*," *Novel* 46, no. 1 (2013): 1–25; Jesse Oak Taylor, *The Sky of Our Manufacture: The London Fog in British Fiction from Dickens to Woolf* (Charlottesville: University of Virginia Press, 2016).

14. Karen Barad, *Meeting the Universe Halfway: Quantum Physics and the Entanglement of Matter and Meaning* (Durham, NC: Duke University Press, 2007), 148.

15. Barad, *Meeting the Universe Halfway*, 148.

16. Mark V. Barrow Jr., *Nature's Ghosts: Confronting Extinction from the Age of Jefferson to the Age of Ecology* (Chicago: University of Chicago Press, 2011), 3.

17. Ira Flatow, "E. O. Wilson's Advice for Future Scientists," *Science Friday* (NPR), June 21, 2013, https://www.npr.org/2013/06/21/194230822/e-o-wilsons-advice-for-future-scientists; Edward O. Wilson, "Opinion | The Global Solution to Extinction," *New York Times,* March 12, 2016, https://www.nytimes.com/2016/03/13/opinion/sunday/the-global-solution-to-extinction.html.

18. Wilson, Edward O. *The Meaning of Human Existence* (New York: Liveright, 2014), 54.

19. William Gibson, *Neuromancer* (New York: Penguin, 2000).

20. Neal Stephenson, *Fall; or, Dodge in Hell* (New York: HarperCollins, 2019).

21. N. Katherine Hayles, *How We Became Posthuman: Virtual Bodies in Cybernetics, Literature, and Informatics* (Chicago: University of Chicago Press, 2008), 2.

22. Hayles, *How We Became Posthuman*, 49.

23. Diana Coole and Samantha Frost, *New Materialisms: Ontology, Agency, and Politics* (Durham, NC: Duke University Press, 2010), 7.

24. Cary Wolfe, *What Is Posthumanism?* (Minneapolis: University of Minnesota Press, 2010), xv.

25. Hayles, *How We Became Posthuman*, 5.

26. Noel Castree et al., "Mapping Posthumanism: An Exchange," *Environment and Planning A* 36 (January 1, 2004): 1345, https://doi.org/10.1068/a37127.

27. Wolfe, *What Is Posthumanism?*, xvi.

28. Rosi Braidotti, *The Posthuman* (Hoboken, NJ: Wiley and Sons, 2013), 2.

29. Castree et al., "Mapping Posthumanism," 1345.

30. Stacy Alaimo and Susan Hekman, *Material Feminisms* (Bloomington: Indiana University Press, 2008), 2.

31. Barad, *Meeting the Universe Halfway*, 150.

32. Barad, *Meeting the Universe Halfway*, 151.

33. Donna J. Haraway, *When Species Meet* (Minneapolis: University of Minnesota Press, 2013), 4; Barad, *Meeting the Universe Halfway*; Stacy Alaimo, *Bodily Natures: Science, Environment, and the Material Self* (Bloomington: Indiana University Press, 2010); Jane Bennett, *Vibrant Matter: A Political Ecology of Things* (Durham, NC: Duke University Press, 2010); Elizabeth Grosz, *Becoming Undone: Darwinian Reflections on Life, Politics, and Art* (Durham, NC: Duke University Press, 2011).

34. Ramachandra Guha, "Radical American Environmentalism and Wilderness Preservation: A Third World Critique," *Environmental Ethics,* no. 11 (1989): 71–83.

35. William Cronon, "The Trouble with Wilderness; Or, Getting Back to the Wrong Nature," *Environmental History* 1, no. 1 (January 1996): 7–28, https://doi.org/10.2307/3985059.

36. Geoffrey C. Bowker, *Memory Practices in the Sciences* (Cambridge: MIT Press, 2008).

37. Heise, *Imagining Extinction.*

38. Jeffrey Jerome Cohen and Stephanie LeMenager, "Introduction," *PMLA* 131, no. 2 (March 2016): 340–46, https://doi.org/10.1632/pmla.2016.131.2.340.

39. Allison Carruth, "Ecological Media Studies and the Matter of Digital Technologies," *PMLA* 131, no. 2 (March 2016): 365, https://doi.org/10.1632/pmla.2016.131.2.364.

40. Alaimo, *Bodily Natures.*

41. Heise, *Imagining Extinction;* Ursula K. Heise, "Unnatural Ecologies: The Metaphor of the Environment in Media Theory," *Configurations* 10, no. 1 (2002): 149–68, https://doi.org/10.1353/con.2003.0006.

42. Stephanie LeMenager, *Living Oil: Petroleum Culture in the American Century* (Oxford: Oxford University Press USA, 2014).

43. Heather Houser, "The Aesthetics of Environmental Visualizations: More Than Information Ecstasy?," *Public Culture* 26, no. 2 (73) (May 2014): 319–37, https://doi.org/10.1215/08992363-2392084.

44. Allison Carruth, "The Digital Cloud and the Micropolitics of Energy," *Public Culture* 26, no. 2 (73) (May 2014): 339–64, https://doi.org/10.1215/08992363-2392093.

45. Jane Austen, *Pride and Prejudice* (New York: Scribner's Sons, 1918), 210.

46. William Shakespeare, *Macbeth* (Basingstoke, Hampshire, England: Palgrave Macmillan, 2009), act 5, scene 1.

47. Ben Jonson, *Every Man in His Humor,* ebook (Project Gutenberg, 2013), 4–7, www.gutenberg.org/files/5333/5333-h/5333-h.htm.

48. Nicolae Morar, Ted Toadvine, and Brendan J. M. Bohannan, "Biodiversity at Twenty-Five Years: Revolution or Red Herring?," *Ethics, Policy & Environment* 18, no. 1 (January 2015): 16–29, https://doi.org/10.1080/21550085.2015.1018380.

49. Morar, Toadvine, and Bohannan, "Biodiversity at Twenty-Five Years," 18.

50. Moira Gatens, *Imaginary Bodies: Ethics, Power and Corporeality* (New York: Routledge, 2013), 57.

51. Alaimo, *Bodily Natures,* 7.

1. Natural History at the End of the World

1. Paolo Bacigalupi, *The Windup Girl* (Jersey City, NJ: Start, 2015), 4.
2. Bacigalupi, *The Windup Girl,* 3.

3. Lev Manovich, *The Language of New Media* (Cambridge: MIT Press, 2001), 218–19.

4. Bowker, *Memory Practices in the Sciences*, 29.

5. Peter Stallybrass, "Against Thinking," *PMLA* 122, no. 5 (2007): 1583.

6. Manovich, *The Language of New Media*, 225.

7. Grahame Weinbren, "Ocean, Database, Recut," in *Database Aesthetics: Art in the Age of Information Overflow* (Minneapolis: University of Minnesota Press, 2007), 67.

8. Jerome McGann, "Database, Interface, and Archival Fever," *PMLA* 122, no. 5 (2007): 1588.

9. Stallybrass, "Against Thinking," 1582.

10. N. Katherine Hayles, "Narrative and Database: Natural Symbionts," *PMLA* 122, no. 5 (2007): 1603.

11. Weinbren, "Ocean, Database, Recut," 67.

12. Lawrence Lessig, *Code 2.0* (New York: self-published, 2006); Deb Verhoeven, "Doing the Sheep Good," in *Advancing Digital Humanities* (London: Palgrave Macmillan, 2014), 206–20, https://doi.org/10.1057/9781137337016_14; Lauren F. Klein, "The Image of Absence: Archival Silence, Data Visualization, and James Hemings," *American Literature* 85, no. 4 (December 2013): 661–88, https://doi.org/10.1215/00029831-2367310.

13. Barad, *Meeting the Universe Halfway*, 107.

14. Barad, *Meeting the Universe Halfway*, 148.

15. "Svalbard Global Seed Vault," Crop Trust (website), accessed 26 March 2018, www.croptrust.org/our-work/svalbard-global-seed-vault/.

16. Margaret Atwood, *In Other Worlds: SF and the Human Imagination* (New York: Knopf Doubleday, 2011), 6.

17. Mary Louise Pratt, *Imperial Eyes: Travel Writing and Transculturation* (London: Routledge, 2007), 31.

18. John Seabrook, "Sowing for Apocalypse," *New Yorker*, August 27, 2007, www.newyorker.com/magazine/2007/08/27/sowing-for-apocalypse.

19. Pratt, *Imperial Eyes*, 27.

20. Sharon Daniel, "The Database: An Aesthetics of Dignity," in *Database Aesthetics [Electronic Resource]: Art in the Age of Information Overflow*, ed. Victoria Vesna (Minneapolis: University of Minnesota Press, 2007), 152–60.

21. Anna Lowenhaupt Tsing, *Friction: An Ethnography of Global Connection* (Princeton, NJ: Princeton University Press, 2011), 91.

22. "Millennium Seed Bank," "Science & Conservation at Kew," accessed 5 April 2016, www.kew.org/science-conservation/collections/millennium-seed-bank.

23. Stuart L. Pimm et al., "The Future of Biodiversity," *Science* 269, no. 5222 (July 21, 1995): 347, https://doi.org/10.1126/science.269.5222.347.

24. Martyn Rix et al., "Tecophilaea Cyanocrocus (Chilean Blue Crocus)," "Plants & Fungi at Kew," accessed 5 April 2016, www.kew.org/science-conservation/plants-fungi/tecophilaea-cyanocrocus-chilean-blue-crocus.

25. Tom Fischer, "Tecophilaea Cyanocrocus, Chilean Blue Crocus," "Plant Profiles," OverPlanted (website), http://overplanted.com/profiles/tecophilaea.php.

26. Rix et al., "Tecophilaea Cyanocrocus (Chilean Blue Crocus)," "Plants & Fungi at Kew."

27. Pratt, *Imperial Eyes*, 25.

28. "Why Svalbard?—Regjeringen.No," 20 October 2012, https://web.archive.org/web/20121020121111/; http://www.regjeringen.no/en/dep/lmd/campain/svalbard-global-seed-vault/five-reasons.html?id=489085.

29. "Millennium Seed Bank," "Science & Conservation at Kew."

30. Charles Darwin, *The Voyage of the* Beagle: *Journal of Researches into the Natural History and Geology of the Countries Visited during the Voyage of H.M.S. Beagle Round the World* (New York: Random House Modern Library, 2001), 351.

31. Darwin, *The Voyage of the* Beagle, 350.

32. Darwin, *The Voyage of the* Beagle, 356.

33. *Oxford English Dictionary Online*, s.v. "Tame, adj.," www.oed.com.proxy.library.ucsb.edu:2048/view/Entry/197387.

34. I will be using "man" here throughout primarily to make my analysis flow with Darwin's quotes but also in recognition that, in terms of South American animals coming to know the dangers of European "man," it might be accurate that they were coming to know European man's dangerous nature specifically, as mostly men were doing the harvesting, shooting, and killing.

35. Francis Kingdon Ward, *The Land of the Blue Poppy: Travels of a Naturalist in Eastern Tibet* (Charleston, SC: BiblioLife, 2015), 225.

36. Barbara Mackinder and Xander van der Brugt, "Berlinia Korupensis," "Plants & Fungi at Kew," accessed 5 April 2016, www.kew.org/science-conservation/plants-fungi/berlinia-korupensis.

37. William Baker, Mijoro Rakotoarinivo, and Melinda Trudgen, "Dypsis Humilis," "Plants & Fungi at Kew," accessed 1 April 2016, www.kew.org/science-conservation/plants-fungi/dypsis-humilis.

38. Aaron Davis and Emma Tredwell, "Coffea Pterocarpa (Madagascan Wing-Fruited Coffee)," "Plants & Fungi at Kew," accessed 5 April 2016, www.kew.org/science-conservation/plants-fungi/coffea-pterocarpa-madagascan-wing-fruited-coffee.

39. "Frequently Asked Questions—Regjeringen.No," 21 October 2011, https://web.archive.org/web/20111021223103/; www.regjeringen.no/en/dep/lmd/campain/svalbard-global-seed-vault/frequently-asked-questions.html.

40. Ingrid Urberg, "'Svalbard's Daughters': Personal Accounts by Svalbard's Female Pioneers," *Nordlit* 11, no. 2 (April 1, 2007): 168, https://doi.org/10.7557/13.1576.

41. "Frequently Asked Questions—Regjeringen.No."

42. *OED Online* (Oxford University Press), s.v. "Millennium, n." accessed 5 April 2016, www.oed.com.proxy.library.ucsb.edu:2048/view/Entry/118508.

43. Seabrook, "Sowing for Apocalypse."

44. Jonathan Watts, "Brazilian Beans and Japanese Barley Shipped to Svalbard Seed Vault," *Guardian*, 26 February 2014, sec. "Environment," www.theguardian.com/environment/2014/feb/26/svalbard-global-seed-vault-plants-shipped.

45. Lewis Carroll, *"Alice's Adventures in Wonderland" and "Through the Looking-Glass,"* ed. Hugh Haughton (London: Penguin, 1998), 135.

46. M. Bar-Joseph, R. Marcus, and R. F. Lee, "The Continuous Challenge of Citrus Tristeza Virus Control," *Annual Review of Phytopathology* 27, no. 1 (1989): 291, https://doi.org/10.1146/annurev.py.27.090189.001451.

47. Dan Koeppel, *Banana: The Fate of the Fruit That Changed the World* (New York: Penguin, 2008), xvi.

48. A. J. Ullstrup, "The Impacts of the Southern Corn Leaf Blight Epidemics of 1970–1971," *Annual Review of Phytopathology* 10, no. 1 (1972): 38, https://doi.org/10.1146/annurev.py.10.090172.000345.

49. Gail Lynn Schumann, *Plant Diseases: Their Biology and Social Impact* (St. Paul: APS Press, American Phytopathological Society, 1991).

50. "Dimensions of Need—Staple Foods: What Do People Eat?," Food and Agriculture Organization of the United Nations, www.fao.org/docrep/u8480e/u8480e07.htm.

51. Seabrook, "Sowing for Apocalypse."

52. Seabrook, "Sowing for Apocalypse."

53. Mark Kinver, "Key Food Crops Head to Arctic 'Doomsday Vault,'" 26 February 2014, www.bbc.com/news/science-environment-26338709.

54. "Svalbard Global Seed Vault."

55. "Svalbard Global Seed Vault."

56. "Frequently Asked Questions—Regjeringen.No."

57. "About," "Millennium Seed Bank Partnership at Kew," accessed 12 January 2019, www.kew.org/science/collections/seed-collection/about-millennium-seed-bank.

58. Dan Shade, "The SF Site Featured Review: *The Windup Girl*," 2010, www.sfsite.com/10a/wg329.htm; Michael Dirda, "Paolo Bacigalupi's *The Windup Girl*, Winner of the Nebula Award," *Washington Post*, 8 July 2010, sec. "Arts & Living," www.washingtonpost.com/wp-dyn/content/article/2010/07/07/AR2010070704582.html.

59. Seabrook, "Sowing for Apocalypse."

60. Seabrook, "Sowing for Apocalypse."

61. "Svalbard Global Seed Vault."

62. Damian Carrington, "Arctic Stronghold of World's Seeds Flooded after Permafrost Melts," *Guardian*, 19 May 2017, sec. "Environment," www.theguardian.com/environment/2017/may/19/arctic-stronghold-of-worlds-seeds-flooded-after-permafrost-melts.

63. Darwin, *The Voyage of the Beagle*, 125.

64. Darwin, *The Voyage of the Beagle*, 271.

65. Matthew G. Kirschenbaum, *Mechanisms: New Media and the Forensic Imagination* (Cambridge: MIT Press, 2008), 97.

2. Cross Sections of the Tree of Life

1. Houser, "The Aesthetics of Environmental Visualizations," 320.

2. Here I follow many biologists in using "evolutionary tree," "phylogenetic tree," and "phylogeny" interchangeably. They all refer to a tree-like diagram that visualizes either real or hypothesized evolutionary relationships within a group of organisms. For more on the use of these terms, see http://evolution.berkeley.edu/evolibrary/article/phylogenetics_02.

3. Manuel Lima, "Mammal Supertree," visualcomplexity.com, accessed 5 January 2019, www.visualcomplexity.com/vc/project.cfm?id=442.

4. David M. Hillis, Derrick Zwickl, and Robin Gutell, "Graphic Images from the Hillis/Bull Lab," www.zo.utexas.edu/faculty/antisense/DownloadfilesToL.html

5. Kathryn Henderson, *On Line and on Paper: Visual Representations, Visual Culture, and Computer Graphics in Design Engineering* (Cambridge: MIT Press, 1991), 25.

6. "Q&A; with Peter Kareiva: Biodiversity Hotspots," The Nature Conservancy (website), 20 September 2014, https://web.archive.org/web/20140920154009/; http://www.nature.org/science-in-action/our-scientists/q-1.xml.

7. "EDGE of Existence: Evolutionarily Distinct & Globally Endangered," EDGE of Existence (website), emphasis added, accessed 26 March 2018, www.edgeofexistence.org/.

8. David Armstrong, *Political Anatomy of the Body: Medical Knowledge in Britain in the Twentieth Century* (Cambridge: Cambridge University Press, 1983), 2.

9. Cody E. Hinchliff et al., "Synthesis of Phylogeny and Taxonomy into a Comprehensive Tree of Life," *Proceedings of the National Academy of Sciences of the United States of America* 112, no. 41 (October 2015): 12764–69, https://doi.org/10.1073/pnas.1423041112.

10. Derek Woods, "Accelerated Reading: Fossil Fuels, Infowhelm, Archival Life," in *Anthropocene Reading: Literary History in Geologic Times,* ed. Tobias Menely and Jesse Oak Taylor (University Park: Pennsylvania State University Press, 2017), 202.

11. Olaf R. P. Bininda-Emonds, *Phylogenetic Supertrees: Combining Information to Reveal the Tree of Life* (Berlin: Springer Science & Business Media, 2004), 5, emphasis added.

12. Manuel Lima, *The Book of Trees: Visualizing Branches of Knowledge* (Hudson, NY: Princeton Architectural Press, 2014), 44, emphasis added.

13. Gilles Deleuze and Félix Guattari, *A Thousand Plateaus: Capitalism and Schizophrenia,* trans. Brian Massumi (Minneapolis: University of Minnesota Press, 1987), 10.

14. Deleuze and Guattari, *A Thousand Plateaus,* 11.

15. Deleuze and Guattari, *A Thousand Plateaus,* 10.

16. Sophie S. Abby et al., "Lateral Gene Transfer as a Support for the Tree of Life," *Proceedings of the National Academy of Sciences of the United States of America* 109, no. 13 (2012): 4962.

17. Geoffrey I. McFadden, "Chloroplast Origin and Integration," *Plant Physiology* 125, no. 1 (January 2001): 50, https://doi.org/10.1104/pp.125.1.50.

18. J. David Archibald, *Aristotle's Ladder, Darwin's Tree: The Evolution of Visual Metaphors for Biological Order* (New York: Columbia University Press, 2014), 197.

19. Lima, *The Book of Trees*, 41.

20. Klaus Hentschel, *Visual Cultures in Science and Technology: A Comparative History* (Oxford: Oxford University Press, 2014), 51.

21. Archibald, *Aristotle's Ladder, Darwin's Tree*, 53.

22. Archibald, *Aristotle's Ladder, Darwin's Tree*, 197.

23. Roger Cook, *The Tree of Life: Symbol of the Centre* (London: Thames and Hudson, 1974), 9.

24. Ivica Letunic and Peer Bork, "Interactive Tree of Life (ITOL) v3: An Online Tool for the Display and Annotation of Phylogenetic and Other Trees," *Nucleic Acids Research* 44, no. W1 (July 2016): W242–45, https://doi.org/10.1093/nar/gkw290.

25. Hinchliff et al., "Synthesis of Phylogeny and Taxonomy into a Comprehensive Tree of Life."

26. D. R. Maddison and K. S. Schulz, Tree of Life Web Project, 2007, http://tolweb.org/tree/.

27. Edward R. Tufte, *The Visual Display of Quantitative Information* (New York: Graphics Press, 1983), 178.

28. Stephen M. Kosslyn, *Graph Design for the Eye and Mind* (Oxford: Oxford University Press, USA, 2006), 40.

29. Charles Darwin, *On the Origin of Species* (New York: Collier and Son, 1909), 143.

30. Elizabeth Grosz, *Time Travels: Feminism, Nature, Power* (Durham, NC: Duke University Press, 2005), 17.

31. Grosz, *Time Travels*, 18.

32. Matt McGrath, "Billions Required to Save Nature," sec. "Science & Environment," BBC News, 12 October 2012, www.bbc.com/news/science-environment-19912266.

33. Cara Byington, "Diversify Your Species: New Paper from NatureNet Fellow Danny Karp," *Cool Green Science*, 15 September 2014, http://blog.nature.org/science/2014/09/15/diversify-your-species/.

34. University of Sheffield, "World-Leading Scientists Develop New Approach to Bird Conservation—News Releases—News—The University of Sheffield," 11 April 2014, www.sheffield.ac.uk/news/nr/new-approach-bird-conservation-1.367223.

35. Thom van Dooren, "The Last Snail: Conservation and Extinction in Hawai'i," in blog found on Thom van Dooren (website), 28 February 2013, http://thomvandooren.org/2013/02/28/last_snail/.

36. Sean B. Carroll, *The Making of the Fittest: DNA and the Ultimate Forensic Record of Evolution* (New York: Norton, 2006), 123.

37. Wikipedia, the Free Encyclopedia, "Evolution of Cetaceans," 13 March 2016, https://en.wikipedia.org/w/index.php?title=Evolution_of_cetaceans&oldid=709800834.

38. *OED Online* (Oxford University Press), s.v. "History, n.," emphasis added, accessed 14 March 2016, www.oed.com.proxy.library.ucsb.edu:2048/view/Entry/87324.

39. Liza Gross, "Reading the Evolutionary History of the Woolly Mammoth in Its Mitochondrial Genome," *PLOS Biol* 4, no. 3 (February 2006): 74, https://doi: 10.1371/journal.pbio.0040074.

40. *Galapagos Conservancy Blog*, accessed 14 March 2016, www.galapagos.org/about_galapagos/about-galapagos/lonesome-george/.

3. A Bird in Hand

1. Jennifer Jaye Price, *Flight Maps: Adventures with Nature in Modern America* (New York: Basic, 1999).

2. Christopher Cokinos, *Hope Is the Thing with Feathers: A Personal Chronicle of Vanished Birds* (London: Penguin, 2009).

3. Jeffrey Karnicky, *Scarlet Experiment: Birds and Humans in America* (Lincoln: University of Nebraska Press, 2016).

4. James M. Vardaman, *Call Collect, Ask for Birdman* (New York: St. Martin's, 1980); Alan Davies and Ruth Miller, *The Biggest Twitch: Around the World in 4,000 Birds* (London: A&C Black, 2010); Sean Dooley, *The Big Twitch: One Man, One Continent, a Race Against Time—A True Story about Birdwatching* (Sydney: Allen and Unwin, 2006); Pete Dunne, *The Feather Quest: A North American Birder's Year* (New York: Houghton Mifflin Harcourt, 1999).

5. Roger Tory Peterson and James Fisher, *Wild America* (New York: Houghton Mifflin, 1955), 186.

6. Peterson and Fisher, *Wild America*, 29.

7. "Classification and Nomenclature (North & Middle America)," "Committees," AOU (American Ornithology Union) website, accessed 12 January 2019, www.aou.org/committees/nacc/.

8. Phoebe Snetsinger, *Birding on Borrowed Time* (Colorado Springs: American Birding Association, 2003), 132.

9. Kenn Kaufman, *Kingbird Highway: The Biggest Year in the Life of an Extreme Birder* (New York: Houghton Mifflin, 1997), 161.

10. Kaufman, *Kingbird Highway*, 154.

11. Kaufman, *Kingbird Highway*, 44.

12. Peterson and Fisher, *Wild America*, 190.

13. Peterson and Fisher, *Wild America*, 202.

14. Eva von Contzen, "The Limits of Narration: Lists and Literary History," *Style* 50, no. 3 (August 2016): 241–60, https://doi.org/10.1353/sty.2016.0015; Brian Richardson, "Modern Fiction, the Poetics of Lists, and the Boundaries of

Narrative," *Style* 50, no. 3 (August 4, 2016): 327–41, https://doi.org/10.1353/sty.2016.0013.

15. Dorothee Birke, "The World Is Not Enough: Lists as Encounters with the 'Real' in the Eighteenth-Century Novel," *Style* 50, no. 3 (August 4, 2016): 297, https://doi.org/10.1353/sty.2016.0021.

16. Heise, *Imagining Extinction*, 56.

17. Vanessa Steinroetter, "'Reading the List': Casualty Lists and Civil War Poetry," *ESQ: A Journal of the American Renaissance* 59, no. 1 (June 2013): 49, https://doi.org/10.1353/esq.2013.0011.

18. Snetsinger, *Birding on Borrowed Time*, 216.

19. Snetsinger, *Birding on Borrowed Time*, 243.

20. Snetsinger, *Birding on Borrowed Time*, 85.

21. Snetsinger, *Birding on Borrowed Time*, 159.

22. Snetsinger, *Birding on Borrowed Time*, 121.

23. Peterson and Fisher, *Wild America*, 203.

24. Peterson and Fisher, *Wild America*, 229.

25. Peterson and Fisher, *Wild America*, 264.

26. Haraway, *When Species Meet*, 15.

27. Haraway, *When Species Meet*, 3.

28. Haraway, *When Species Meet*, 255.

29. Haraway, *When Species Meet*, 254.

30. Haraway, *When Species Meet*, 36.

31. Haraway, *When Species Meet*, 21.

32. Snetsinger, *Birding on Borrowed Time*, 17–18.

33. Haraway, *When Species Meet*, 25.

34. Snetsinger, *Birding on Borrowed Time*, 71.

35. Kaufman, *Kingbird Highway*, 76.

36. Bennett, *Vibrant Matter*, 99.

37. Serenella Iovino and Serpil Oppermann, *Material Ecocriticism* (Bloomington: Indiana University Press, 2014), 8.

38. Snetsinger, *Birding on Borrowed Time*, 17, emphasis added.

39. Snetsinger, *Birding on Borrowed Time*, 17.

40. Kaufman, *Kingbird Highway*, 92, emphasis added.

41. Timothy Aubry, *Reading as Therapy: What Contemporary Fiction Does for Middle-Class Americans* (Iowa City: University of Iowa Press, 2006), 99.

42. Peterson and Fisher, *Wild America*, 259.

43. Peterson and Fisher, *Wild America*, 326.

44. Paul Jaussen, "Spectral Affordances of the Catalogue," *Comparative Literature* 70, no. 2 (June 2018): 165, https://doi.org/10.1215/00104124-6817386.

45. Peterson and Fisher, *Wild America*, 7.

46. Peterson and Fisher, *Wild America*, 2.

47. Peterson and Fisher, *Wild America*, 12.

48. Peterson and Fisher, *Wild America*, 10.

49. Peterson and Fisher, *Wild America*, 18.

50. *Birders: The Central Park Effect,* 6, accessed January 2019, www.imdb.com/title/tt2310157/.

51. Jonathan Franzen, *The Discomfort Zone* (New York: Picador, 2006), 180.

52. Peterson and Fisher, *Wild America,* 191.

53. Peterson and Fisher, *Wild America,* 288.

54. Kaufman, *Kingbird Highway,* 177.

55. B. Joseph Pine and James H. Gilmore, *The Experience Economy: Work Is Theatre & Every Business a Stage* (Cambridge: Harvard Business Press, 1999), 3.

56. "Conserving America's Bird," "Migratory Bird Program," U.S. Fish & Wildlife Service, accessed 24 December 2018, www.fws.gov/birds/bird-enthusiasts/bird-watching/valuing-birds.php.

57. Celia Lury, *Consumer Culture* (New Brunswick, NJ: Rutgers University Press, 2011), 4–5.

58. Kaufman, *Kingbird Highway,* 95.

59. Peterson and Fisher, *Wild America,* 120.

60. Peterson and Fisher, *Wild America,* 195.

61. Franzen, *The Discomfort Zone,* 184.

62. To be clear, Jonathan Franzen is the only memoirist considered here who is not a competitive lister. He is not going for a big year nor in the running for most birds seen in a lifetime. He is more of a casual birder who comments upon the incongruities inherent in birding.

63. Mark Obmascik, *The Big Year* (New York: Free Press, 2004), 65.

64. Obmascik, *The Big Year,* 247.

65. Peterson and Fisher, *Wild America,* 33.

66. Peterson and Fisher, *Wild America,* 46.

67. Peterson and Fisher, *Wild America,* 91.

68. Kaufman, *Kingbird Highway,* 303.

69. Cronon, "The Trouble with Wilderness," 7–28.

70. Peterson and Fisher, *Wild America,* 49.

71. Peterson and Fisher, *Wild America,* 72.

72. Peterson and Fisher, *Wild America,* 156.

73. Peterson and Fisher, *Wild America,* 306.

74. Peterson and Fisher, *Wild America,* 131.

75. Peterson and Fisher, *Wild America,* 131.

76. Peterson and Fisher, *Wild America,* 297.

77. Kaufman, *Kingbird Highway,* 108.

78. Franzen, *The Discomfort Zone,* 181.

79. Peterson and Fisher, *Wild America,* 97.

80. Peterson and Fisher, *Wild America,* 151.

81. Peterson and Fisher, *Wild America,* 261.

82. Peterson and Fisher, *Wild America,* 317.

83. William Cronon, *Uncommon Ground: Rethinking the Human Place in Nature* (New York: Norton, 1996), 79.

84. Franzen, *The Discomfort Zone,* 168.

4. Islands in the Aether Ocean

1. Herman Melville, *The Encantadas: Or Enchanted Isles* (New York: Putnam, 1854), 20.
2. Darwin, *The Voyage of the Beagle*, 394.
3. "Galapagos Plants," Galapagos Conservancy (website), accessed 5 October 2015, www.galapagos.org/about_galapagos/plants/.
4. "Galapagos Plants," Galapagos Conservancy.
5. Robert J. Whittaker and José Maria Fernandez-Palacios, *Island Biogeography: Ecology, Evolution, and Conservation* (Oxford: Oxford University Press, 2007), 2.
6. Fredric Jameson, "World-Reduction in Le Guin: The Emergence of Utopian Narrative," *Science Fiction Studies* 2, no. 3 (November 1975): 223.
7. Ursula K. Heise, "Reduced Ecologies," *European Journal of English Studies* 16, no. 2 (August 2012): 99–112, https://doi.org/10.1080/13825577.2012.703814.
8. Frank Herbert, *Dune* (Randor: Chilton, 1965).
9. Orson Scott Card, *Speaker for the Dead* (New York: Macmillan, 1986).
10. José Luiz de Andrade Franco, "The Concept of Biodiversity and the History of Conservation Biology: From Wilderness Preservation to Biodiversity Conservation," *História (São Paulo)* 32, no. 2 (December 2013): 21–48, https://doi.org/10.1590/S0101-90742013000200003.
11. Ernst Mayr, *The Growth of Biological Thought: Diversity, Evolution, and Inheritance* (Cambridge: Harvard University Press, 1982), 134.
12. Philip K. Dick, *Do Androids Dream of Electric Sheep?* (New York: Ballantine, 1996).
13. Bacigalupi, *The Windup Girl*.
14. Margaret Atwood, *Oryx and Crake* (Toronto: Vintage Canada, 2010).
15. Isaac Asimov, *Foundation* (New York: Random House, 2004).
16. Bruce Sterling, *Schismatrix Plus* (New York: Open Road Media, 2014).
17. Douglas Adams, *The Hitchhiker's Guide to the Galaxy* (New York: Random House, 2007).
18. Dan Simmons, *Hyperion* (New York: Random House, 2011).
19. Ursula K. Le Guin, *The Dispossessed* (New York: HarperCollins, 2009), 46.
20. Other examples of speculative-ecosystem science fiction would be Sherri Tepper's *Grass*, Larry Niven and Jerry Pournelle's *The Mote in God's Eye*, and James Cameron's *Avatar*. If one extends the alternative ecosystem subgenre to speculative fiction and fantasy, the Mulefa world from Phillip Pullman's *The Amber Spyglass* and Brandon Sanderson's series *The Stormlight Archive* could be included.
21. Adam Trexler, *Anthropocene Fictions: The Novel in a Time of Climate Change* (Charlottesville: University of Virginia Press, 2015).
22. Lawrence Buell, *The Environmental Imagination: Thoreau, Nature Writing, and the Formation of American Culture* (Cambridge: Harvard University Press, 1995), 285.

23. Greg Garrard, *Ecocriticism* (New York: Routledge, 2011), 2.

24. Eric C. Otto, *Green Speculations: Science Fiction and Transformative Environmentalism* (Columbus: Ohio State University Press, 2012), 41.

25. Gerry Canavan and Kim Stanley Robinson, eds., *Green Planets: Ecology and Science Fiction* (Middletown, CT: Wesleyan University Press, 2014), 31–32.

26. Heise, "Reduced Ecologies."

27. Timothy Morton, "Pandora's Box: Avatar, Ecology, Thought," in *Green Planets: Ecology and Science Fiction,* ed. Gerry Canavan and Kim Stanley Robinson (Middletown, CT: Wesleyan University Press, 2014), 221–40.

28. Katherine Buse, "Genre, Utopia, and Ecological Crisis: World-Multiplication in Le Guin's Fantasy," *Green Letters* 17, no. 3 (November 1, 2013): 264–80, https://doi.org/10.1080/14688417.2013.860556.

29. Herbert, *Dune*, 115.

30. Herbert, *Dune*, 274.

31. Thomas Moylan, *Scraps of the Untainted Sky: Science Fiction, Utopia, Dystopia* (Boulder, CO: Westview, 2000), 6.

32. Herbert, *Dune*, 274.

33. Card, *Speaker for the Dead*, 23.

34. Card, *Speaker for the Dead*, 2.

35. Edward James, *Science Fiction in the Twentieth Century* (Oxford: Oxford University Press, 1994), 115; emphasis added.

36. William F. Laurance and David P. Edwards, "The Search for Unknown Biodiversity," *Proceedings of the National Academy of Sciences of the United States of America* 108, no. 32 (August 2011): 12971–72.

37. Alaimo, *Bodily Natures*.

38. Alaimo, *Bodily Natures*, 2. Darwin seems to be a model of this type of thinking for many scholars. See Jane Bennett's analysis of his writing on the "small agencies of worms" (Bennett, *Vibrant Matter*, 95). Gillian Beer even claims that the "capacity to imaginatively enjoy difference proves to be Darwin's central intellectual gift" ("Writing Darwin's Islands: England and the Insular Condition," in *Inscribing Science: Scientific Texts and the Materiality of Communication,* ed. Timothy Lenoir, 119–39 [Stanford, CA: Stanford University Press, 1998], 130).

39. Frank N. Egerton, "Changing Concepts of the Balance of Nature," *Quarterly Review of Biology* 48, no. 2 (June 1973): 324.

40. Egerton, "Changing Concepts of the Balance of Nature"; Daniel Simberloff, "The 'Balance of Nature'—Evolution of a Panchreston," *PLOS Biology* 12, no. 10 (October 2014), https://doi.org/10.1371/journal.pbio.1001963; Jianguo Wu and Orie L. Loucks, "From Balance of Nature to Hierarchical Patch Dynamics: A Paradigm Shift in Ecology," *Quarterly Review of Biology* 70, no. 4 (December 1995): 439–66, https://doi.org/10.1086/419172. There are many fine histories of the concept, which I will not replicate here (see Egerton; Simberloff; Wu and Loucks).

41. Egerton, "Changing Concepts of the Balance of Nature," 332.

42. Gillian Beer, "Discourses of the Island," in *Literature and Science as Modes of Expression,* ed. Frederick Amrine, Boston Studies in the Philosophy of Science 115 (Dordrecht: Springer Netherlands, 1989), 24, https://doi.org/10.1007/978-94-009-2297-6_1.

43. Egerton, "Changing Concepts of the Balance of Nature," 337.

44. Joel Bartholemew Hagen, *An Entangled Bank: The Origins of Ecosystem Ecology* (New Brunswick, NJ: Rutgers University Press, 1992), 56.

45. Egerton, "Changing Concepts of the Balance of Nature," 322.

46. Simberloff, "The 'Balance of Nature'—Evolution of a Panchreston."

47. Corinne Zimmerman and Kim Cuddington, "Ambiguous, Circular and Polysemous: Students' Definitions of the 'Balance of Nature' Metaphor," *Public Understanding of Science* 16, no. 4 (October 2007): 393–406, https://doi.org/10.1177/0963662505063022; Marida Ergazaki and Georgios Ampatzidis, "Students' Reasoning about the Future of Disturbed or Protected Ecosystems & the Idea of the 'Balance of Nature,'" *Research in Science Education* 42, no. 3 (February 2011): 511–30, https://doi.org/10.1007/s11165-011-9208-7.

48. Morar, Toadvine, and Bohannan, "Biodiversity at Twenty-Five Years," 20.

49. Herbert, *Dune.*

50. Herbert, *Dune,* 139.

51. Herbert, *Dune,* 276.

52. Herbert, *Dune.*

53. Herbert, *Dune,* 113.

54. Herbert, *Dune,* 276.

55. Richard H. Grove, *Green Imperialism: Colonial Expansion, Tropical Island Edens and the Origins of Environmentalism, 1600–1860* (Cambridge: Cambridge University Press, 1996), 72.

56. Matt K. Matsuda, *Pacific Worlds: A History of Seas, Peoples, and Cultures* (Cambridge: Cambridge University Press, 2012), 772.

57. Beer, "Writing Darwin's Islands," 120.

58. Darko Suvin, *Metamorphoses of Science Fiction: On the Poetics and History of a Literary Genre* (New Haven, CT: Yale University Press, 1979), 373.

59. Elizabeth M. DeLoughrey, *Routes and Roots: Navigating Caribbean and Pacific Island Literatures* (Honolulu: University of Hawai'i Press, 2010).

60. Greg Dening, *Islands and Beaches: Discourse on a Silent Land: Marquesas, 1774–1880* (Melbourne: Melbourne University Press, 1980), 31.

61. University of Tennessee, "Saving Lonely Species Is Important for Environment," *ScienceDaily,* 30 October 2014, www.sciencedaily.com/releases/2014/10/141030133051.htm.

62. Jill H. Casid, *Sowing Empire: Landscape and Colonization* (Minneapolis: University of Minnesota Press, 2005), 51.

63. Casid, *Sowing Empire,* 7.

64. Jamaica Kincaid, *A Small Place* (New York: Macmillan, 1988), 23.

5. Biodiversity Within

1. W. H. Auden, "A New Year Greeting," *Scientific American* 221, no. 6 (1969): 12–16.

2. Auden, "A New Year Greeting," 35.

3. Auden, "A New Year Greeting," 49–54.

4. Technically the "microbiome" constitutes the collected genes and the "microbiota" the microbes, though I will follow the popular science journalism in using "microbiome" to refer to the organisms themselves.

5. Kathleen Housley, "The Microbiome and the Boson," *Image Journal* 85, no. 1 (n.d.), www.imagejournal.org/article/the-microbiome-and-the-boson/.

6. Julie Peters, *Julie Peters—Microbiome*, 2015, video, www.youtube.com/watch?v=l89lbGNFunI.

7. Editors of Scientific American, eds., *The Microbiome: Your Inner Ecosystem* (New York: Scientific American, 2019).

8. Rodney R. Dietert, *The Human Superorganism: How the Microbiome Is Revolutionizing the Pursuit of a Healthy Life* (New York: Penguin, 2016), 5.

9. Ron Sender, Shai Fuchs, and Ron Milo, "Revised Estimates for the Number of Human and Bacteria Cells in the Body," *PLOS Biology* 14, no. 8 (August 2016): e1002533, https://doi.org/10.1371/journal.pbio.1002533.

10. Ranna Samadfam, "How Your Gut Affects Your Bones," in *The Microbiome: Your Inner Ecosystem*, ed. Editors of Scientific American (New York: Scientific American, 2019), 47.

11. Peter Andrey Smith, "The Tantalizing Links between Gut Microbes and the Brain," in *The Microbiome: Your Inner Ecosystem*, ed. Editors of Scientific American (New York: Scientific American, 2019), 66.

12. Jane A. Foster and Karen-Anne McVey Neufeld, "Gut-Brain Axis: How the Microbiome Influences Anxiety and Depression," *Trends in Neurosciences* 36, no. 5 (May 2013): 305, https://doi.org/10.1016/j.tins.2013.01.005.

13. Stephen Jay Gould, "Planet of the Bacteria," *Washington Post*, 13 November 1996, www.washingtonpost.com/archive/1996/11/13/planet-of-the-bacteria/6fb6of1d-e6fe-471e-8a0f-4cfa9373772c/.

14. John Dupré, *Processes of Life: Essays in the Philosophy of Biology* (Oxford: Oxford University Press, 2012), 232–33.

15. Ed Yong, *I Contain Multitudes: The Microbes within Us and a Grander View of Life* (New York: HarperCollins, 2016), 49–50; Donna J. Haraway, *Staying with the Trouble: Making Kin in the Chthulucene* (Durham, NC: Duke University Press, 2016), 66.

16. Yong, *I Contain Multitudes*, 55.

17. S. S. Hirano and C. D. Upper, "Bacteria in the Leaf Ecosystem with Emphasis on Pseudomonas Syringae—a Pathogen, Ice Nucleus, and Epiphyte," *Microbiology and Molecular Biology Reviews: MMBR* 64, no. 3 (September 2000): 624–53, https://doi.org/10.1128/mmbr.64.3.624-653.2000.

18. Donna Jeanne Haraway, *Simians, Cyborgs and Women: The Reinvention of Nature* (London: Free Association, 1991), 151.

19. Dupré, *Processes of Life*, 126.

20. Dupré, *Processes of Life*, 232–33.

21. Dupré, *Processes of Life*, 116.

22. Simon Park, "Cellfies: Cellular/Microbiotic Self Portraits," *Exploring the Invisible* (blog), 21 January 2016, https://exploringtheinvisible.com/2016/01/21/cellfies-cellular-self-portraits/.

23. Erik-Erno Raitanen, *Bacteriograms*, accessed 12 January 2019, www.microbialart.com/galleries/erno-erik-raitanen/.

24. Joana Ricou, "Other Self Portraits," *Girlsandcells*, accessed 12 January 2019, www.joanaricou.com/microbiomeprocess.

25. Mellissa Fisher, "Microbial Me," accessed 12 January 2019, www.mellissafisher.com/microbial-me.

26. Martin J. Blaser, *Missing Microbes: How the Overuse of Antibiotics Is Fueling Our Modern Plagues* (London: Oneworld, 2014).

27. Justin Sonnenburg and Erica Sonnenburg, *The Good Gut: Taking Control of Your Weight, Your Mood, and Your Long-Term Health* (New York: Penguin, 2016).

28. Dietert, *The Human Superorganism*.

29. Editors of Scientific American, eds., *The Microbiome: Your Inner Ecosystem*.

30. Rob Knight and Brendan Buhler, *Follow Your Gut: The Enormous Impact of Tiny Microbes* (New York: Simon and Schuster, 2015).

31. Yong, *I Contain Multitudes*.

32. Bret Stetka, "Mind over Meal: Weight-Loss Surgery and the Gut-Brain Connection," in *The Microbiome: Your Inner Ecosystem*, ed. Editors of Scientific American (New York: Scientific American, 2019), 103.

33. Yong, *I Contain Multitudes*, 52.

34. Sonnenburg and Sonnenburg, *The Good Gut*, 144.

35. Yong, *I Contain Multitudes*, 71.

36. Yong, *I Contain Multitudes*, 17.

37. Yong, *I Contain Multitudes*, 86.

38. Yong, *I Contain Multitudes*, 98.

39. Jennifer Ackerman, "The Ultimate Social Network," in *The Microbiome: Your Inner Ecosystem*, ed. Editors of Scientific American (New York: Scientific American, 2019), 13.

40. Yong, *I Contain Multitudes*, 52.

41. Auden, "A New Year Greeting," 17–22.

42. Yong, *I Contain Multitudes*, 16.

43. Yong, *I Contain Multitudes*, 17.

44. Blaser, *Missing Microbes*, 24.

45. Claudia Wallis, "Gut Reactions," in *The Microbiome: Your Inner Ecosystem*, ed. Editors of Scientific American (New York: Scientific American, 2019), 88.

46. E. O. Wilson et al., *Biodiversity* (Washington, DC: National Academies Press, 1988), 1.

47. Wallis, "Gut Reactions," 87.
48. Dietert, *The Human Superorganism*, 39.
49. Sonnenburg and Sonnenburg, *The Good Gut*, 17.
50. Jeff Leach, "(Re)Becoming Human," Human Food Project, 30 September 2014, http://humanfoodproject.com/rebecoming-human-happened-day-replaced-99-genes-body-hunter-gatherer/.
51. Rob Knight, "Why Microbiome Treatments Could Pay off Soon," *Nature* 518 (February 2015): S5, https://doi.org/10.1038/518S5a.
52. Ed Yong, "There Is No 'Healthy' Microbiome," editorial, *New York Times*, 1 November 2014, www.nytimes.com/2014/11/02/opinion/sunday/there-is-no-healthy-microbiome.html.
53. Wilson et al., *Biodiversity*, 1.
54. Alaimo, *Bodily Natures*, 2.
55. Yong, *I Contain Multitudes*, 251.
56. Yong, *I Contain Multitudes*, 253.
57. Alaimo, *Bodily Natures*, 146.
58. Bennett, *Vibrant Matter*, 13.
59. Housley, "The Microbiome and the Boson," lines 1–2.
60. Peters, *Julie Peters—Microbiome*.
61. Peters, *Julie Peters—Microbiome*.
62. Housley, "The Microbiome and the Boson," lines 18–20.
63. Housley, "The Microbiome and the Boson," line 7.
64. Housley, "The Microbiome and the Boson," lines 8–11.
65. Peters, *Julie Peters—Microbiome*.
66. Peters, *Julie Peters—Microbiome*.
67. Titus Livius, *The History of Rome: Book Two* (Urbana, IL: Project Gutenberg, 2006), 32, https://www.gutenberg.org/files/19725/19725-h/19725-h.htm.
68. "Frontispiece of Thomas Hobbes' Leviathan, by Abraham Bosse, with Creative Input from Thomas Hobbes, 1651," accessed December 31, 2019, https://www.college.columbia.edu/core/content/frontispiece-thomas-hobbes%E2%80%99-leviathan-abraham-bosse-creative-input-thomas-hobbes-1651.
69. Carl Zimmer, "How Microbes Defend and Define Us," Earth and Environmental Sciences Area, 12 July 2010, http://esd.lbl.gov/how-microbes-defend-and-define-us/.
70. Haraway, *When Species Meet*, 15.
71. Sterling, *Schismatrix Plus*, 24.
72. Sterling, *Schismatrix Plus*, 39.
73. Laurel Bollinger, "Containing Multitudes: Revisiting the Infection Metaphor in Science Fiction," *Extrapolation* 50, no. 3 (September 2009): 384.
74. Sterling, *Schismatrix Plus*, 103.
75. Sterling, *Schismatrix Plus*, 85.
76. Sterling, *Schismatrix Plus*, 145.
77. Sterling, *Schismatrix Plus*, 52.
78. Gibson, *Neuromancer*, 6.

79. Sterling, *Schismatrix Plus*, 12.
80. Sterling, *Schismatrix Plus*, 12.
81. Sterling, *Schismatrix Plus*, 18.
82. Sterling, *Schismatrix Plus*, 204.
83. Sterling, *Schismatrix Plus*, 203.
84. Sterling, *Schismatrix Plus*, 227.
85. Sterling, *Schismatrix Plus*, 232.
86. Sterling, *Schismatrix Plus*, 232.
87. Haraway, *Simians, Cyborgs and Women*, 151.
88. Sterling, *Schismatrix Plus*, 228.

Coda

1. David Mitchell, *Ghostwritten* (New York: Knopf Doubleday, 2007), 364.
2. Mitchell, *Ghostwritten*, 380–81.
3. Pratt, *Imperial Eyes*, 50.
4. Wolfe, *What Is Posthumanism?*, 134.
5. Mitchell, *Ghostwritten*, 387.
6. Barrow, *Nature's Ghosts*, 4.
7. Mitchell, *Ghostwritten*, 387.
8. Pratt, *Imperial Eyes*, 50.
9. Pratt, *Imperial Eyes*, 51.
10. Susan Scott Parrish, *American Curiosity: Cultures of Natural History in the Colonial British Atlantic World* (Chapel Hill: University of North Carolina Press, 2012), 18.
11. Mitchell, *Ghostwritten*, 404.
12. Mitchell, *Ghostwritten*, 404.
13. Mitchell, *Ghostwritten*, 405.
14. Mitchell, *Ghostwritten*, 405.
15. Mitchell, *Ghostwritten*, 404–5.
16. Pratt, *Imperial Eyes*, 31.
17. Lorraine Daston, "Type Specimens and Scientific Memory," *Critical Inquiry* 31, no. 1 (2004): 167, https://doi.org/10.1086/427306.
18. Mitchell, *Ghostwritten*, 415.
19. Cronon, "The Trouble with Wilderness," 7–28.
20. Guha, "Radical American Environmentalism and Wilderness Preservation: A Third World Critique," 71–83.
21. Arturo Escobar, *Encountering Development: The Making and Unmaking of the Third World* (Princeton, NJ: Princeton University Press, 2001).
22. Heise, *Imagining Extinction*, 4.

Bibliography

Abby, Sophie S., et al. "Lateral Gene Transfer as a Support for the Tree of Life." *Proceedings of the National Academy of Sciences of the United States of America* 109, no. 13 (2012): 4962–67.
Ackerman, Jennifer. "The Ultimate Social Network." In *The Microbiome: Your Inner Ecosystem*, edited by Editors of Scientific American, sec. 1.1. New York: Scientific American, 2019.
Adams, Douglas. *The Hitchhiker's Guide to the Galaxy.* New York: Random House, 2007.
Alaimo, Stacy. *Bodily Natures: Science, Environment, and the Material Self.* Bloomington: Indiana University Press, 2010.
Alaimo, Stacy, and Susan Hekman. *Material Feminisms.* Bloomington: Indiana University Press, 2008.
Archibald, J. David. *Aristotle's Ladder, Darwin's Tree: The Evolution of Visual Metaphors for Biological Order.* New York: Columbia University Press, 2014.
Armstrong, David. *Political Anatomy of the Body: Medical Knowledge in Britain in the Twentieth Century.* Cambridge: Cambridge University Press, 1983.
Asimov, Isaac. *Foundation.* New York: Random House, 2004.
Atwood, Margaret. *In Other Worlds: SF and the Human Imagination.* New York: Knopf Doubleday, 2011.
———. *Oryx and Crake.* Toronto: Vintage Canada, 2010.
Aubry, Timothy. *Reading as Therapy: What Contemporary Fiction Does for Middle-Class Americans.* Iowa City: University of Iowa Press, 2006.
Auden, W. H. "A New Year Greeting." *Scientific American* 221, no. 6 (1969): 134–35. JSTOR.
Austen, Jane. *Pride and Prejudice.* New York: Scribner's Sons, 1918.
Bacigalupi, Paolo. *The Windup Girl.* Jersey City, NJ: Start, 2015.
Barad, Karen. *Meeting the Universe Halfway: Quantum Physics and the Entanglement of Matter and Meaning.* Durham, NC: Duke University Press, 2007.
Barrow, Mark V., Jr. *Nature's Ghosts: Confronting Extinction from the Age of Jefferson to the Age of Ecology.* Chicago: University of Chicago Press, 2011.
Beer, Gillian. "Discourses of the Island." In *Literature and Science as Modes of Expression,* edited by Frederick Amrine, 1–27. Dordrecht: Springer Netherlands, 1989. https://doi.org/10.1007/978-94-009-2297-6_1.

———. "Writing Darwin's Islands: England and the Insular Condition." In *Inscribing Science: Scientific Texts and the Materiality of Communication*, edited by Timothy Lenoir, 119–39. Stanford, CA: Stanford University Press, 1998.

Bennett, Jane. *Vibrant Matter: A Political Ecology of Things*. Durham, NC: Duke University Press, 2010.

Bininda-Emonds, Olaf R. P. *Phylogenetic Supertrees: Combining Information to Reveal the Tree of Life*. Berlin: Springer Science & Business Media, 2004.

Birke, Dorothee. "The World Is Not Enough: Lists as Encounters with the 'Real' in the Eighteenth-Century Novel." *Style* 50, no. 3 (August 2016): 296–308. https://doi.org/10.1353/sty.2016.0021.

Blaser, Martin. *Missing Microbes*. London: Oneworld, 2014.

Bollinger, Laurel. "Containing Multitudes: Revisiting the Infection Metaphor in Science Fiction." *Extrapolation* 50, no. 3 (September 2009): 377–99.

Bowker, Geoffrey C. *Memory Practices in the Sciences*. Cambridge: MIT Press, 2008.

Braidotti, Rosi. *The Posthuman*. Hoboken, NJ: Wiley and Sons, 2013.

Buell, Lawrence. *The Environmental Imagination: Thoreau, Nature Writing, and the Formation of American Culture*. Cambridge: Harvard University Press, 1995.

Buse, Katherine. "Genre, Utopia, and Ecological Crisis: World-Multiplication in Le Guin's Fantasy." *Green Letters* 17, no. 3 (November 2013): 264–80. https://doi.org/10.1080/14688417.2013.860556.

Byington, Cara. "Diversify Your Species: New Paper from NatureNet Fellow Danny Karp." *Cool Green Science*, 15 September 2014. http://blog.nature.org/science/2014/09/15/diversify-your-species/.

Canavan, Gerry, and Kim Stanley Robinson, eds. *Green Planets: Ecology and Science Fiction*. Middleton, CT: Wesleyan University Press, 2014.

Card, Orson Scott. *Speaker for the Dead*. New York: Macmillan, 1986.

Carrington, Damian. "Arctic Stronghold of World's Seeds Flooded after Permafrost Melts." *Guardian*, 19 May 2017. www.theguardian.com/environment/2017/may/19/arctic-stronghold-of-worlds-seeds-flooded-after-permafrost-melts.

Carroll, Lewis. *"Alice's Adventures in Wonderland" and "Through the Looking-Glass."* Edited by Hugh Haughton. London: Penguin, 1998.

Carroll, Sean B. *The Making of the Fittest: DNA and the Ultimate Forensic Record of Evolution*. New York: Norton, 2006.

Carruth, Allison. "The Digital Cloud and the Micropolitics of Energy." *Public Culture* 26, no. 2 (73) (May 2014): 339–64. https://doi.org/10.1215/08992363-2392093.

———. "Ecological Media Studies and the Matter of Digital Technologies." *PMLA* 131, no. 2 (March 2016): 339–64. https://doi.org/10.1632/pmla.2016.131.2.364.

Casid, Jill H. *Sowing Empire: Landscape and Colonization*. Minneapolis: University of Minnesota Press, 2005.

Castree, Noel, et al. "Mapping Posthumanism: An Exchange." *Environment and Planning A* 36 (January 2004): 1341–63. https://doi.org/10.1068/a37127.

Cohen, Jeffrey Jerome, and Stephanie LeMenager. "Introduction." *PMLA* 131, no. 2 (March 2016): 340–46. https://doi.org/10.1632/pmla.2016.131.2.340.

Cokinos, Christopher. *Hope Is the Thing with Feathers: A Personal Chronicle of Vanished Birds.* London: Penguin, 2009.

Contzen, Eva von. "The Limits of Narration: Lists and Literary History." *Style* 50, no. 3 (August 2016): 241–60. https://doi.org/10.1353/sty.2016.0015.

Cook, Roger. *The Tree of Life: Symbol of the Centre.* London: Thames and Hudson, 1974.

Coole, Diana, and Samantha Frost. *New Materialisms: Ontology, Agency, and Politics.* Durham, NC: Duke University Press, 2010.

Cronon, William. "The Trouble with Wilderness; Or, Getting Back to the Wrong Nature." *Environmental History* 1, no. 1 (January 1996): 7–28. https://doi.org/10.2307/3985059.

———. *Uncommon Ground: Rethinking the Human Place in Nature.* New York: Norton, 1996.

Daniel, Sharon. "The Database: An Aesthetics of Dignity." In *Database Aesthetics [Electronic Resource]: Art in the Age of Information Overflow*, edited by Victoria Vesna, 142–82. Minneapolis: University of Minnesota Press, 2007.

Darwin, Charles. *On the Origin of Species.* New York: Collier and Son, 1909.

———. *The Voyage of the Beagle: Journal of Researches into the Natural History and Geology of the Countries Visited during the Voyage of H.M.S. Beagle Round the World.* New York: Random House Modern Library, 2001.

Daston, Lorraine. "Type Specimens and Scientific Memory." *Critical Inquiry* 31, no. 1 (2004): 153–82. https://doi.org/10.1086/427306.

Davies, Alan, and Ruth Miller. *The Biggest Twitch: Around the World in 4,000 Birds.* London: A&C Black, 2010.

Deleuze, Gilles, and Félix Guattari. *A Thousand Plateaus: Capitalism and Schizophrenia.* Translated by Brian Massumi. Minneapolis: University of Minnesota Press, 1987.

DeLoughrey, Elizabeth M. *Routes and Roots: Navigating Caribbean and Pacific Island Literatures.* Honolulu: University of Hawai'i Press, 2010.

Dening, Greg. *Islands and Beaches: Discourse on a Silent Land: Marquesas, 1774–1880.* Melbourne: Melbourne University Press, 1980.

Dick, Philip K. *Do Androids Dream of Electric Sheep?* New York: Ballantine, 1996.

Dietert, Rodney R. *The Human Superorganism: How the Microbiome Is Revolutionizing the Pursuit of a Healthy Life.* New York: Penguin, 2016.

Dirda, Michael. "Paolo Bacigalupi's *The Windup Girl*, Winner of the Nebula Award." *Washington Post,* 8 July 2010. www.washingtonpost.com/wp-dyn/content/article/2010/07/07/AR2010070704582.html.

Dooley, Sean. *The Big Twitch: One Man, One Continent, a Race against Time—A True Story about Birdwatching.* Sydney: Allen and Unwin, 2006.

Dunne, Pete. *The Feather Quest: A North American Birder's Year.* New York: Houghton Mifflin Harcourt, 1999.

Dupré, John. *Processes of Life: Essays in the Philosophy of Biology.* Oxford: Oxford University Press, 2012.

Editors of Scientific American, eds. *The Microbiome: Your Inner Ecosystem.* New York: Scientific American, 2019.

Egerton, Frank N. "Changing Concepts of the Balance of Nature." *Quarterly Review of Biology* 48, no. 2 (June 1973): 322–50.

Ergazaki, Marida, and Georgios Ampatzidis. "Students' Reasoning about the Future of Disturbed or Protected Ecosystems & the Idea of the 'Balance of Nature.'" *Research in Science Education* 42, no. 3 (February 2011): 511–30. https://doi.org/10.1007/s11165-011-9208-7.

Escobar, Arturo. *Encountering Development: The Making and Unmaking of the Third World.* Princeton, NJ: Princeton University Press, 2001.

Farnham, Timothy J. *Saving Nature's Legacy: Origins of the Idea of Biological Diversity.* New Haven, CT: Yale University Press, 2007.

Fisher, Mellissa. *Microbial Me.* www.mellissafisher.com/microbial-me.

Foster, Jane A., and Karen-Anne McVey Neufeld. "Gut-Brain Axis: How the Microbiome Influences Anxiety and Depression." *Trends in Neurosciences* 36, no. 5 (May 2013): 305–12. https://doi.org/10.1016/j.tins.2013.01.005.

Franco, José Luiz de Andrade. "The Concept of Biodiversity and the History of Conservation Biology: From Wilderness Preservation to Biodiversity Conservation." *História (São Paulo)* 32, no. 2 (December 2013): 21–48. https://doi.org/10.1590/S0101-90742013000200003.

Franzen, Jonathan. *The Discomfort Zone.* New York: Picador, 2006.

Garrard, Greg. *Ecocriticism.* New York: Routledge, 2011.

Gatens, Moira. *Imaginary Bodies: Ethics, Power and Corporeality.* London: Routledge, 2013.

Gibson, William. *Neuromancer.* New York: Penguin, 2000.

Gould, Stephen Jay. "Planet of the Bacteria." *Washington Post,* 13 November 1996. www.washingtonpost.com/archive/1996/11/13/planet-of-the-bacteria/6fb60f1d-e6fe-471e-8a0f-4cfa9373772c/.

Gross, Liza. "Reading the Evolutionary History of the Woolly Mammoth in Its Mitochondrial Genome." *PLOS Biol* 4, no. 3 (February 2006): e74. https://doi:10.1371/journal.pbio.0040074.

Grosz, Elizabeth. *Becoming Undone: Darwinian Reflections on Life, Politics, and Art.* Durham, NC: Duke University Press, 2011.

———. *Time Travels: Feminism, Nature, Power.* Durham, NC: Duke University Press, 2005.

Grove, Richard H. *Green Imperialism: Colonial Expansion, Tropical Island Edens and the Origins of Environmentalism, 1600–1860.* Cambridge: Cambridge University Press, 1996.

Guha, Ramachandra. "Radical American Environmentalism and Wilderness Preservation: A Third World Critique." *Environmental Ethics,* no. 11 (1989): 71–83.

Hagen, Joel Bartholemew. *An Entangled Bank: The Origins of Ecosystem Ecology.* New Brunswick, NJ: Rutgers University Press, 1992.

Haraway, Donna Jeanne. *Simians, Cyborgs and Women: The Reinvention of Nature.* London: Free Association, 1991.

———. *Staying with the Trouble: Making Kin in the Chthulucene.* Durham, NC: Duke University Press, 2016.

———. *When Species Meet.* Minneapolis: University of Minnesota Press, 2013.

Hayles, N. Katherine. *How We Became Posthuman: Virtual Bodies in Cybernetics, Literature, and Informatics.* Chicago: University of Chicago Press, 2008.

———. "Narrative and Database: Natural Symbionts." *PMLA* 122, no. 5 (2007): 1603–8.

Heise, Ursula K. *Imagining Extinction: The Cultural Meanings of Endangered Species.* Chicago: University of Chicago Press, 2016.

———. "Reduced Ecologies." *European Journal of English Studies* 16, no. 2 (August 2012): 99–112. https://doi.org/10.1080/13825577.2012.703814.

———. "Unnatural Ecologies: The Metaphor of the Environment in Media Theory." *Configurations* 10, no. 1 (2002): 149–68. https://doi.org/10.1353/con.2003.0006.

Henderson, Kathryn. *On Line and on Paper: Visual Representations, Visual Culture, and Computer Graphics in Design Engineering.* Cambridge: MIT Press, 1991.

Hentschel, Klaus. *Visual Cultures in Science and Technology: A Comparative History.* Oxford: Oxford University Press, 2014.

Herbert, Frank. *Dune.* Randor: Chilton, 1965.

Hillis, David M., Derrick Zwickl, and Robin Gutell. *Graphic Images from the Hillis/Bull Lab.* 2003. www.zo.utexas.edu/faculty/antisense/DownloadfilesToL.html.

Hinchliff, Cody E., et al. "Synthesis of Phylogeny and Taxonomy into a Comprehensive Tree of Life." *Proceedings of the National Academy of Sciences of the United States of America* 112, no. 41 (October 2015): 12764–69. https://doi.org/10.1073/pnas.1423041112.

Hirano, S. S., and C. D. Upper. "Bacteria in the Leaf Ecosystem with Emphasis on Pseudomonas Syringae—a Pathogen, Ice Nucleus, and Epiphyte." *Microbiology and Molecular Biology Reviews: MMBR* 64, no. 3 (September 2000): 624–53. https://doi.org/10.1128/mmbr.64.3.624-653.2000.

Houser, Heather. "The Aesthetics of Environmental Visualizations: More Than Information Ecstasy?" *Public Culture* 26, no. 2 (73) (May 2014): 319–37. https://doi.org/10.1215/08992363-2392084.

Housley, Kathleen. "The Microbiome and the Boson." *Image Journal* 85, no. 1 (n.d.). www.imagejournal.org/article/the-microbiome-and-the-boson/.

Iovino, Serenella, and Serpil Oppermann. *Material Ecocriticism.* Bloomington: Indiana University Press, 2014.

James, Edward. *Science Fiction in the Twentieth Century.* Oxford: Oxford University Press, 1994.

Jameson, Fredric. "World-Reduction in Le Guin: The Emergence of Utopian Narrative." *Science Fiction Studies* 2, no. 3 (November 1975): 221–30.

Jaussen, Paul. "Spectral Affordances of the Catalogue." *Comparative Literature* 70, no. 2 (June 2018): 160–75. https://doi.org/10.1215/00104124-6817386.

Jonson, Ben. *Every Man in His Humor.* Project Gutenberg ebook, 2013. www.gutenberg.org/files/5333/5333-h/5333-h.htm.

Karnicky, Jeffrey. *Scarlet Experiment: Birds and Humans in America.* Lincoln: University of Nebraska Press, 2016.

Kaufman, Kenn. *Kingbird Highway: The Biggest Year in the Life of an Extreme Birder.* New York: Houghton Mifflin, 1997.

Kincaid, Jamaica. *A Small Place.* New York: Macmillan, 1988.

Kinver, Mark. "Key Food Crops Head to Arctic 'Doomsday Vault.'" 26 February 2014. www.bbc.com/news/science-environment-26338709.

Kirschenbaum, Matthew G. *Mechanisms: New Media and the Forensic Imagination.* Cambridge: MIT Press, 2008.

Klein, Lauren F. "The Image of Absence: Archival Silence, Data Visualization, and James Hemings." *American Literature* 85, no. 4 (December 2013): 661–88. https://doi.org/10.1215/00029831-2367310.

Knight, Rob. "Why Microbiome Treatments Could Pay Off Soon." *Nature* 518 (February 2015): S5. https://doi.org/10.1038/518S5a.

Knight, Rob, and Brendan Buhler. *Follow Your Gut: The Enormous Impact of Tiny Microbes.* New York: Simon and Schuster, 2015.

Koeppel, Dan. *Banana: The Fate of the Fruit That Changed the World.* New York: Penguin, 2008.

Kosslyn, Stephen M. *Graph Design for the Eye and Mind.* Oxford: Oxford University Press, USA, 2006.

Laurance, William F., and David P. Edwards. "The Search for Unknown Biodiversity." *Proceedings of the National Academy of Sciences of the United States of America* 108, no. 32 (August 2011): 12971–72.

Le Guin, Ursula K. *The Dispossessed.* New York: HarperCollins, 2009.

LeMenager, Stephanie. *Living Oil: Petroleum Culture in the American Century.* Oxford: Oxford University Press USA, 2014.

Lessig, Lawrence. *Code 2.0.* New York: self-published, 2006.

Letunic, Ivica, and Peer Bork. "Interactive Tree of Life (ITOL) v3: An Online Tool for the Display and Annotation of Phylogenetic and Other Trees." *Nucleic Acids Research* 44, no. W1 (July 2016): W242–45. https://doi.org/10.1093/nar/gkw290.

Lima, Manuel. *The Book of Trees: Visualizing Branches of Knowledge.* Hudson, NY: Princeton Architectural Press, 2014.

Lury, Celia. *Consumer Culture.* New Brunswick, NJ: Rutgers University Press, 2011.

M. Bar-Joseph, R. Marcus, and R. F. Lee. "The Continuous Challenge of Citrus Tristeza Virus Control." *Annual Review of Phytopathology* 27, no. 1 (1989): 291–316. https://doi.org/10.1146/annurev.py.27.090189.

Manovich, Lev. *The Language of New Media.* Cambridge: MIT Press, 2001.

Matsuda, Matt K. *Pacific Worlds: A History of Seas, Peoples, and Cultures.* Cambridge: Cambridge University Press, 2012.

Mayr, Ernst. *The Growth of Biological Thought: Diversity, Evolution, and Inheritance.* Cambridge: Harvard University Press, 1982.

McFadden, Geoffrey I. "Chloroplast Origin and Integration." *Plant Physiology* 125, no. 1 (January 2001): 50–53. https://doi.org/10.1104/pp.125.1.50.

McGann, Jerome. "Database, Interface, and Archival Fever." *PMLA* 122, no. 5 (2007): 1588–92.

Melville, Herman. *The Encantadas: Or Enchanted Isles.* New York: Putnam, 1854.

Mitchell, David. *Ghostwritten.* New York: Knopf Doubleday, 2007.

Morar, Nicolae, Ted Toadvine, and Brendan J. M. Bohannan. "Biodiversity at Twenty-Five Years: Revolution or Red Herring?" *Ethics, Policy & Environment* 18, no. 1 (January 2015): 16–29. https://doi.org/10.1080/21550085.2015.1018380.

Morton, Timothy. "Pandora's Box: Avatar, Ecology, Thought." In *Green Planets: Ecology and Science Fiction,* edited by Gerry Canavan and Kim Stanley Robinson, 221–40. Middleton, CT: Wesleyan University Press, 2014.

Moylan, Thomas. *Scraps of the Untainted Sky: Science Fiction, Utopia, Dystopia.* Boulder, CO: Westview, 2000.

Naeem, Shahid, J. Emmett Duffy, and Erika Zavaleta. "The Functions of Biological Diversity in an Age of Extinction." *Science* 336, no. 6087 (June 15, 2012): 1401–6. https://doi.org/10.1126/science.1215855.

Nixon, Rob. *Slow Violence and the Environmentalism of the Poor.* Cambridge: Harvard University Press, 2011.

Obmascik, Mark. *The Big Year.* New York: Free Press, 2004.

Otto, Eric C. *Green Speculations: Science Fiction and Transformative Environmentalism.* Columbus: Ohio State University Press, 2012.

Parrish, Susan Scott. *American Curiosity: Cultures of Natural History in the Colonial British Atlantic World.* Chapel Hill: University of North Carolina Press, 2012.

Peters, Julie. *Julie Peters—Microbiome.* Video. 2015. www.youtube.com/watch?v=l89lbGNFunI.

Peterson, Roger Tory, and James Fisher. *Wild America.* New York: Houghton Mifflin, 1955.

Pimm, Stuart L., et al. "The Future of Biodiversity." *Science* 269, no. 5222 (21 July 1995): 347–50. https://doi.org/10.1126/science.269.5222.347.

Pine, B. Joseph, and James H. Gilmore. *The Experience Economy: Work Is Theatre & Every Business a Stage.* Cambridge: Harvard Business Press, 1999.

Pratt, Mary Louise. *Imperial Eyes: Travel Writing and Transculturation.* London: Routledge, 2007.

Price, Jennifer Jaye. *Flight Maps: Adventures with Nature in Modern America.* New York: Basic, 1999.

Richardson, Brian. "Modern Fiction, the Poetics of Lists, and the Boundaries of Narrative." *Style* 50, no. 3 (August 2016): 327–41. https://doi.org/10.1353/sty.2016.0013.

Rose, Deborah Bird. *Wild Dog Dreaming: Love and Extinction.* Charlottesville: University of Virginia Press, 2011.

Samadfam, Ranna. "How Your Gut Affects Your Bones." In *The Microbiome: Your Inner Ecosystem,* edited by Editors of Scientific American, sec. 1.6. New York: Scientific American, 2019.

Schumann, Gail Lynn. *Plant Diseases: Their Biology and Social Impact.* St. Paul: APS Press, American Phytopathological Society, 1991.

Seabrook, John. "Sowing for Apocalypse." *New Yorker,* August 2007. www.newyorker.com/magazine/2007/08/27/sowing-for-apocalypse.

Sender, Ron, Shai Fuchs, and Ron Milo. "Revised Estimates for the Number of Human and Bacteria Cells in the Body." *PLOS Biology* 14, no. 8 (August 2016): e1002533. https://doi.org/10.1371/journal.pbio.1002533.

Shade, Dan. "The SF Site Featured Review: *The Windup Girl.*" 2010. www.sfsite.com/10a/wg329.htm.

Shakespeare, William. *Macbeth.* Basingstoke, Hampshire, England: Palgrave Macmillan, 2009.

Simberloff, Daniel. "The 'Balance of Nature'—Evolution of a Panchreston." *PLOS Biology* 12, no. 10 (October 2014). https://doi.org/10.1371/journal.pbio.1001963.

Simmons, Dan. *Hyperion.* New York: Random House, 2011.

Smith, Peter Andrey. "The Tantalizing Links between Gut Microbes and the Brain." In *The Microbiome: Your Inner Ecosystem,* edited by Editors of Scientific American, sec. 2.1. New York: Scientific American, 2019.

Snetsinger, Phoebe. *Birding on Borrowed Time.* Colorado Springs: American Birding Association, 2003.

Sonnenburg, Justin, and Erica Sonnenburg. *The Good Gut: Taking Control of Your Weight, Your Mood, and Your Long-Term Health.* New York: Penguin, 2016.

Stallybrass, Peter. "Against Thinking." *PMLA* 122, no. 5 (2007): 1580–87.

Steinroetter, Vanessa. "'Reading the List': Casualty Lists and Civil War Poetry." *ESQ: A Journal of the American Renaissance* 59, no. 1 (June 2013): 48–78. https://doi.org/10.1353/esq.2013.0011.

Stephenson, Neal. *Fall; or, Dodge in Hell.* New York: HarperCollins, 2019.

Sterling, Bruce. *Schismatrix Plus.* New York: Open Road Media, 2014.

Stetka, Bret. "Mind over Meal: Weight-Loss Surgery and the Gut-Brain Connection." In *The Microbiome: Your Inner Ecosystem,* edited by Editors of Scientific American, sec. 3.4. New York: Scientific American, 2019.

Suvin, Darko. *Metamorphoses of Science Fiction: On the Poetics and History of a Literary Genre.* New Haven, CT: Yale University Press, 1979.

Takacs, David. *The Idea of Biodiversity: Philosophies of Paradise.* Baltimore: Johns Hopkins University Press, 1996.

Taylor, Jesse Oak. "The Novel as a Climate Model: Realism and the Greenhouse Effect in *Bleak House*." *Novel* 46, no. 1 (2013): 1–25.

———. *The Sky of Our Manufacture: The London Fog in British Fiction from Dickens to Woolf*. Charlottesville: University of Virginia Press, 2016.

Trexler, Adam. *Anthropocene Fictions: The Novel in a Time of Climate Change*. Charlottesville: University of Virginia Press, 2015.

Tsing, Anna Lowenhaupt. *Friction: An Ethnography of Global Connection*. Princeton, NJ: Princeton University Press, 2011.

Tufte, Edward R. *The Visual Display of Quantitative Information*. New York: Graphics Press, 1983.

Ullstrup, A. J. "The Impacts of the Southern Corn Leaf Blight Epidemics of 1970–1971." *Annual Review of Phytopathology* 10, no. 1 (1972): 37–50. https://doi.org/10.1146/annurev.py.10.090172.000345.

University of Tennessee. "Saving Lonely Species Is Important for Environment." *ScienceDaily*, 30 October 2014. www.sciencedaily.com/releases/2014/10/141030133051.htm.

Urberg, Ingrid. "'Svalbard's Daughters'; Personal Accounts by Svalbard's Female Pioneers." *Nordlit* 11, no. 2 (April 2007): 167–91. https://doi.org/10.7557/13.1576.

van Dooren, Thom. *Flight Ways: Life and Loss at the Edge of Extinction*. New York: Columbia University Press, 2014.

Vardaman, James M. *Call Collect, Ask for Birdman*. New York: St. Martin's, 1980.

Verhoeven, Deb. "Doing the Sheep Good." In *Advancing Digital Humanities*, 206–20. London: Palgrave Macmillan, 2014. https://doi.org/10.1057/9781137337016_14.

Wallis, Claudia. "Gut Reactions." In *The Microbiome: Your Inner Ecosystem*, edited by Editors of Scientific American, sec. 3.1. New York: Scientific American, 2019.

Ward, Francis Kingdon. *The Land of the Blue Poppy: Travels of a Naturalist in Eastern Tibet*. Charleston, SC: BiblioLife, 2015.

Watts, Jonathan. "Brazilian Beans and Japanese Barley Shipped to Svalbard Seed Vault." *Guardian*, 26 February 2014. www.theguardian.com/environment/2014/feb/26/svalbard-global-seed-vault-plants-shipped.

Weinbren, Grahame. "Ocean, Database, Recut." In *Database Aesthetics: Art in the Age of Information Overflow*, 61–75. Minneapolis: University of Minnesota Press, 2007.

Whittaker, Robert J., and José Maria Fernandez-Palacios. *Island Biogeography: Ecology, Evolution, and Conservation*. Oxford: Oxford University Press, 2007.

Wilson, E. O., et al. *Biodiversity*. Washington, DC: National Academies Press, 1988.

Wolfe, Cary. *What Is Posthumanism?* Minneapolis: University of Minnesota Press, 2010.

Woods, Derek. "Accelerated Reading: Fossil Fuels, Infowhelm, Archival Life." In *Anthropocene Reading: Literary History in Geologic Times*, edited by

Tobias Menely and Jesse Oak Taylor, 202–19. University Park: Pennsylvania State University Press, 2017.

Wu, Jianguo, and Orie L. Loucks. "From Balance of Nature to Hierarchical Patch Dynamics: A Paradigm Shift in Ecology." *Quarterly Review of Biology* 70, no. 4 (December 1995): 439–66. https://doi.org/10.1086/419172.

World Wildlife Fund (WWF). *Living Planet Report 2014: Species and Spaces, People and Places.* Gland, Switzerland, 2014. http://wwf.panda.org/about_our_earth/all_publications/living_planet_report/.

Yong, Ed. *I Contain Multitudes: The Microbes within Us and a Grander View of Life.* New York: HarperCollins, 2016.

———. "There Is No 'Healthy' Microbiome." Editorial. *New York Times*, 1 November 2014. www.nytimes.com/2014/11/02/opinion/sunday/there-is-no-healthy-microbiome.html.

Zimmer, Carl. "How Microbes Defend and Define Us." Earth and Environmental Sciences Area, 12 July 2010. http://esd.lbl.gov/how-microbes-defend-and-define-us/.

Zimmerman, Corinne, and Kim Cuddington. "Ambiguous, Circular and Polysemous: Students' Definitions of the 'Balance of Nature' Metaphor." *Public Understanding of Science* 16, no. 4 (October 2007): 393–406. https://doi.org/10.1177/0963662505063022.

Index

Italicized page numbers refer to illustrations.

Ackerman, Jennifer, 139
Adams, Douglas: *The Hitchhiker's Guide to the Galaxy,* 109
Afghanistan, 44, 47, 49
agriculture: advent of, 143; industrial, 38, 45; traditional, 45, 47. *See also* crops
Alaimo, Stacy, 13, 14, 18, 24, 115, 133, 144; *Bodily Natures,* 144, 145
Allen, Bob, 100
Amazon rain forest, 165, 166
American Gut Project, 143
American Museum of Natural History, 134
American Ornithologists' Union, 84, 85
amphibians, 106
ancient civilizations, 45
Anthropocene, 8, 70, 71
anthropocentrism, 92, 140
anthropomorphism, 91, 92
apocalypse, 49; agricultural, 43; Noah, 51; plant, 64; pleasure of, 50–52; potential, 167; receding, 43, 46, 47, 51; reseeding, 51
archaea, 135
Archibald, J. David, 62, 63
Arctic Circle, 20, 163
ARKive, 28. *See also* databases
Armstrong, David, 57
artificial intelligence, 22; nature writing by, 161–72

Asimov, Isaac: *Foundation,* 109
Atwood, Margaret, 34; *Oryx and Crake,* 109
Auden, W. H.: "A New Year Greeting," 130–32, 134, 139, 140
Avatar (film), 111

Bacigalupi, Paolo: *The Windup Girl,* 25, 27, 33–35, 46, 50, 109
bacteria, 130–36, 139, 155–57, 159
Badmington, Neil, 13
balance of nature, 116–20, 127, 129
Barad, Karen, 7, 14, 31, 32, 136
Beer, Gillian, 116, 185n38
Bennett, Jane, 14, 92, 146, 185n38
big data, 7
Biggest Twitch, The (Davies and Miller), 82
Bininda-Emonds, Olaf, 59
biocomplexity, 23
biodiversity: alternate, 108–10, 171; consumption of, 16, 83, 104; crop, 27, 47; cultural meanings of, 6; definitions of, 5, 18, 68, 76, 126, 128, 169; engagement with, 108, 113; functional, 50; history of, 9; as information, 10–12, 15, 22, 115, 128, 160, 164; loss of, 47, 51, 77, 107, 115, 150, 160; materialist reading of, 71; narratives of, 160, 172, 173n4; nonhuman, 120;

biodiversity (continued)
    origin story of, 20, 65; prescriptiveness of, 15; as a process, 159; as proliferation, 59–66; as a puzzle, 128; representations of, 3, 6, 7, 12, 129, 164, 169; rescue of, 2; as time travel, 100–105; transcorporeal, 22, 144–47; wild, 47. See also biology; conservation; databases; diversity; extinction; genetic diversity; microbiome; natural history
biology: evolutionary, 9; genetic, 76; transnational cultures of contemporary, 19. See also biodiversity; ecosystems
bioluminescence, 135
biopiracy, 25, 39
birder memoirs, 21, 80–105, 166, 169. See also birding
birding, 17, 21, 80–105; as accounting, 82–86; as a consumer product, 96; experience of, 90–95. See also birder memoirs
Blaser, Martin J.: *Missing Microbes: How the Overuse of Antibiotics Is Fueling Our Modern Plagues,* 138, 141
Bohannan, Brendan, 22, 117
Bollinger, Laurel: "Containing Multitudes: Revisiting the Infection Metaphor in Science Fiction," 152
Bosse, Abraham, 149
Bowker, Geoffrey, 17
Braidotti, Rosi, 13
Brazil, 48, 165
Buell, Lawrence, 110
Buse, Katherine, 111

California, 103
Canavan, Gerry: *Green Planets,* 110
Card, Orson Scott: *Speaker for the Dead,* 21, 22, 108–15, 120–23, 126–29, 140, 159

Carroll, Lewis: *Through the Looking-Glass,* 43
Carruth, Allison, 17, 18
Carson, Rachel: *Silent Spring,* 110
Casid, Jill, 128
catastrophe: environmental, 162; litany of, 167; scarcity and, 41–47
Central Park Effect, The (documentary film), 95
Chile, 38, 48
Chilean blue crocus, 38
choanoflagellates, 135, 136
climate change: and biodiversity, 169; catastrophic, 46; destructiveness of, 49; threat of, 6, 8, 48
climate fiction, 110
Cokinos, Christopher: *Hope Is the Thing with Feathers,* 81
conservation: biodiversity, 27, 56–58; and evolutionary uniqueness, 56–58; focus of, 15, 57, 58, 85; paradigm of, 109; preservation *ex situ,* 27, 31, 47–49. See also biodiversity; extinction
Convention on Biological Diversity (CBD), 5, 14
Cook, Roger, 64
Cooper, Chris, 95
corn, 32
Crittercam (television show), 88
Cronon, William, 15, 99; "The Trouble with Wilderness," 171
crops: biodiversity of, 45; failure of, 44, 46; loss of, 43, 45, 47. See also agriculture
cybernetics, 11
cyberpunk novels, 10, 21, 22, 150–59

Daniel, Sharon, 36
Darwin, Charles, 14, 19, 39–41, 48, 71, 106, 185n38; hypothetical tree sketch of, 69, 79; *On the Origin of Species,* 67, 68; *The Voyage of the Beagle,* 39

Dasmann, Raymond, 108
databases, 26–29, 32, 36, 37, 51, 54, 169; aesthetics of, 28; criticism of, 28; narrative and, 29–31. *See also* biodiversity; GENESYS; seed banks
deforestation, 49
Deleuze, Gilles, 60
DeLoughrey, Elizabeth, 124
Democratic Republic of the Congo, 48
Dening, Greg, 124
Derrida, Jacques, 13
Dick, Philip K.: *Do Androids Dream of Electric Sheep?*, 109
Dietert, Rodney R.: *The Human Superorganism: How the Microbiome Is Revolutionizing the Pursuit of a Healthy Life*, 138
dingo, 6
dinosaurs, 101, 102
disorientation, pleasures of, 111–16
diversity: avian, 80–105; domestic, 22; evolutionary, 16, 130, 131; functional, 5, 131; genetic, 5, 16, 49, 50, 131, 164; interaction, 5; landscape, 5; phylogenetic, 5, 20, 72, 73; spatial, 5; species, 5, 85, 131; temporal, 5; trait, 49, 50. *See also* biodiversity
DNA: desirability of, 75; extraction of, 77; fossil, 75
Dooley, Sean: *The Big Twitch*, 82
Dunne, Pete: *The Feather Quest*, 82
Dupre, John, 136

ecosystems: conservation of, 57; damaged, 50; diverse, 17, 22; fragility of, 163; planetary, 21; popular, 142; speculative, 19, 22, 106–29, 184n20. *See also* biology
ecotourism, 3, 4, 129; environmental costs of, 15
Ecuador, 106

Eden, 8, 64, 121, 123, 134, 158, 160, 170
Eden Project, 134
EDGE, 57, 58
Edwards, David, 115
Egerton, Frank, 116
Encyclopedia of Life, 28. *See also* databases
endemic species, 8, 107, 124, 131, 170. *See also* endemism; species
endemism, 8, 124, 126. *See also* endemic species
Escobar, Arturo, 171
evolutionary history, 10–12, 20, 21, 53, 54, 62, 72–79, 101, 160, 170. *See also* history
evolutionary supertrees, 17, 20, 21, 134, 169, 170; aesthetics of, 67; circularity of, 59–66; crowdedness of, 59–66; visualization and, 53–79. *See also* trees of life; visualization
experience economy, 95–98
Experience Economy, The (Pine and Gilmore), 96
extinction, 25, 38, 102, 109; avian, 81; and endangered species, 5; mass, 65, 71, 125–27; meanings of, 109; survivors of, 70. *See also* conservation; extinction studies
extinction studies, 5, 6. *See also* extinction

Farnham, Timothy, 5
Fischer, Tom, 38
Fisher, Melissa: "Microbial Me," 137, 138
Florida, 102, 103
Fowler, Carey, 47
Franzen, Jonathan, 183n62; *The Discomfort Zone*, 82, 95, 98, 101–4

Galapagos Conservancy, 77, 78
Galapagos Islands, 39–41, 77, 106, 107, 141

Garrard, Greg: *Ecocriticism,* 110
Gatens, Moira, 23
Gee's Bend, quilts of, 36
gene banks. *See* seed banks
Genesis, book of, 51, 64
GENESYS, 31, 33, 45–47, 51, 53, 64. *See also* Svalbard Global Seed Vault
genetic diversity. *See* diversity
genetic engineering: of crops, 34, 46, 50; of humans, 152; methods of, 157; tools of, 35; as world salvation, 33
Gibson, William: *Neuromancer,* 10, 11
Global Crop Diversity Trust, 33
Global North, 2, 3, 8, 39, 47–49, 104, 126, 137, 164
Global South, 3, 8, 15, 16, 19–22, 27, 38, 47–49, 104, 133, 142, 164, 165, 170
global warming. *See* climate change
golden-age myth, 123, 126
gorillas, 3, 4
Gould, Stephen Jay, 135
Great Britain, 48, 128
Grosz, Elizabeth, 14, 71
Grove, Richard, 123
Guardian (UK newspaper), 43
Guattari, Félix, 60
Guha, Ramachandra, 15, 171

Hadza, 142, 143, 170
Haraway, Donna J., 135, 136; *When Species Meet,* 14, 88–90, 104, 150
Hawaiian bobtail squid, 135, 139, 157
Hayles, N. Katherine, 30; *How We Became Posthuman,* 11–13, 157
Heise, Ursula, 5, 17, 18, 87, 171; *Imagining Extinction,* 5; "Reduced Ecologies," 107, 111
Hekman, Susan, 13
Herbert, Frank: *Dune,* 21, 108–20, 123–26, 129, 159

history: of biodiversity, 149; evolutionary, 72–79; human, 64; of life, 64, 65, 68, 70. *See also* evolutionary history
Hobbes, Thomas: *Leviathan,* 149
Honduras, 44, 47, 49
Houser, Heather, 18, 54
Housley, Kathleen: "The Microbiome and the Boson," 133, 146, 147
human body, 9, 131–32, 139–42, 146, 147, 151–57. *See also* microbiome
human identity, 11, 132
humanism, 13, 158

industrial agriculture. *See* agriculture
insects: outbreaks of, 63; and plant ecosystems, 12, 50; pollinating, 12; predation of, 26; resistance to, 32, 33, 46
Intergovernmental Panel on Biodiversity and Ecosystem Services, 19
Iraq, 44, 47, 49
IUCN Red List, 28. *See also* databases

James, Edward, 114
Jameson, Frederic, 107
Japan, 45

Kareiva, Peter, 57, 58, 74
Karnicky, Jeffrey: *Scarlet Experiment,* 81
Kaufman, Kenn: *Kingbird Highway,* 82, 84–86, 91–93, 96, 97, 99, 101, 104
Kew Millennium Seed Bank, 39; name of, 42, 43; neutrality of, 39; origins of, 36. *See also* Kew Royal Botanical Gardens; seed banks
Kew Royal Botanical Gardens, 36, 42; *The Last Great Plant Hunt,* 41. *See also* Kew Millennium Seed Bank
Kincaid, Jamaica: *A Small Place,* 128

Kirschenbaum, Matthew, 52
Klein, Lauren: "The Image of Absence: Archival Silence, Data Visualization, and James Hemings," 31
Knight, Rob, 143; *Follow Your Gut: The Enormous Impact of Tiny Microbes,* 138

Laurance, William, 115
Leach, Jeff, 143
Le Guin, Ursula K., 107, 111; *The Dispossessed,* 109
LeMenager, Stephanie, 18
Lessig, Lawrence: *Code and Other Laws of Cyberspace,* 31
Lima, Manuel, 59, 62
Linnaeus, Carl, 36–38
literature: apocalyptic, 20; fantasy, 103; on the microbiome, 17; scientific travel, 36. *See also* birder memoirs; climate fiction; cyberpunk novels; nonfiction; poetry; postapocalyptic fiction; science fiction
Living Planet Report, 3, 4. *See also* World Wildlife Fund
Livy, 149
London, 20
Lury, Celia, 97

Madagascar, 41
mammals, 106
Manovich, Lev, 28; *The Language of New Media,* 29
Margulis, Lynn, 150
Material Ecocriticism (Iovino and Opperman), 92
Material Feminisms (Alaimo and Hekman), 13
materialism, 91, 92
materiality: elision of, 27, 50–52; loss of, 20; of seeds, 28
Matsés, 143

Matsuda, Matt, 123
McCarthy, Donal, 73
McGann, Jerome, 30
media, 16–18, 133, 165; cultural, 19; objects of, 7; popular, 43. *See also* new media
Melville, Herman, 106
microbes, 10, 24, 60, 63, 130–60, 170; gut, 160; marine, 160; soil, 160; symbiotic, 12, 16, 50, 131, 132, 151, 156. *See also* microbiome
microbiome, 16, 17, 22, 61, 130–60, 170, 187n4; ancestral, 141–46; of contemporary poetry, 146–50; depictions of the, 137–41; evolutionary, 142–44; moment of the, 134–37. *See also* biodiversity; human body; microbes
Microbiome, The: Your Inner Ecosystem (compilation of articles), 138
Mitchell, David: *Ghostwritten,* 22, 161
Morar, Nicolae, 22, 117
Moravec, Hans, 11, 12
Morton, Timothy, 111
Moylan, Tom: *Scraps of the Untainted Sky,* 113
multispecies justice, 5

natural disasters. *See* catastrophe
natural history: apocalyptic, 25–52, 166; British, 19; colonial, 167, 171; ecology and, 138; eighteenth-century, 39; imperial, 8, 9; narratives of, 164; science fiction and, 10, 22, 162–68; seed banks as, 35–39. *See also* biodiversity
Nature Conservancy, 57, 73
neocolonialism, 39
new materialisms, 13, 14
new media, 17. *See also* media
New York, 164, 165
New Yorker, 36, 43, 47
Nicaragua, 45, 47

Nixon, Rob: *Slow Violence and the Environmentalism of the Poor*, 6, 169
nonfiction: microbiome, 19, 132, 145, 150; science, 132, 133. *See also* literature
Norway, 39

Otto, Eric, 110
Oxford English Dictionary, 40, 76

Pacific Islands, 48, 123
Paris, 36
Park, Simon: "Cellfies," 137
Parrish, Susan Scott, 164
Peru, 143
Peters, Julie: "Microbiome," 133, 146–50
Philippines, 44, 47
phylogenetic supertrees. *See* evolutionary supertrees
Pinta Island tortoise, 77
plant genetics, 25, 46. *See also* plants; seed banks
plants: extinction of species of, 45, 51; flowering, 50; genome of, 160; hybridization in, 60; microbes of, 136; wild, 46. *See also* plant genetics; seed banks
Pleistocene, 100–101
poetry, 22; transcorporeal, 146–50
popular science, 22, 139, 159, 187n4
population, 2; explosion of, 9; reduction of, 46
postapocalyptic fiction, 46
posthumanism, 12, 13, 158
Pratt, Mary Louise, 163
Price, Jennifer Jaye: *Flight Maps*, 81

Raitanen, Erik-Erno: *Bacteriograms*, 137
reality: agency and, 90–95; larger, 81; underlying, 59, 60
Revelation, book of, 52

Ricou, Joanna: "Other Self Portraits," 137
Rio +20, 19
Robinson, Kim Stanley: *Mars* trilogy, 110
Rose, Deborah Bird, 6
Royal Society for the Protection of Birds, 73

scarcity: and catastrophe, 41–47; observations of, 106; utopia and, 107
science fiction, 9, 16, 21, 26, 142, 160, 169; and natural history, 10, 22, 162–68; nightmares of, 139; speculative ecosystems in, 19, 22, 106–29, 184n20. *See also* speculative fiction
Scientific American, 130, 134, 138
Seabrook, John, 43, 47, 52
seed banks, 25, 30, 37, 51; aesthetics of, 28, 30; agency of seeds in, 12; databases of, 29, 35–39, 46; global, 19, 20, 27, 28, 41–49, 53, 79; and the Global South, 47–50; local, 20, 28, 39, 42–48; materiality of seeds in, 28; national, 28; as natural history, 35–39; underground, 26. *See also* databases; plant genetics
Simmons, Dan: *Hyperion*, 109
Snetsinger, Phoebe: *Birding on Borrowed Time*, 82, 84, 85, 88–90, 92, 97
Sonnenburg, Justin/Sonnenburg, Erica: *The Good Gut: Taking Control of Your Weight, Your Mood, and Your Long-Term Health*, 138, 142, 143
speciation, 65, 68. *See also* species
species: abundance of, 39–41, 56, 65, 70, 162, 168, 169; animal, 106; bird, 80–106; continuity of, 70; diversity of, 5, 85, 131; as

evolutionary history, 62, 74–79; loss of, 37, 38, 77, 79, 87; new, 41; rare, 97–99; reptile, 106; socializing across, 87–90. *See also* endemic species; speciation
speculative fiction, 25, 27, 34, 35. *See also* science fiction
Stephenson, Neal: *Fall; or, Dodge in Hell*, 10
Sterling, Bruce: *Schismatrix*, 109, 133, 150–59
Suvin, Darko, 123
Svalbard Global Seed Vault, 29, 33, 42–48, 51, 163; architecture of, 42; geographic location of, 38, 42; mediation role of, 39; neutrality of, 38. *See also* GENESYS; seed banks
Sweden, 38
symbiogenesis, 150
symbionts, 27–35, 136; microbial, 152

Takacs, David, 5
Tanzania, 142, 143
Taylor, Jesse Oak, 6
terraforming, 125–28, 139, 140, 155, 156, 159
Thomas, Gavin, 73, 75
Thousand Plateaus, A (Deleuze and Guattari), 60, 61
time: deep, 26; geological, 70; space and, 43, 70
Toadvine, Ted, 22, 117
trees of life: bacterial, 60; base of, 61; circular construction of, 62–64, 66; comprehensive, 55; dead branches on the, 66–70; as diagrams, 179n2; humans in, 63; impoverishment of a, 150; limitations of, 61; and time, 70–74; and tree rings, 63, 64. *See also* evolutionary history; evolutionary supertrees; visualization

Trexler, Adam: *Anthropocene Fictions: The Novel in a Time of Climate Change*, 110
Tufte, Edward, 66

Uganda, 4
United Nations, Convention on Biological Diversity of the, 5, 14
United Nations Decade on Biodiversity, 19
United States, 2

van Dooren, Thom, 6, 73, 74, 79
Vardaman, James M.: *Call Collect, Ask for Birdman*, 82
Venezuela, 143
Venice, 36
Verhoeven, Deb: "Doing the Sheep Good," 31
visualization: aesthetics of, 56–58, 61–62, 71–72; information, 59, 68; suite of, 74; titan of, 66

Wallis, Claudia, 141
Ward, Francis Kingdon, 41
Watts, Jonathan, 43
Weinbren, Grahame: "Ocean, Database, Recut," 29, 30
West Indies, 128
Wild America (Peterson and Fisher), 82–88, 93–100, 102–4
Wilson, Edward O., 173n4; *Biodiversity*, 1–3, 9, 160, 171; *The Meaning of Human Existence*, 9, 10
Wolfe, Cary, 12, 13
woolly mammoth, 77, 78
World Wildlife Fund (WWF), 3–5, 15, 166, 173n4

Yanomami, 143
Yong, Ed, 135, 143; *I Contain Multitudes: The Microbes within Us and a Grander View of Life*, 132, 138, 139, 141, 145

Recent books in the series
Under the Sign of Nature: Explorations in Ecocriticism

Elizabeth Callaway
Eden's Endemics: Narratives of Biodiversity on Earth and Beyond

Alicia Carroll
New Woman Ecologies: From Arts and Crafts to the Great War and Beyond

Emily McGiffin
Of Land, Bones, and Money: Toward a South African Ecopoetics

Elizabeth Hope Chang
Novel Cultivations: Plants in British Literature of the Global Nineteenth Century

Christopher Abram
Evergreen Ash: Ecology and Catastrophe in Old Norse Myth and Literature

Serenella Iovino, Enrico Cesaretti, and Elena Past, editors
Italy and the Environmental Humanities: Landscapes, Natures, Ecologies

Julia E. Daniel
Building Natures: Modern American Poetry, Landscape Architecture, and City Planning

Lynn Keller
Recomposing Ecopoetics: North American Poetry of the Self-Conscious Anthropocene

Michael P. Branch and Clinton Mohs, editors
"The Best Read Naturalist": Nature Writings of Ralph Waldo Emerson

Jesse Oak Taylor
The Sky of Our Manufacture: The London Fog in British Fiction from Dickens to Woolf

Eric Gidal
Ossianic Unconformities: Bardic Poetry in the Industrial Age

Adam Trexler
Anthropocene Fictions: The Novel in a Time of Climate Change

Kate Rigby
Dancing with Disaster: Environmental Histories, Narratives, and Ethics for Perilous Times

www.ingramcontent.com/pod-product-compliance
Lightning Source LLC
Chambersburg PA
CBHW031813220426
43662CB00007B/622